Linked

for Beginners

A Step-by-Step Guide

Kiet Huynh

Table of Contents

Introduction

1.1 Why LinkedIn Matters in Today's World

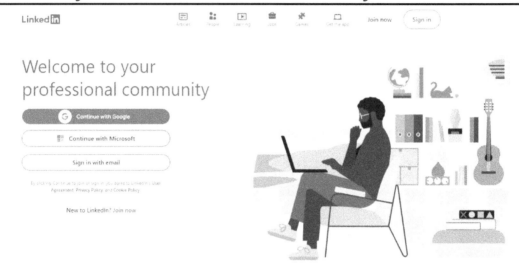

In an age where digital connections often hold as much value as face-to-face interactions, LinkedIn has emerged as a critical tool for professionals. Its importance is underscored by its ability to connect individuals across industries, foster career growth, and serve as a platform for thought leadership. This chapter delves into the multifaceted reasons LinkedIn is essential in today's professional landscape.

The Shift Toward a Digital-First Professional World

The world has experienced a massive shift toward digitization in recent decades. This transformation has impacted nearly every aspect of professional life, from job searching to networking and personal branding. LinkedIn sits at the heart of this shift, providing a digital ecosystem where professionals can establish their presence, showcase their skills, and connect with others.

1. **Global Connectivity:** LinkedIn enables users to connect with professionals worldwide, breaking down geographical barriers that once limited networking

opportunities. Whether you're in a small town or a bustling metropolis, LinkedIn allows you to interact with industry leaders, recruiters, and like-minded peers from any location.

2. **Remote Work and Virtual Collaboration:** The rise of remote work has emphasized the need for robust professional networks that aren't tied to physical spaces. LinkedIn helps bridge this gap, ensuring professionals can maintain and grow their networks regardless of where they work.

Networking in the Digital Age

In today's interconnected world, who you know often matters as much as what you know. Networking is no longer confined to in-person events or conferences. LinkedIn offers a virtual alternative that is equally impactful, if not more so.

1. **Expanding Your Network:** LinkedIn enables users to connect with people they wouldn't typically meet in their daily lives. For example, you can connect with a recruiter in another country, follow a CEO of a company you admire, or join industry-specific groups to meet like-minded professionals.

2. **Staying Connected:** Unlike traditional networking methods that often rely on sporadic contact, LinkedIn allows you to stay continuously updated on your connections' professional activities. Updates on promotions, job changes, and skill acquisitions keep relationships active and relevant.

3. **Opportunities Through Connections:** Many job opportunities arise through referrals and recommendations. LinkedIn's structured platform makes it easy for professionals to identify potential opportunities within their network.

Building a Personal Brand

LinkedIn serves as a platform for individuals to craft and showcase their personal brand. A well-maintained LinkedIn profile acts as a digital resume, portfolio, and business card all rolled into one.

1. **Showcasing Your Expertise:** Through a comprehensive profile, you can highlight your skills, achievements, and experiences. LinkedIn's features, such as the ability to upload media, share articles, or publish long-form posts, provide avenues to demonstrate your expertise.

2. **Thought Leadership:** By consistently engaging with content, sharing insights, or publishing original articles, you can establish yourself as a thought leader in your field. This not only boosts your professional credibility but also helps attract career opportunities.

3. **Visibility to Recruiters:** LinkedIn is a primary tool for recruiters and hiring managers. By optimizing your profile with relevant keywords and a clear summary, you can increase your chances of appearing in recruiter searches.

Access to Knowledge and Resources

LinkedIn is more than just a networking site—it is a hub for professional development and learning. The platform offers a wealth of resources that can help users stay updated and grow their knowledge.

1. **LinkedIn Learning:** The platform's educational offerings include thousands of courses covering everything from technical skills to soft skills. These courses are led by industry experts and are tailored to help professionals stay competitive.

2. **Industry Insights:** LinkedIn feeds are filled with articles, news, and updates from companies and professionals. This makes it an excellent platform for staying informed about industry trends and innovations.

3. **Peer-to-Peer Learning:** Engaging in discussions, joining groups, and following influencers can expose users to diverse perspectives and practical advice from peers across the globe.

Job Hunting Made Easier

For job seekers, LinkedIn is a game-changer. It simplifies the job search process and provides tools that make it easier to find and secure employment.

1. **Search Tools:** LinkedIn's advanced job search filters allow users to find roles based on location, industry, experience level, and more. These tools make the job-hunting process efficient and targeted.

2. **Direct Applications:** Many companies allow candidates to apply for roles directly through LinkedIn. The "Easy Apply" feature, for example, streamlines the application process by allowing users to submit their profile with just a few clicks.

3. **Recruiter Access:** By marking your profile as "open to work," you can signal to recruiters that you're looking for new opportunities. This feature increases your visibility to hiring professionals who use LinkedIn to find talent.

Community and Engagement

LinkedIn isn't just about individuals—it's also about communities. By joining and participating in groups, users can foster a sense of belonging and engage with others who share similar interests or goals.

1. **Finding Your Niche:** LinkedIn groups cover a wide range of industries, topics, and interests. Joining these groups allows you to connect with professionals who share your goals and challenges.

2. **Engaging Through Content:** Regularly interacting with posts, sharing updates, or writing articles can help you build rapport with your network and keep your profile active and engaging.

3. **Collaborative Opportunities:** The platform provides ample opportunities to collaborate, whether through shared projects, group discussions, or direct outreach.

Conclusion: LinkedIn's Role in Your Success

In today's world, LinkedIn is more than just a professional networking platform—it's a critical tool for career development, personal branding, and staying connected in a digital-first environment. Whether you're a student looking for internships, a professional seeking new opportunities, or an entrepreneur aiming to grow your business, LinkedIn provides the resources and connections needed to succeed.

By understanding its value and leveraging its features effectively, you can position yourself for long-term professional growth and success.

1.2 Who This Book is For

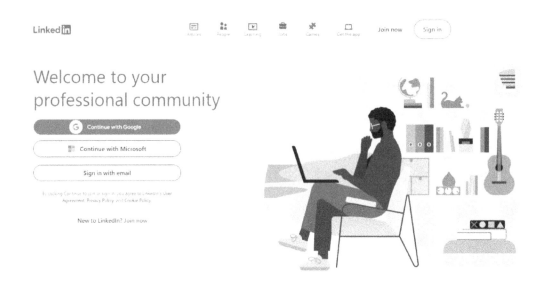

LinkedIn is one of the most powerful tools for professionals today, offering a unique platform where individuals can showcase their skills, connect with others in their industry, and open doors to countless opportunities. This book, **"LinkedIn for Beginners: A Step-by-Step Guide,"** has been crafted with care and precision to address the needs of those who are just starting their LinkedIn journey. Whether you're a fresh graduate, a career changer, or simply someone looking to maximize your professional online presence, this guide is for you.

Recent Graduates: Entering the Workforce

If you've just graduated and are eager to start your professional career, this book will be your go-to manual for establishing a robust online presence. As a recent graduate, you may have limited work experience, but LinkedIn allows you to highlight your education, internships, volunteer work, and transferable skills. This book will guide you on:

- Crafting a professional profile that stands out to recruiters.
- Using LinkedIn to explore job opportunities and internships.
- Networking with alumni from your school to build valuable connections.

- Learning how to approach recruiters and employers confidently.

For graduates, LinkedIn isn't just about finding a job—it's about planting the seeds for a successful career.

Professionals Transitioning to a New Industry

If you're considering a career change, this guide will help you position yourself effectively on LinkedIn to attract opportunities in your desired field. Transitioning careers can feel daunting, but LinkedIn provides tools to showcase your transferable skills and market yourself in a new light. In this book, you'll learn:

- How to update your profile to reflect your future career aspirations.

- Strategies to connect with professionals in your target industry.

- Ways to leverage LinkedIn Learning to acquire new skills.

- Tips for positioning your past experience as relevant and valuable to your new career path.

LinkedIn bridges the gap between your old career and your new one, and this book will help you cross that bridge with confidence.

Entrepreneurs and Freelancers

For entrepreneurs, small business owners, and freelancers, LinkedIn is more than just a networking site—it's a platform to build your personal and professional brand. Whether you're looking for clients, collaborators, or simply want to showcase your expertise, this guide will show you how to make LinkedIn work for your business. Here's what you'll discover:

- How to optimize your profile to showcase your products, services, or expertise.

- Strategies for creating engaging content that builds credibility.

- Tips for networking with potential clients and business partners.

- Ways to use LinkedIn analytics to measure the effectiveness of your efforts.

By following the strategies outlined in this book, you'll transform LinkedIn into a lead-generation tool and a hub for building relationships that matter.

Job Seekers: Looking for New Opportunities

If you're actively looking for a job, LinkedIn is one of the best platforms to help you find your next opportunity. This book is tailored to job seekers who want to maximize their chances of landing their dream role. Here's how this guide will help you:

- Learn how to craft a compelling headline and summary that attract recruiters.

- Discover how to set up job alerts and use advanced search features to find the perfect role.

- Understand how to use the "Open to Work" feature effectively.

- Master the art of reaching out to recruiters and hiring managers.

No matter your field or experience level, LinkedIn opens the door to opportunities, and this book will ensure you make the most of it.

Students: Preparing for the Future

Students who are still in school or university can use LinkedIn to lay the groundwork for their future careers. Even if you're not actively searching for a job, creating a LinkedIn profile early allows you to start building your professional network and learning about your field of interest. In this book, students will find guidance on:

- How to build a strong LinkedIn profile even with limited experience.

- Ways to showcase academic achievements, projects, and extracurricular activities.

- Tips for connecting with professors, mentors, and industry professionals.

- The importance of joining LinkedIn groups related to your field of study.

By starting early, students can position themselves as proactive and driven individuals, which will benefit them immensely when they enter the workforce.

Professionals Looking to Expand Their Network

LinkedIn isn't just for job seekers; it's also for established professionals who want to grow their network and stay informed about their industry. If you're already in a job but looking to build connections, find collaborators, or stay updated on industry trends, this book has you covered. You'll learn:

- How to identify and connect with industry leaders and peers.

- The value of participating in LinkedIn groups and discussions.

- Strategies for creating content that establishes you as a thought leader.

- How to use LinkedIn to keep your professional skills and knowledge up to date.

For professionals, LinkedIn is an invaluable tool for continuous growth and networking.

Recruiters and Hiring Managers

Even if your primary focus on LinkedIn is to find top talent for your organization, this book can help you optimize your use of the platform. LinkedIn offers a treasure trove of features for recruiters and hiring managers, and this guide will cover:

- How to create a professional profile that attracts job seekers.

- Tips for posting effective job listings.

- Strategies for identifying and reaching out to passive candidates.

- Ways to use LinkedIn Recruiter (if applicable) to streamline your hiring process.

By leveraging LinkedIn effectively, recruiters can find the right candidates faster and build a strong talent pipeline for their organizations.

Anyone New to Social Media

Finally, this book is for anyone who feels overwhelmed by the concept of social media or doesn't consider themselves "tech-savvy." LinkedIn is one of the most user-friendly platforms out there, and this guide will break down everything you need to know in simple, step-by-step instructions. You'll learn:

- How to navigate LinkedIn's interface with ease.

- Tips for avoiding common mistakes or pitfalls.

- Strategies to stay professional while engaging with others online.

Even if you've never used a social media platform before, this book will help you get started on LinkedIn with confidence.

Conclusion

This book is designed to meet the needs of a diverse audience, from students and job seekers to professionals and entrepreneurs. No matter your background, LinkedIn has something valuable to offer, and this guide will ensure you unlock its full potential. Let's dive in and start building your professional online presence today!

1.3 How to Use This Guide

LinkedIn is a platform full of possibilities, whether you're looking to network with professionals, explore job opportunities, or establish your personal brand. However, understanding how to effectively use this platform can feel overwhelming, especially for beginners. This guide is designed to take you from the very basics to becoming confident in navigating and leveraging LinkedIn for your personal and professional goals. In this section, we will walk you through how to best use this book, breaking down its structure and highlighting what you can expect from each chapter. Let this guide be your companion as you embark on your LinkedIn journey.

Understanding the Book's Structure

This book is divided into carefully designed chapters, each focusing on a specific aspect of LinkedIn. Here's how the structure works and what each part aims to achieve:

- **Introduction**: The introduction provides a foundation for understanding LinkedIn's role in today's professional world. It also identifies who can benefit the most from this book and how you can maximize its potential.

- **Getting Started with LinkedIn (Chapter 1)**: This chapter is perfect for absolute beginners. It explains what LinkedIn is, how it works, and how to create your account. By the end of this chapter, you will be familiar with the basic interface and ready to start building your profile.

- **Crafting a Winning Profile (Chapter 2)**: Your LinkedIn profile is your digital resume. This chapter dives into crafting a strong profile that attracts recruiters, potential employers, or collaborators. From selecting the right profile picture to writing an impactful summary, you'll learn step-by-step how to create a profile that stands out.

- **Building Your Network (Chapter 3)**: Networking is at the heart of LinkedIn. This chapter focuses on expanding your connections, finding and joining professional groups, and engaging meaningfully with others in your industry.

- **Engaging with Content (Chapter 4)**: LinkedIn is not just about networking but also about engaging with content. You'll learn how to create posts, interact with others' content, and publish articles to establish thought leadership.

- **Job Searching on LinkedIn (Chapter 5)**: If you're looking for a job, this chapter will guide you through the job search process on LinkedIn. From using job boards to optimizing your profile for recruiters, you'll find actionable tips to enhance your job search.

- **Growing Your Personal Brand (Chapter 6)**: LinkedIn is a powerful tool for personal branding. This chapter explores strategies for building your professional image, establishing authority in your niche, and leveraging analytics to track your progress.

- **Advanced Tips for Beginners (Chapter 7)**: Once you've mastered the basics, this chapter will provide tips and strategies for advanced use, including SEO optimization, privacy settings, and avoiding common mistakes.

The chapters build upon each other, creating a comprehensive journey from setting up your account to becoming a confident LinkedIn user.

How to Navigate the Book

This book is structured to provide value whether you read it cover to cover or skip to the sections most relevant to your needs. Here's how you can navigate it effectively:

- **For Complete Beginners**: If you're entirely new to LinkedIn, start with Chapter 1 and move sequentially through the book. Each chapter builds on the knowledge of the previous one, giving you a solid foundation to explore LinkedIn.

- **For Experienced Users**: If you've already set up a LinkedIn account but feel like you're not using it to its full potential, you can jump straight to chapters on profile optimization, networking, or personal branding.

- **For Job Seekers**: Focus on Chapter 5 to learn how to use LinkedIn's job search features effectively. Pair this with Chapter 2 for optimizing your profile to catch recruiters' attention.

- **For Entrepreneurs or Professionals Looking to Network**: Chapters 3, 4, and 6 will help you build a strong network and establish your personal brand, allowing you to grow your professional presence on LinkedIn.

Leveraging Actionable Steps

This guide includes practical steps at the end of many sections to help you implement what you've learned. These actionable steps are designed to encourage you to apply the tips and strategies immediately. For example:

- **Profile Optimization Checklists**: After reading Chapter 2, you'll find a checklist to evaluate and improve your LinkedIn profile.

- **Networking Exercises**: In Chapter 3, you'll be guided through exercises like writing a personalized connection request or joining a LinkedIn group.

- **Content Creation Tips**: Chapter 4 provides templates for writing engaging posts or articles to help you get started with content creation.

Make use of these steps as you read to see immediate progress in your LinkedIn journey.

Key Features to Look For

Throughout this book, you'll notice additional features that are designed to enhance your learning:

- **Pro Tips**: Quick insights or advanced strategies for making the most of LinkedIn.

- **Common Mistakes**: Highlighting errors to avoid, ensuring you don't make rookie mistakes.

- **Case Studies**: Real-life examples of LinkedIn users who've achieved success by applying the strategies outlined in the book.

- **FAQs**: Frequently asked questions to address common concerns or confusion related to LinkedIn usage.

These features make the guide more interactive and tailored to real-world applications.

Using the Book Alongside LinkedIn

The best way to learn LinkedIn is by doing. As you read through this book, it's highly recommended that you follow along on your LinkedIn account. For example:

- When reading about profile setup, open your LinkedIn profile and make adjustments in real-time.

- When learning about connecting with others, practice sending personalized connection requests immediately.

- Experiment with creating posts or articles after reading Chapter 4.

By combining learning with action, you'll develop confidence and see results faster.

Adapting the Guide to Your Goals

Finally, remember that LinkedIn can be used in different ways depending on your goals. Whether you're:

- A student looking for internships

- A professional seeking new job opportunities

- An entrepreneur aiming to connect with potential clients

- A freelancer showcasing your portfolio

This guide can be tailored to suit your needs. Keep your goals in mind as you read through the book and prioritize the sections most relevant to you.

CHAPTER I
Getting Started with LinkedIn

1.1 Understanding LinkedIn: An Overview

1.1.1 What is LinkedIn?

LinkedIn is the world's largest professional networking platform, designed to connect professionals across industries, geographies, and job functions. Launched in 2003, LinkedIn has become the go-to platform for building and maintaining professional relationships, showcasing skills and expertise, and exploring career opportunities. Unlike social platforms such as Facebook or Instagram, LinkedIn focuses specifically on professional growth and career advancement, offering tools and features tailored to individuals and organizations seeking to establish their presence in the professional world.

At its core, LinkedIn serves as a digital résumé, a professional networking tool, and a platform for career development. It allows users to present their professional profiles online, highlighting their skills, experiences, and accomplishments. Employers and recruiters use LinkedIn to find talent, while job seekers leverage the platform to connect with potential employers, research companies, and discover job openings. However, LinkedIn is much more than just a job search engine—it is a hub for thought leadership, industry insights, and meaningful professional connections.

The Purpose of LinkedIn

LinkedIn was created to bridge the gap between professionals, enabling them to connect in a way that wasn't possible before. In a globalized world where opportunities span across countries and industries, LinkedIn makes it easier for professionals to find each other and work together. The platform's primary goals include:

1. **Networking:** LinkedIn helps individuals connect with colleagues, mentors, industry leaders, and potential business partners. It provides a way to grow your

network beyond face-to-face interactions by connecting digitally with professionals you may never meet in person.

2. **Career Development:** Whether you're looking for your first job, aiming for a promotion, or exploring a career change, LinkedIn offers resources to help you grow professionally. You can find job postings, build your personal brand, and engage with content that aligns with your career interests.

3. **Learning and Skill Building:** LinkedIn is not just for job seekers and recruiters. The platform also serves as a learning hub with LinkedIn Learning, offering thousands of courses to help professionals upskill and stay competitive in their industries.

4. **Knowledge Sharing:** By publishing posts, articles, and multimedia content, LinkedIn users can establish themselves as thought leaders, sharing insights and fostering discussions on industry trends.

Who Uses LinkedIn?

LinkedIn caters to a diverse audience, including professionals at all levels of their careers, students, educators, and organizations. Here are the primary user groups:

- **Job Seekers:** Individuals looking for employment opportunities or career advancement use LinkedIn to showcase their skills and experience, connect with recruiters, and apply for jobs.

- **Employers and Recruiters:** Companies and hiring professionals use LinkedIn to find qualified candidates, post job openings, and promote their company culture.

- **Entrepreneurs and Business Owners:** LinkedIn helps small business owners and entrepreneurs build their personal brands, attract clients, and network with potential collaborators.

- **Students and Educators:** Students use LinkedIn to begin building their professional profiles, while educators connect with industry leaders and potential collaborators for academic projects.

- **Industry Leaders and Influencers:** These users leverage LinkedIn to share their expertise, build their reputation, and contribute to professional conversations.

LinkedIn's Global Reach

LinkedIn operates in over 200 countries and has more than 900 million members as of 2024. Its global presence makes it a valuable tool for professionals looking to expand their networks internationally. Whether you're a software engineer in Silicon Valley, a marketing manager in London, or a supply chain expert in Singapore, LinkedIn offers a platform to connect with like-minded individuals around the world.

Key Benefits of LinkedIn

To fully understand what LinkedIn is, it's important to recognize its benefits and how it can add value to your professional journey. Here are the most notable advantages:

1. **Building a Professional Online Presence:** LinkedIn acts as your online business card. It's a place where you can showcase your experience, skills, and achievements in a structured and visually appealing format. Unlike a traditional résumé, your LinkedIn profile is dynamic and can include rich media like videos, presentations, and certifications.

2. **Expanding Your Network:** LinkedIn makes it easy to connect with professionals in your industry or related fields. It also helps you stay in touch with past colleagues, classmates, and mentors, fostering relationships that might lead to future opportunities.

3. **Access to Job Opportunities:** One of the most significant advantages of LinkedIn is its extensive job board, which includes millions of listings worldwide. With features like job alerts and "Easy Apply," job seekers can efficiently apply for positions that match their qualifications.

4. **Learning and Development:** LinkedIn Learning offers courses on a wide range of topics, from technical skills like coding and graphic design to soft skills like communication and leadership. This feature makes LinkedIn a valuable resource for continuous learning and self-improvement.

5. **Establishing Thought Leadership:** Professionals can write articles, share insights, and participate in discussions to build their authority in their fields. This feature is particularly useful for consultants, entrepreneurs, and industry leaders.

How LinkedIn is Different from Other Platforms

While LinkedIn shares some similarities with other social platforms, it stands out for its professional focus. Here's how LinkedIn differs:

- **Professional Intent:** LinkedIn is designed for professional interactions, whereas platforms like Facebook and Instagram are primarily for personal or social engagement.

- **Content Relevance:** Most of the content on LinkedIn revolves around career development, industry insights, and professional achievements, making it a valuable tool for learning and networking.

- **Searchability:** LinkedIn profiles are optimized for search engines, allowing recruiters and other professionals to find you based on keywords in your profile.

- **Networking Opportunities:** Unlike traditional networking events, LinkedIn allows you to connect with people globally, expanding your reach and potential opportunities.

Conclusion

Understanding what LinkedIn is and its purpose is the first step in leveraging it effectively. It's more than just a platform for job seekers—it's a tool for lifelong career development, networking, and professional growth. Whether you're a recent graduate, a seasoned professional, or an entrepreneur, LinkedIn provides the resources you need to succeed in today's competitive job market.

1.1.2 Key Features and Benefits

LinkedIn is a professional social networking platform with a variety of features designed to help users connect, share, and grow in their careers or businesses. Understanding these key features and their benefits is essential for leveraging LinkedIn effectively. Let's break them down in detail.

1. Professional Profiles: Your Online Resume

One of LinkedIn's primary features is the professional profile. This acts as your online resume or portfolio, showcasing your work experience, skills, education, and accomplishments.

Benefits:

- **Visibility to Employers and Clients:** A complete LinkedIn profile can significantly improve your visibility to recruiters, hiring managers, and potential clients. When optimized with relevant keywords, your profile can appear in search results for specific roles or industries.

- **Showcase Your Achievements:** Unlike a traditional resume, LinkedIn allows you to expand on your accomplishments with multimedia such as videos, presentations, and certifications.

- **Customizable URL:** You can personalize your LinkedIn profile URL to make it easy to share and more professional for resumes, business cards, or email signatures.

2. Networking: Building Professional Connections

LinkedIn's core strength lies in its ability to facilitate professional networking. You can connect with colleagues, mentors, industry leaders, and even friends.

Benefits:

- **Expanding Your Network:** LinkedIn allows you to reach beyond your immediate circle, connecting you with 2nd- and 3rd-degree contacts through mutual connections. This is invaluable for expanding your professional reach.

- **Opportunities for Mentorship:** You can connect with experienced professionals in your field who may be willing to guide you or share industry insights.

- **Staying Updated:** By connecting with professionals, you gain access to their shared content, helping you stay informed about industry trends.

3. Job Search Tools: Accessing Opportunities

LinkedIn has robust tools specifically for job seekers. The platform allows you to browse job postings, research companies, and even apply directly.

Benefits:

- **Personalized Job Recommendations:** LinkedIn provides job suggestions based on your profile, skills, and interests.

- **"Easy Apply" Feature:** This function simplifies the application process by allowing users to submit their profile details directly for jobs without the need for lengthy forms.

- **Open to Work:** By enabling the "Open to Work" badge, you can signal to recruiters that you're actively seeking new opportunities.

4. Groups and Communities: Joining Conversations

LinkedIn Groups are spaces for professionals with shared interests to engage in discussions, ask questions, and share resources.

Benefits:

- **Knowledge Sharing:** Groups are excellent for learning from others in your industry or gaining insights into unfamiliar topics.

- **Expanding Influence:** Active participation in groups can establish you as a thought leader in your field.

- **Networking in Specific Niches:** Joining industry-specific groups helps you connect with professionals who share your interests or work in your target roles.

5. Content Creation and Sharing: Showcasing Expertise

LinkedIn allows you to create posts, share updates, and even publish long-form articles directly on the platform.

Benefits:

- **Building Your Personal Brand:** Sharing valuable content helps you establish your expertise and build credibility in your field.

- **Reaching a Wider Audience:** Your content can be seen by your network and beyond if others engage with or share your posts.

- **Staying Relevant:** Consistently creating and sharing content keeps you visible and top-of-mind for your network.

6. Endorsements and Recommendations: Validating Your Skills

LinkedIn includes features for others to endorse your skills or provide recommendations for your work.

Benefits:

- **Credibility:** Endorsements and recommendations act as social proof, reinforcing your expertise and trustworthiness.

- **Career Advancement:** Recruiters often look for candidates who have validated skills and glowing recommendations from colleagues or supervisors.

- **Professional Relationships:** Writing or receiving recommendations strengthens relationships within your network.

7. LinkedIn Learning: Upskilling Made Easy

LinkedIn Learning offers a vast library of courses across various fields, including business, technology, and personal development.

Benefits:

- **Continuous Learning:** Stay ahead of industry trends by acquiring new skills or certifications.

- **Certifications:** Courses often provide certificates of completion, which you can display on your profile to enhance your credibility.

- **On-Demand Access:** The courses are available anytime, making it convenient for busy professionals.

8. Analytics and Insights: Measuring Your Impact

LinkedIn provides analytics for your profile, posts, and articles.

Benefits:

- **Understanding Your Audience:** Analytics reveal who is viewing your profile, where they're from, and what roles they hold.

- **Tracking Engagement:** You can measure how your posts and articles are performing, helping you refine your content strategy.

- **Identifying Opportunities:** By analyzing who interacts with your content, you can identify potential networking or business opportunities.

9. Company Pages: Exploring Businesses

Company Pages on LinkedIn allow businesses to showcase their culture, job openings, and updates.

Benefits:

- **Researching Employers:** Learn about companies you're interested in, including their mission, values, and recent news.

- **Networking with Employees:** Identify employees of a company you're targeting and connect with them to gain insights or build relationships.

- **Following Industry Leaders:** Stay updated on trends by following thought-leading organizations.

10. Advanced Search Filters: Finding the Right People

LinkedIn's search tools allow you to locate professionals, companies, or jobs based on specific criteria.

Benefits:

- **Targeted Networking:** Use filters like location, industry, or job title to find the right connections.

- **Recruiter Insights:** Recruiters can use advanced filters to find candidates that match their specific needs.

- **Efficient Job Search:** Search for roles tailored to your skills and preferences, saving time and effort.

Conclusion

Understanding the key features and benefits of LinkedIn is the foundation for using the platform effectively. Whether you're building your network, searching for jobs, or establishing your personal brand, LinkedIn's tools offer endless possibilities for career growth. By utilizing these features, you can position yourself as a competitive professional in the modern workforce.

1.2 Creating Your Account

1.2.1 Signing Up for LinkedIn

Creating a LinkedIn account is the first step in building your professional online presence. In this section, we will walk you through each step of the sign-up process, providing detailed guidance to ensure that your account is set up correctly and efficiently. Whether you're a job seeker, student, or professional looking to network, LinkedIn is an invaluable tool for achieving your career goals. Let's dive into how you can create your LinkedIn account.

Step 1: Visit LinkedIn's Website or Download the App

LinkedIn is accessible via its website or mobile app, which is available for both iOS and Android devices. Follow these steps:

1. Open your preferred browser and visit www.linkedin.com.

2. Alternatively, go to the App Store (iOS) or Google Play Store (Android), search for "LinkedIn," and download the app.

3. Once the app is installed, open it to begin the registration process.

☞ **Tip:** If you plan to use LinkedIn frequently on the go, the app is highly convenient and user-friendly. However, the website offers a more comprehensive interface for setting up your account.

Step 2: Start the Registration Process

Once you've accessed LinkedIn, you'll see the option to sign up for a new account. Click the "Join Now" button or similar prompts on the homepage.

1. **Provide Your Basic Information:**

    o Enter your **first name** and **last name** in the respective fields. Use your full professional name to ensure credibility.

    o Input a **valid email address** that you frequently check. This will be used for account verification and important updates.

    o Create a **strong password** that is at least eight characters long and includes a mix of uppercase, lowercase, numbers, and special characters for security.

Make the most of your professional life

Email

Password

Show

☑ Remember me

By clicking Agree & Join or Continue, you agree to the LinkedIn
User Agreement, Privacy Policy, and Cookie Policy.

Agree & Join

or

G Continue with Google

▦ Continue with Microsoft

Already on LinkedIn? Sign in

Looking to create a page for a business? Get help

2. **Agree to LinkedIn's Terms of Service:**

- o Review the terms of service and privacy policy before proceeding.

- o Check the box to confirm that you agree to these terms, then click "Agree & Join."

☞ **Tip:** Use an email address that is professional and easy to recognize. If you don't have one, consider creating a new email specifically for your LinkedIn activity. Avoid using outdated or unprofessional email addresses.

Step 3: Verify Your Email Address

After completing the initial registration, LinkedIn will send a verification email to the address you provided. Follow these steps to verify your account:

1. Open the email from LinkedIn in your inbox.

2. Click the **verification link** within the email to confirm your address.

3. If you don't see the email, check your spam or junk folders.

☞ **Tip:** To ensure you receive future notifications from LinkedIn, add their email address to your safe sender list.

Step 4: Add Your Location and Job Preferences

To customize your LinkedIn experience, you'll need to provide some additional details during the sign-up process.

1. **Country and ZIP Code:**

   o Select your **country** from the dropdown menu.

   o Enter your **ZIP code** to help LinkedIn show you local job opportunities and networking events.

2. **Current Employment Status:**

   o Indicate whether you are a student, job seeker, employed professional, or business owner.

   o If you're a student, provide information about your school and expected graduation year.

Tip: Providing accurate information helps LinkedIn tailor its features to suit your career stage and goals.

Step 5: Choose Your Interests

LinkedIn will ask you about your interests to personalize your news feed and suggestions.

1. Select topics or industries that align with your career goals, such as "Technology," "Marketing," or "Finance."

2. Follow companies, thought leaders, or organizations that interest you.

☞ **Tip:** Choosing relevant interests ensures that your LinkedIn experience is customized to deliver valuable content and connections.

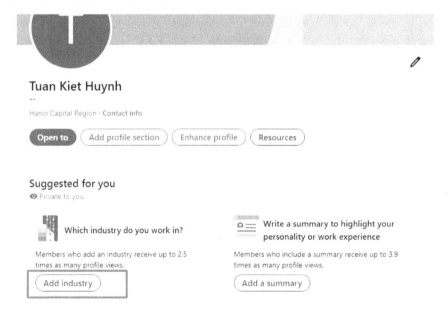

Step 6: Add a Professional Profile Photo

While this step can be skipped initially, it's highly recommended to upload a profile photo during the sign-up process. Profiles with photos receive significantly more views and connection requests.

1. Select a **clear, high-quality photo** of yourself.

   o Use a neutral or professional background.

o Dress in attire suitable for your industry.

2. Make sure your face is clearly visible, with the photo cropped to show your head and shoulders.

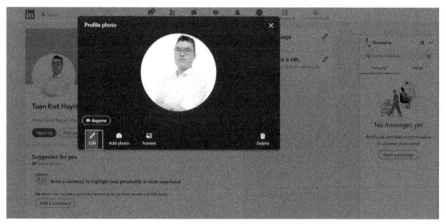

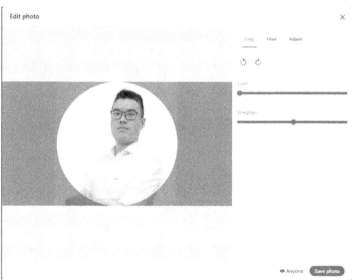

☞ **Tip:** Avoid selfies, group photos, or heavily edited pictures. Aim for a clean, professional look.

Step 7: Set a Strong Headline

Your headline is one of the first things people notice when they view your profile. LinkedIn will auto-fill this field based on your current role, but you can edit it later.

1. If you are currently employed, include your job title and company name (e.g., "Marketing Specialist at ABC Corp").

2. If you're a student or job seeker, highlight your career goals (e.g., "Aspiring Software Developer | Computer Science Graduate 2025").

☞ **Tip:** A compelling headline makes you stand out in search results and encourages others to view your profile.

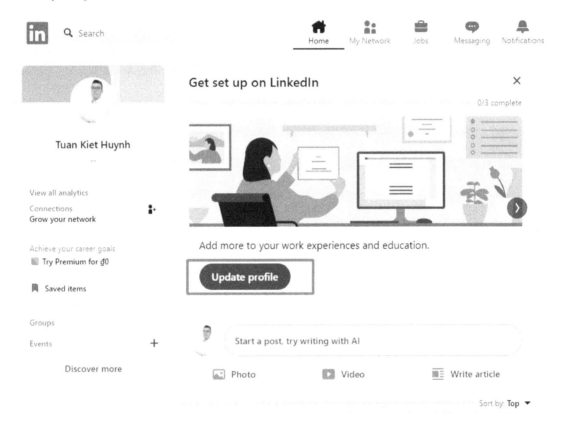

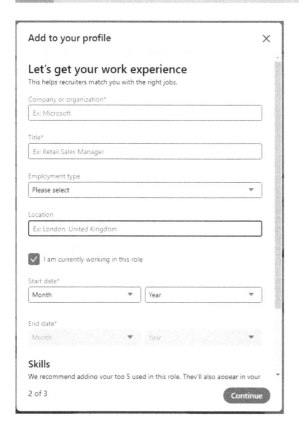

Step 8: Import Contacts (Optional)

LinkedIn may prompt you to import your email contacts to find people you already know on the platform.

1. Skip this step if you're not ready to connect immediately.

2. You can always return to this option later by navigating to the "My Network" tab.

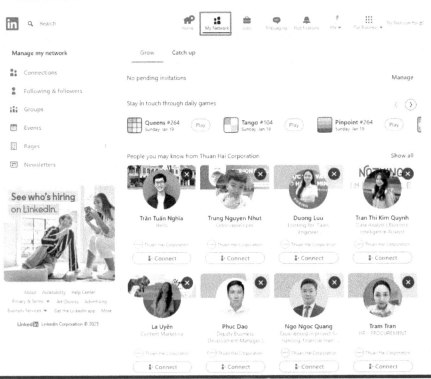

☞ **Tip:** While importing contacts can be helpful, take your time to curate your network thoughtfully.

Step 9: Complete the Onboarding Checklist

LinkedIn provides an onboarding checklist to help you set up your profile. This includes adding:

- Your education background.

- Skills and certifications.

- A personalized summary.

☞ **Tip:** Completing your profile during the initial setup will help you achieve "All-Star" profile status, which increases visibility in search results.

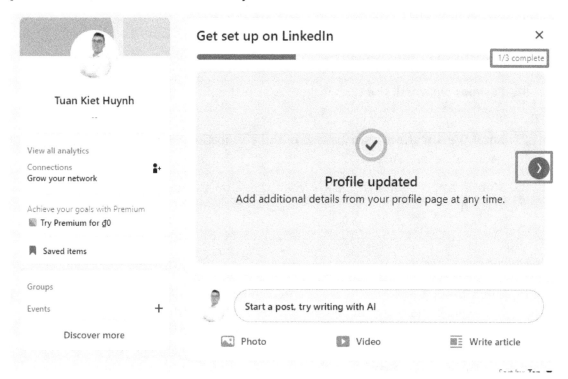

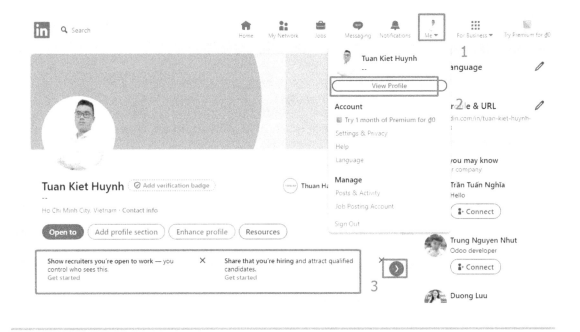

Common Troubleshooting Tips

1. **Forgot Password:** Use the "Forgot Password" link on the login page to reset it via email.

2. **Email Verification Issues:** Resend the verification email if you don't receive it within a few minutes.

3. **Mobile App Problems:** Ensure your app is up to date or switch to the desktop version.

Conclusion

By following these steps, you've successfully created your LinkedIn account! Take a moment to explore the platform and familiarize yourself with its features. Remember, a fully optimized profile is the key to maximizing LinkedIn's potential. In the next section, we'll guide you on navigating the LinkedIn interface, so you can confidently use the platform to achieve your goals.

1.2.2 Choosing the Right Membership (Free vs. Premium)

Join the millions of LinkedIn members using Premium to get ahead.

Millions of members use Premium

Start your free 1-month trial today. Cancel anytime. We'll send you a reminder 7 days before your trial ends.

Choose plan   90%

Career

Get hired and get ahead

✓ See jobs where you'll be a top applicant based on your skills

✓ Boost your chances of hearing back by marking your top choice jobs

✓ Directly message hiring managers with 5 InMail credits per month

Learn more

Business

Grow your network and find the right people

✓ Find key industry contacts and decision-makers with unlimited people browsing

✓ Grow your business with exclusive profile customizations and add a custom call to action

✓ Access exclusive growth and hiring trends with company insights

Learn more

Sales Navigator Core

Drive more leads and sales opportunities

✓ Find new leads with over 50 search filters

✓ Get conversations started with 50 InMail credits each per month

✓ Save time with smart lead recommendations and saved searches

Learn more

Recruiter Lite

Find and hire talent

✓ Find qualified candidates faster with 20+ advanced search filters

✓ Get more responses with 30 InMail credits per month

✓ Save time with daily candidate recommendations and search alerts

Learn more

When setting up your LinkedIn account, one of the most important decisions you will face is whether to use a **Free Account** or subscribe to one of LinkedIn's **Premium Memberships**. Both options have distinct advantages depending on your needs, goals, and how you plan to use the platform. This section provides an in-depth guide to help you make an informed choice.

Understanding LinkedIn Membership Tiers

LinkedIn offers several membership options that cater to different users, including job seekers, professionals looking to grow their networks, salespeople, recruiters, and businesses. Broadly, these are categorized into **Free Membership** and **Premium Memberships**, which include the following tiers:

- **LinkedIn Premium Career** (for job seekers)

- **LinkedIn Premium Business** (for professionals growing their network)

- **LinkedIn Sales Navigator** (for sales professionals)
- **LinkedIn Recruiter Lite** (for recruiters and hiring managers)

1. The Free LinkedIn Account: What It Offers

The **Free Membership** is an excellent starting point for beginners, offering a variety of tools and features. Here's what you can do with a free account:

Build and Maintain Your Profile

- Create a detailed LinkedIn profile with a professional photo, headline, summary, work experience, and skills.
- Display your achievements, certifications, and endorsements to showcase your expertise.
- Add links to portfolios, websites, or projects to highlight your work.

Network with Professionals

- Send up to **100 connection requests** per week to expand your professional network.
- Join **up to 100 LinkedIn Groups**, where you can interact with like-minded professionals.
- View profiles of other users in your **1st- and 2nd-degree connections** for free.

Job Search Features

- Access **LinkedIn Jobs** to search and apply for job postings.
- Save job alerts and monitor applications.

Content Engagement

- Post and share updates, articles, photos, and videos.
- Engage with others' posts through likes, comments, and shares.

Basic Insights

- View who has visited your profile (limited to the **last five viewers** in the past 90 days).

- Access limited information about profile viewers and limited insights into connections.

2. LinkedIn Premium Membership: What's Different?

Premium Membership adds advanced features designed to boost your profile visibility, enhance networking, and achieve specific career goals. Each premium tier offers a unique set of tools.

LinkedIn Premium Career

This plan is ideal for job seekers and professionals aiming to increase their visibility to recruiters. Key features include:

- **InMail Messages**: Send direct messages to people who are not your connections (up to **5 InMails per month**).

- **Who Viewed Your Profile**: Unlock the full list of everyone who viewed your profile in the past 90 days.

- **Job Insights**: Access detailed data about jobs, including company growth trends, salary insights, and job application statistics.

- **Applicant Status**: See how you rank among other applicants and get tips to stand out.

- **Learning Courses**: Unlimited access to LinkedIn Learning for skill development.

LinkedIn Premium Business

This plan suits professionals looking to grow their network and enhance their online presence. Key features include:

- **Unlimited People Browsing**: Access to profiles beyond your 2nd-degree connections.

- **Business Insights**: View expanded information about company pages and industry trends.

- **Enhanced Analytics**: Gain more insights into how people interact with your profile.

LinkedIn Sales Navigator

This tier is built for sales professionals who want to generate leads and build relationships. Features include:

- **Advanced Search Filters**: Refine searches based on criteria like company size, industry, and job title.

- **Lead Recommendations**: Get suggestions for potential leads based on your target audience.

- **InMail Credits**: Includes more InMails per month (starting at **20 messages**).

- **CRM Integration**: Sync LinkedIn with customer relationship management tools like Salesforce.

LinkedIn Recruiter Lite

Designed for recruiters and hiring managers, this plan helps with talent acquisition. Features include:

- **Recruiting Insights**: Gain access to talent pools and track candidates.

- **InMail Messages**: Send up to **30 InMails per month** to potential candidates.

- **Applicant Tracking**: Keep track of your hiring pipelines within LinkedIn.

3. Comparing Free and Premium Memberships

To help you decide whether to stick with the free version or upgrade to premium, here's a side-by-side comparison of key features:

Feature	Free Account	Premium Account
Profile Visibility	Limited (only 1st & 2nd degree)	Unlimited
InMail Messages	Not Available	5–30 per month (depending on plan)
Who Viewed Your Profile	Last 5 viewers only	Full list with detailed insights
Job Insights	Not Available	Available
LinkedIn Learning Access	Not Available	Unlimited
Advanced Search Filters	Basic Filters	Industry, Job Title, Company Size, etc.

Recruiter Analytics	Not Available	Detailed stats on job performance
Salary Insights	Limited	Detailed with benchmarking data

4. How to Decide: Free vs. Premium

Choosing the right plan depends on your goals and how you intend to use LinkedIn. Here's a quick guide:

Stick with Free If:

- You are new to LinkedIn and still learning the platform.

- Your goal is to create a professional profile and build a small network.

- You're looking for free tools to explore job opportunities.

Upgrade to Premium If:

- You're actively seeking a job and want access to **advanced job insights** and recruiter visibility.

- You're in a competitive field and need to **stand out among applicants**.

- You're a professional aiming to **expand your network** and gain insights into companies and industries.

- You want access to **LinkedIn Learning** to enhance your skills.

5. How to Upgrade to Premium

If you decide that Premium is the right choice for you, here's how to upgrade:

1. **Log into LinkedIn** and click on the "Try Premium for Free" button (usually available in your profile menu).

2. Choose a **plan** based on your goals (Career, Business, Sales Navigator, or Recruiter Lite).

3. Enter your **payment details** (LinkedIn often provides a free trial for the first month).

4. Start exploring Premium features immediately!

Conclusion

Choosing between a free and premium LinkedIn account is a critical step in leveraging the platform to its fullest potential. While the **Free Membership** provides robust tools for beginners, **Premium Membership** unlocks advanced features that can significantly enhance your career prospects. Assess your goals, start small, and consider upgrading when you're ready to take your LinkedIn experience to the next level.

1.3 Navigating the LinkedIn Interface

1.3.1 Home Page Overview

The LinkedIn Home Page is your central hub for engaging with your professional network, accessing updates, and discovering opportunities. Understanding its layout and features is essential for effectively navigating the platform and maximizing its potential. In this section, we will break down each element of the Home Page to help you navigate with ease and confidence.

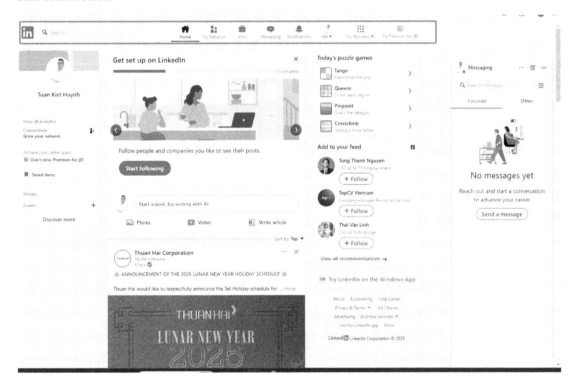

1. Understanding the Layout of the LinkedIn Home Page

The Home Page is the first thing you see after logging into your LinkedIn account. It's designed to provide quick access to essential updates, content from your network, and tools for professional engagement. Here's a detailed breakdown of its key sections:

1. **The Top Navigation Bar**: The top navigation bar is a constant feature across all LinkedIn pages. It contains several important tools and shortcuts:

   o **LinkedIn Logo**: Clicking on the LinkedIn logo in the top left corner will always return you to the Home Page. This is useful when you're exploring other areas of LinkedIn and need to quickly return to your feed.

   o **Search Bar**: The search bar is where you can look for people, companies, jobs, groups, and content. You can type in specific names, keywords, or phrases to find what you need. Advanced search filters, such as location and industry, help refine your search.

   o **Navigation Icons**: These icons lead to different sections of LinkedIn:

      ▪ **Home**: This icon brings you back to the Home Page.

      ▪ **My Network**: Displays your connections, connection requests, and suggested contacts.

      ▪ **Jobs**: Takes you to LinkedIn's job search section.

      ▪ **Messaging**: Opens your inbox for direct messages and chats.

      ▪ **Notifications**: Shows alerts about activity relevant to you, such as likes, comments, and connection requests.

      ▪ **Me**: Clicking on this icon shows your profile and account settings.

2. **The Feed**: The central portion of the Home Page is the feed, which displays updates and content shared by your network, companies you follow, and posts recommended by LinkedIn based on your activity. Key features include:

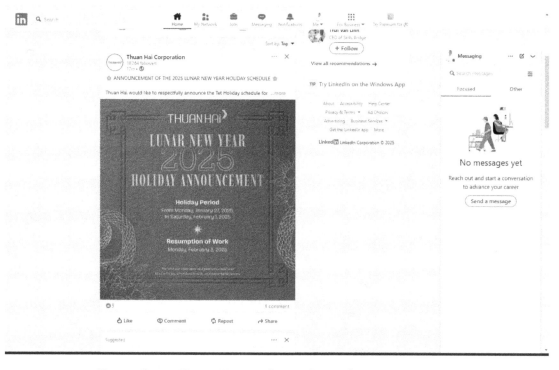

- ○ **Posts from Your Network**: Updates from your connections, such as articles, photos, videos, and professional achievements.

- ○ **Engagement Options**: You can like, comment, or share posts directly from your feed. Engaging with posts increases your visibility within your network.

- ○ **Sponsored Content**: Ads and promoted posts appear occasionally in your feed. These are typically marked as "Promoted" or "Sponsored" to differentiate them from regular updates.

- ○ **Show More Button**: LinkedIn allows you to expand content previews using the "Show More" option on longer posts.

3. **The Left Sidebar**: The left sidebar contains personalized information about your LinkedIn activity and shortcuts to key areas:

- **Profile Snapshot**: Displays your profile picture, headline, and the number of views or searches your profile has received. Clicking on it takes you directly to your profile.

- **Quick Links**: Links to sections like "My Items" (saved articles or jobs) and "Groups."

- **Who's Viewed Your Profile**: This metric allows you to see how many people have visited your profile recently, with more detailed insights available for premium users.

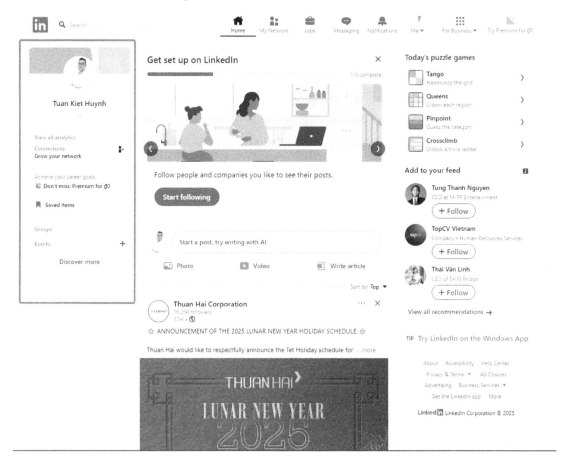

4. **The Right Sidebar**: The right sidebar offers additional tools and insights tailored to your interests:

- **LinkedIn News**: A curated list of trending news and articles relevant to your industry. Clicking on a headline opens the full article.

- **Suggested Connections**: Displays potential new connections based on your profile, current network, and shared interests.

- **Job Recommendations**: Suggested job postings tailored to your skills, experience, and preferences.

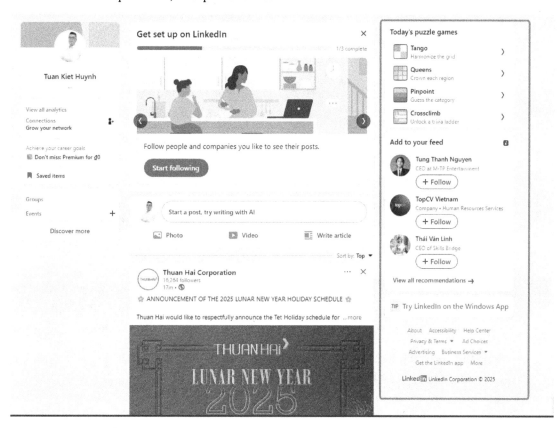

2. How to Use the Home Page Features Effectively

Now that we've explored the Home Page's layout, let's discuss how to use its features to maximize your LinkedIn experience.

Engaging with Your Feed

- **Interacting with Posts**: Regularly engage with posts by liking, commenting, or sharing to stay visible in your network. Meaningful comments, rather than generic ones, help you build stronger connections.

- **Posting Updates**: Use the "Start a post" option at the top of your feed to share updates, articles, or personal achievements. Keep your posts professional and relevant to your industry.

- **Customizing Your Feed**: LinkedIn allows you to hide posts or unfollow individuals whose content you don't find relevant, ensuring your feed remains valuable and focused.

Managing Notifications

- **Viewing Notifications**: Click on the notifications bell icon in the top navigation bar to view alerts about your connections' activities, such as work anniversaries or shared content.

- **Customizing Notifications**: Use the settings menu to manage the types of notifications you receive, ensuring they align with your professional goals.

Building Your Network from the Home Page

- **Accepting Connection Requests**: Regularly check the "My Network" icon for new requests. Always send a personalized thank-you message after accepting a request.

- **Sending Invitations**: Use the "People You May Know" section in the right sidebar to find and connect with individuals relevant to your field.

3. Tips for Beginners: Navigating with Confidence

To make the most of the LinkedIn Home Page, keep these best practices in mind:

- **Log in Regularly**: Aim to check LinkedIn at least a few times a week to stay updated on your network and opportunities.

- **Focus on Quality Engagement**: Instead of passively scrolling, actively engage with posts, share valuable insights, and contribute to discussions.

- **Use LinkedIn on Mobile**: Download the LinkedIn mobile app to access your Home Page on the go, ensuring you don't miss important updates.

- **Stay Organized**: Use features like bookmarks and saved items to keep track of posts, jobs, or articles you want to revisit later.

Conclusion

The LinkedIn Home Page is more than just a newsfeed; it's a dynamic workspace designed to help you connect, engage, and grow. By mastering its layout and using its features effectively, you can unlock new opportunities and take the first step toward building a strong professional presence.

1.3.2 Menu and Navigation Basics

Navigating LinkedIn's interface can initially feel overwhelming, but once you understand its layout, you'll be able to move around the platform efficiently and make the most of its features. This section provides a detailed guide to each menu item and explains how to use LinkedIn's navigation tools effectively.

Understanding the Main Menu

The main menu bar on LinkedIn is your gateway to all its features. Located at the top of the page on desktop (or as a collapsible menu on mobile), it includes key sections such as **Home**, **My Network**, **Jobs**, **Messaging**, **Notifications**, and **Me**. Each menu item is designed to help you manage specific aspects of your LinkedIn experience.

1. Home

- **Purpose**: The **Home** tab is your LinkedIn dashboard, where you can see updates from your connections, companies you follow, and groups you've joined.

- **What You'll See**:

- **News Feed**: A dynamic list of posts, articles, and updates from your network.

- **Start a Post**: A quick way to share updates, articles, photos, or videos with your network.

- **Suggestions**: LinkedIn often suggests people, companies, or content to follow based on your interests and activity.

- **Key Tips**:

  - Use the search bar at the top of the page to find people, companies, or jobs directly from the Home tab.

  - Interact with posts in your feed by liking, commenting, or sharing to boost engagement.

---

2. My Network

- **Purpose**: The **My Network** section focuses on building and maintaining your professional connections.

- **What You'll See**:

  - **Connection Requests**: View and accept (or ignore) pending invitations to connect.

  - **Suggestions**: LinkedIn recommends people you may know or might want to connect with, often based on shared industries, companies, or education.

  - **Manage Connections**: A complete list of your connections, which you can sort or search through.

- **Key Actions**:

  - Use the **Manage My Network** feature to see a summary of your connections, groups, and contacts.

  - Send personalized connection requests to make a positive impression.

  - Regularly check for new connection suggestions to expand your network strategically.

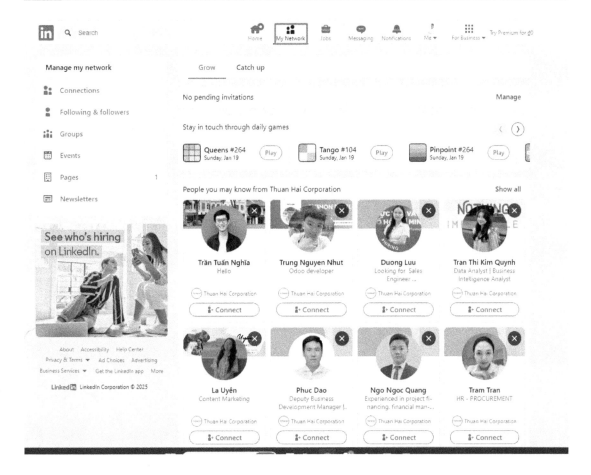

3. Jobs

- **Purpose**: The **Jobs** section helps you search for and apply to job opportunities.

- **What You'll See**:

    o **Job Search Bar**: Enter keywords, job titles, or locations to find relevant positions.

    o **Job Alerts**: Set up custom alerts to receive notifications about new opportunities that match your preferences.

    o **Applied Jobs**: Track the status of jobs you've applied for directly on LinkedIn.

- **Key Tips**:

  o Regularly update your job preferences to ensure LinkedIn suggests relevant openings.

  o Use the **Easy Apply** feature for quick applications with your LinkedIn profile.

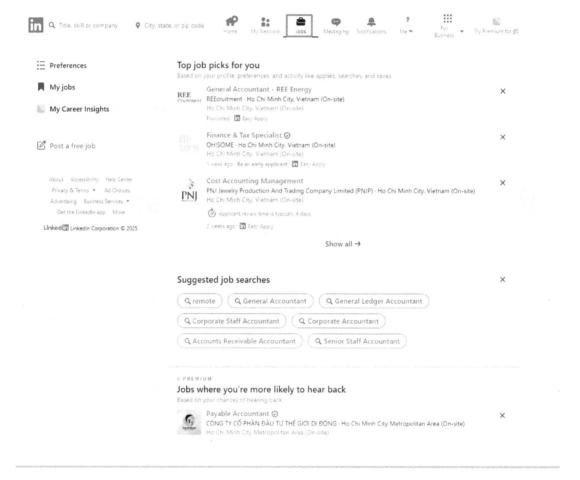

4. Messaging

- **Purpose**: The **Messaging** section allows you to communicate directly with your connections.

- **What You'll See**:

- o **Inbox**: A list of your conversations, including connection messages, recruiter inquiries, and networking discussions.

- o **Search Bar**: Find specific conversations by typing keywords or names.

- o **Smart Replies**: LinkedIn's automated suggestions for quick responses.

- **Key Actions**:

  - o Start conversations by clicking the **Compose Message** button.

  - o Use messaging to thank new connections, follow up after events, or explore job opportunities.

  - o Be professional and concise in your messages to make a good impression.

5. Notifications

- **Purpose**: The **Notifications** tab keeps you updated on activity relevant to your network.

- **What You'll See**:
    - Alerts about profile views, connection milestones, job changes, and post engagements.
    - Event invitations or reminders for webinars and virtual meetups.

- **Key Tips**:
    - Regularly check your notifications to stay informed about new opportunities and maintain relationships.
    - Customize your notification settings to prioritize alerts that matter most to you.

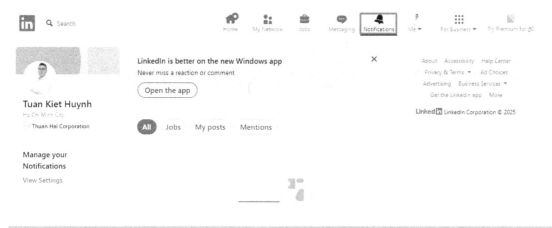

6. Me (Profile Settings)

- **Purpose**: The **Me** section is where you manage your LinkedIn profile and account settings.

- **What You'll See**:
    - **Profile View**: A snapshot of how your profile appears to others.

- o **Settings & Privacy**: Options to manage account security, visibility, and notifications.

- o **Activity Dashboard**: Insights into who's viewed your profile and what content you've shared.

- **Key Actions**:

  - o Edit your profile regularly to reflect your current skills and achievements.

  - o Review your privacy settings to control who can see your activity, connections, and personal information.

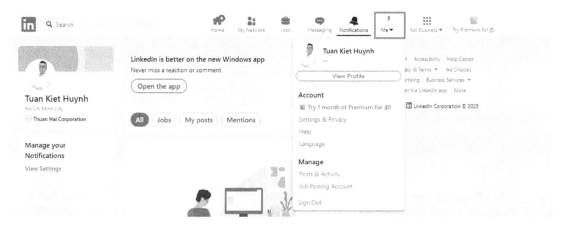

Additional Features in the Navigation Bar

7. Work (Grid Icon)

- **Purpose**: The **Work** icon, represented by a grid, provides access to additional LinkedIn tools and features.

- **What You'll See**:

  - o **LinkedIn Learning**: Online courses to develop new skills.

  - o **Post a Job**: Tools for hiring managers to find candidates.

  - o **Groups**: Communities based on shared interests or industries.

- **Key Tips**:

- o Use LinkedIn Learning to upskill in areas relevant to your career.

- o Explore groups to network with like-minded professionals.

Customizing Your Navigation Experience

LinkedIn allows you to tailor some aspects of the navigation to suit your needs:

1. **Reordering Tabs**: Drag and drop tabs to prioritize those you use most frequently.

2. **Hiding Tabs**: Certain tabs, like "Work," can be minimized if they're not relevant.

3. **Mobile vs. Desktop**: The layout on the LinkedIn app is slightly different but mirrors the core functionality. Familiarize yourself with both for a seamless experience.

Practical Tips for Efficient Navigation

- **Keyboard Shortcuts**: Use shortcuts (e.g., pressing / to focus on the search bar) to save time.

- **Search Bar Power**: The search bar is one of the most powerful tools. Use filters to find people, jobs, or content quickly.

- **Stay Organized**: Bookmark frequently visited sections or save searches for quicker access in the future.

With these navigation basics mastered, you're well on your way to becoming comfortable with LinkedIn's interface. The next chapter will guide you through crafting a standout profile that attracts attention and opportunities.

CHAPTER II
Crafting a Winning Profile

2.1 The Anatomy of a LinkedIn Profile

2.1.1 Profile Photo: Choosing a Professional Image

A LinkedIn profile photo is the first impression you make on recruiters, potential employers, or business connections. Your photo is a critical component of your profile, as it immediately communicates professionalism, approachability, and credibility. This section provides a comprehensive guide to choosing the right profile photo, from understanding its importance to practical tips for taking and selecting a great picture.

Why a Profile Photo Matters on LinkedIn

Your LinkedIn profile photo is not just an image; it is part of your personal brand. Here's why it matters:

- **First Impressions:** Studies show that people form opinions about you within seconds of seeing your profile photo. A professional photo can immediately convey that you are trustworthy and serious about your career.

- **Increased Profile Views:** Profiles with photos are 14 times more likely to be viewed than those without. Recruiters are more likely to click on a profile with a photo when browsing candidates.

- **Human Connection:** A friendly, confident photo makes your profile more relatable. People are more inclined to connect with someone they can visually identify with.

Key Characteristics of a Great LinkedIn Profile Photo

A great LinkedIn profile photo should follow these guidelines to ensure you present yourself in the best possible way:

1. **Professional Attire:**

   o   Dress as you would for an interview in your industry. For corporate roles, a formal suit or blouse works well, while more casual attire may be acceptable for creative industries.

   o   Avoid busy patterns, overly bright colors, or clothing with logos (unless it's part of your professional identity).

2. **Neutral Background:**

   o   Choose a clean, uncluttered background to keep the focus on you. A plain wall, office setting, or softly blurred outdoor background works well.

   o   Avoid busy, distracting environments like crowded cafes or messy rooms.

3. **Framing and Composition:**

   o   Your face should take up about 60% of the frame. This means cropping from the top of your head to just below your shoulders.

   o   Center yourself in the frame for a balanced composition.

4. **Facial Expression:**

   o   Aim for a natural, friendly smile. A smile communicates approachability and confidence.

   o   Avoid overly serious or staged expressions that may come across as uninviting.

5. **High-Quality Image:**

   o   Use a high-resolution photo that is not pixelated or blurry. A poorly taken photo can detract from your professionalism.

   o   Ensure proper lighting to avoid shadows or overexposure. Natural light is ideal.

Dos and Don'ts for Your Profile Photo

Dos:

- **Invest in Professional Photography:** If possible, hire a professional photographer who specializes in headshots. They can guide you on posing, lighting, and expression.

- **Test Multiple Options:** Take several photos in different outfits, angles, and lighting conditions. Review them and ask for feedback from trusted colleagues or friends.

- **Use Natural Light:** Outdoor or window lighting provides a soft, flattering effect on your face. Position yourself facing the light source for even illumination.

- **Keep it Updated:** Ensure your profile photo reflects your current appearance. Avoid using an outdated photo from several years ago.

Don'ts:

- **Avoid Group Photos:** Your profile photo should only feature you. Group photos or cropped images where other people are visible look unprofessional.

- **No Selfies:** Selfies, especially those taken in informal settings, lack the polish needed for LinkedIn.

- **Steer Clear of Filters:** Avoid heavy photo filters or editing that make you appear unnatural or overly airbrushed.

- **Don't Use Logos or Symbols:** Your photo should focus on you, not your company logo or any unrelated imagery.

Step-by-Step Guide to Taking the Perfect LinkedIn Photo

1. **Prepare Your Look:**

   o Groom yourself appropriately. Neatly styled hair, subtle makeup, and well-ironed clothes contribute to a polished appearance.

   o Avoid accessories or jewelry that may distract from your face.

2. **Choose the Right Location:**

- o Find a spot with ample natural light, such as near a window or in an outdoor setting during daytime.

- o If indoors, ensure the background is clean and professional.

3. **Set Up the Camera:**

- o Use a tripod or a stable surface to avoid shaky, uneven photos.

- o Use the rear camera of your smartphone or a DSLR camera for better quality.

4. **Position Yourself:**

- o Stand or sit with good posture, keeping your shoulders relaxed.

- o Face the camera directly or at a slight angle for a natural look.

5. **Take Multiple Shots:**

- o Experiment with different angles, smiles, and lighting conditions.

- o Review the photos and select the one where you look confident and approachable.

6. **Edit Sparingly:**

- o Use basic editing tools to adjust brightness, contrast, or crop the image.

- o Avoid excessive touch-ups that make your photo appear artificial.

Common Mistakes to Avoid

- **Over-Casual Attire:** Wearing casual clothing like t-shirts, tank tops, or hoodies can undermine your professionalism.

- **Distracting Backgrounds:** A cluttered background, like a kitchen or bedroom, can shift the focus away from you.

- **Overly Formal Expression:** A stiff or overly serious expression can make you seem unapproachable.

- **Ignoring Proportion:** A poorly cropped photo that cuts off your head or focuses too much on your torso looks awkward.

Examples of Effective LinkedIn Profile Photos

1. **Corporate Professional:**

   o Wearing a tailored suit with a neutral background and a confident smile.

2. **Creative Professional:**

   o Lightly casual attire with a softly blurred outdoor background and a warm, approachable expression.

3. **Freelancer/Entrepreneur:**

   o Business-casual attire with a relaxed yet professional posture in a co-working space or home office.

Reviewing and Updating Your Profile Photo

Your profile photo is not a "set it and forget it" feature. Review and update it periodically to reflect any changes in your appearance or career growth. Ideally, you should update your photo every 2–3 years or when you take on a significant career change.

Conclusion

A well-chosen LinkedIn profile photo can set the tone for how others perceive you on the platform. By following the guidelines and steps outlined in this section, you'll create an image that portrays professionalism, confidence, and approachability. Remember, your profile photo is the foundation of your LinkedIn presence—investing time and effort into getting it right is well worth it.

2.1.2 Headline: Crafting Your Personal Tagline

Your LinkedIn headline is one of the most critical elements of your profile. It's often the first thing people notice when they view your profile, appearing prominently beneath your name. Think of your headline as a personal tagline — a concise, impactful statement that defines who you are, what you do, and what you bring to the table. A well-crafted headline can make a powerful first impression, helping you stand out in a crowded professional landscape.

Why Your Headline Matters

Before diving into the steps to create an effective headline, let's discuss why it's so important:

1. **First Impressions:** Your headline is the first thing recruiters, potential employers, or connections see when they search for you or view your profile. It shapes their initial perception of you.

2. **Search Optimization:** LinkedIn uses keywords in your headline to rank you in search results. A strategic headline increases your visibility.

3. **Branding Opportunity:** Your headline is a chance to define yourself and communicate your unique value proposition.

Key Elements of an Effective LinkedIn Headline

To craft a compelling headline, include the following elements:

1. **Your Current Role or Goal:** Highlight your job title, profession, or career aspirations. For example, "Marketing Manager" or "Aspiring Data Scientist."

2. **Key Skills or Expertise:** Showcase your specialized skills or areas of expertise. For example, "Content Marketing Specialist | SEO Expert" or "Software Developer | Full-Stack Experience."

3. **Value Proposition:** Explain how you add value. For example, "Helping Businesses Drive Sales Through Data Analysis."

4. **Industry or Niche:** If applicable, mention your specific industry. For example, "Tech Enthusiast | SaaS Growth Strategist."

Step-by-Step Guide to Crafting Your Headline

Step 1: Understand Your Target Audience

- Ask yourself, "Who do I want to attract with my profile?"

- Consider your industry, role, and career goals. If you're a job seeker, think about the types of roles and employers you're targeting.

Step 2: Brainstorm Keywords

- Identify keywords that reflect your skills, roles, and industry.

- Examples of effective keywords include "Project Management," "Digital Marketing," "Java Developer," or "Customer Success."

Step 3: Define Your Unique Value Proposition

- What sets you apart? What impact do you make in your role?

- For example: "Helping companies save time with automated solutions" or "Transforming raw data into actionable business insights."

Step 4: Keep It Concise

- LinkedIn headlines have a 220-character limit, so every word matters.

- Aim for clarity and brevity without sacrificing important details.

Examples of Strong LinkedIn Headlines

Here are some examples tailored to different industries and roles:

For Job Seekers:

- "Aspiring Data Scientist | Skilled in Python, Machine Learning, and Statistical Analysis"

- "Marketing Graduate | Passionate About Brand Strategy and Social Media"

For Experienced Professionals:

- "Sales Manager | Driving Revenue Growth Through Customer-Centric Solutions"

- "Product Designer | Creating User-Centered Experiences in FinTech"

For Entrepreneurs:

- "Founder at XYZ Startup | Empowering Small Businesses with Digital Tools"

- "Startup Mentor | Helping Entrepreneurs Build Scalable Businesses"

For Freelancers:

- "Freelance Content Writer | Specializing in SEO and B2B Copywriting"

- "Graphic Designer | Transforming Brands with Creative Visuals"

Tips for an Attention-Grabbing Headline

1. **Use Action Words:** Incorporate dynamic verbs like "driving," "creating," "transforming," or "empowering." Action-oriented language conveys confidence and proactivity.

2. **Highlight Key Achievements:** If space permits, mention a notable accomplishment. For example, "Award-Winning Journalist | Published in Forbes and The Guardian."

3. **Avoid Overused Phrases:** Generic statements like "Hardworking Professional" or "Seeking Opportunities" lack specificity. Focus on what makes you unique.

4. **Leverage Industry Jargon:** Use relevant terminology to demonstrate expertise in your field. For example, a digital marketer might mention "PPC Campaigns" or "Google Ads Certified."

5. **Focus on the Reader:** Frame your headline from the perspective of your audience. Instead of saying, "Experienced Accountant," you could write, "Helping Small Businesses Optimize Their Financial Processes."

6. **Keep It Professional:** While creativity is welcome, ensure your tone remains professional and appropriate for LinkedIn's audience.

How to Test and Optimize Your Headline

1. **Ask for Feedback:** Share your draft headline with trusted colleagues or mentors to get their perspective.

2. **Use LinkedIn Search:** Search for profiles similar to yours and see which headlines stand out.

3. **Experiment with Variations:** Try different combinations of keywords, skills, and value propositions. Monitor your profile views to determine what resonates.

4. **Utilize Analytics:**Check LinkedIn's dashboard to see how many people are viewing your profile. An increase in visibility could indicate that your headline is working.

Common Mistakes to Avoid

1. **Vague or Generic Headlines:** Avoid headlines like "Unemployed" or "Looking for Work." Focus on skills and value instead.

2. **Keyword Stuffing:** Using too many unrelated keywords can make your headline confusing and less impactful.

3. **Outdated Information:** Ensure your headline reflects your current role or aspirations.

4. **Ignoring the Audience:** Your headline should be tailored to appeal to your target audience, whether it's recruiters, clients, or collaborators.

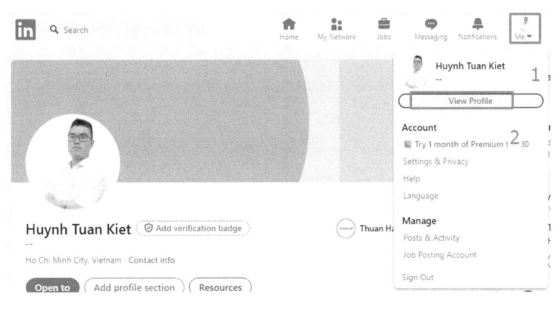

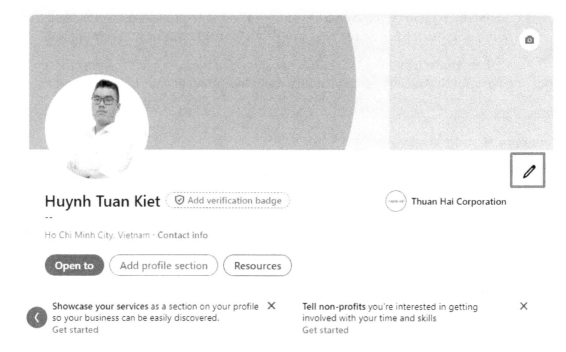

Huynh Tuan Kiet ⊘ Add verification badge

--

Ho Chi Minh City, Vietnam · Contact info

[**Open to**] [Add profile section] [Resources]

Showcase your services as a section on your profile ✕
so your business can be easily discovered.
Get started

Tell non-profits you're interested in getting ✕
involved with your time and skills
Get started

Thuan Hai Corporation

Exercise: Write Your Own Headline

Take 10 minutes to draft three versions of your LinkedIn headline using the tips above. Compare them and choose the one that best reflects your goals and skills. Here's a simple formula to get started:

[Current Role or Goal] | [Key Skills or Expertise] | [Value Proposition]

For example:

- "Marketing Specialist | Social Media and Content Expert | Driving Engagement for Global Brands"

- "Customer Service Manager | Passionate About Delivering Exceptional Experiences"

By crafting a well-thought-out LinkedIn headline, you're taking a crucial step toward building a professional online presence that attracts opportunities and connections. Remember, your headline is more than just a title — it's your story, your value, and your brand in one concise line.

2.2 Writing an Impactful Summary

2.2.1 Structuring Your Summary

Your LinkedIn summary is one of the most important parts of your profile. It provides an opportunity to showcase your personality, skills, achievements, and career goals in a way that engages your audience. A well-written summary can capture the attention of recruiters, employers, and potential collaborators. Below, we'll explore a detailed guide on how to structure your LinkedIn summary effectively.

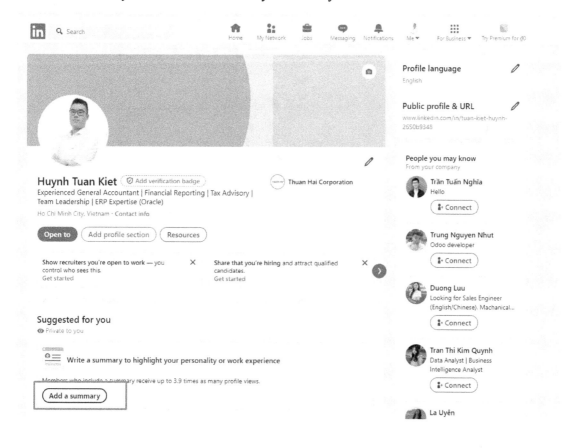

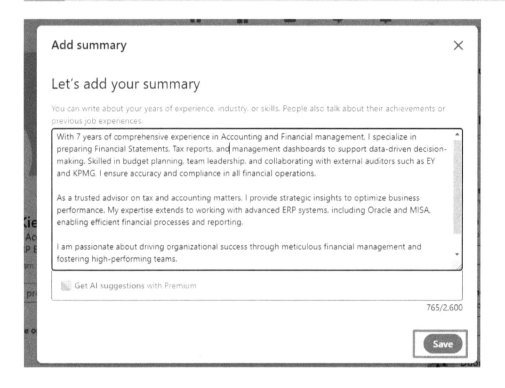

Why is a LinkedIn Summary Important?

Before diving into the structure, it's essential to understand the importance of this section. Unlike the headline or job descriptions, the summary allows you to go beyond the basics and tell your professional story. It's a space to explain what makes you unique, what you bring to the table, and what you're looking for in your career.

A strong summary should:

- Highlight your key strengths and achievements.

- Show your personality and professionalism.

- Include relevant keywords for LinkedIn's search algorithms.

- Provide a clear call to action.

Step 1: Start with a Captivating Opening Statement

The first sentence of your summary is critical. It's the hook that determines whether someone continues reading or moves on to another profile. A compelling opening should be attention-grabbing, concise, and relevant to your professional identity.

Tips for Crafting Your Opening Statement:

- Use a strong and confident tone.
  Example: *"As a marketing professional with over five years of experience, I specialize in crafting data-driven campaigns that drive measurable results."*

- Highlight a key strength or achievement.
  Example: *"I've helped companies increase their social media engagement by 200% through strategic content planning and audience analysis."*

- Reflect your personality or passion.
  Example: *"I'm passionate about helping startups scale their operations through innovative supply chain strategies."*

What to Avoid:

- Starting with generic phrases like "I'm a hardworking professional."

- Writing in a way that doesn't reflect your unique value.

Step 2: Outline Your Career Highlights

After hooking the reader, transition into the main body of your summary by showcasing your professional achievements and expertise. This is where you provide evidence of your skills and experience.

Key Elements to Include:

1. **Experience and Skills:** Mention your current role and summarize your key responsibilities. Highlight the skills you've mastered in this role.
   Example: *"Currently, I work as a software engineer at XYZ Corp., where I design and implement scalable web applications. My expertise includes Python, JavaScript, and cloud-based solutions."*

2. **Achievements and Results:** Quantify your accomplishments whenever possible to demonstrate your impact.

Example: *"In my previous role, I reduced system downtime by 30% by streamlining backend processes."*

3. **Specialization or Industry Focus:** Share your area of expertise or niche within your industry.

   Example: *"I specialize in cybersecurity and have a strong track record of mitigating risks for global enterprises."*

4. **Unique Value Proposition:** Explain what sets you apart from others in your field. Example: *"What makes me unique is my ability to bridge the gap between technical teams and business stakeholders, ensuring projects are delivered on time and within budget."*

Step 3: Show Your Personality and Passion

Your summary isn't just a list of skills and accomplishments. It's also an opportunity to show your personality and what drives you professionally. This helps you connect with your audience on a deeper level.

Questions to Answer:

- Why do you love what you do? Example: *"I find immense satisfaction in transforming complex data into actionable insights that help businesses thrive."*

- What are you passionate about in your industry? Example: *"I'm passionate about sustainable architecture and creating designs that minimize environmental impact."*

- How do you approach your work or challenges? Example: *"I approach every project with curiosity, a collaborative mindset, and a focus on delivering excellence."*

Pro Tip: Consider adding a personal touch, such as a hobby or interest, that aligns with your professional identity. For instance, a data analyst could mention their love for puzzles or problem-solving.

Step 4: Include a Call to Action

A great LinkedIn summary ends with a clear call to action. This encourages your audience to take the next step, whether that's connecting with you, visiting your portfolio, or reaching out about opportunities.

Examples of Effective Calls to Action:

- *"Let's connect! Feel free to send me a message if you'd like to discuss collaboration opportunities."*

- *"Looking for a dynamic marketer to join your team? I'd love to chat!"*

- *"Check out my portfolio at [insert link] to see examples of my work."*

What to Avoid:

- Being vague or not including a call to action at all.

- Using overly aggressive language like "Hire me now!"

Step 5: Use Keywords Strategically

Your summary plays a significant role in LinkedIn's search algorithms. Recruiters and employers often search for candidates using specific keywords related to skills, industries, and job roles.

Tips for Keyword Optimization:

- Identify keywords relevant to your industry and role (e.g., "project management," "data analysis," or "content strategy").

- Naturally integrate these keywords throughout your summary.

- Avoid keyword stuffing, which can make your summary feel unnatural.

Example of Keyword Integration: *"As a certified project manager (PMP), I specialize in leading cross-functional teams to deliver enterprise-level solutions. My expertise includes Agile methodologies, risk management, and stakeholder communication."*

Step 6: Keep it Concise and Well-Organized

While LinkedIn allows up to 2,600 characters for the summary, it's important to strike a balance between detail and readability. Break your text into short paragraphs or use bullet points to make it easy to scan.

Best Practices for Formatting:

- Limit paragraphs to 2-3 sentences.

- Use bullet points for key achievements or skills.

- Avoid large blocks of text.

Final Example: A Well-Structured LinkedIn Summary

Here's a sample summary based on the steps above:

"As a marketing strategist with over 8 years of experience, I help brands connect with their audiences through data-driven campaigns and innovative storytelling. My expertise lies in content marketing, SEO, and social media management, and I've successfully increased client engagement by an average of 40% year-over-year.

Currently, I lead a dynamic team at XYZ Agency, where we've launched award-winning campaigns for global brands. I'm passionate about staying ahead of industry trends and leveraging analytics to drive impactful results.

Let's connect! Whether you're looking to collaborate on a project or share insights about the latest marketing trends, feel free to send me a message."

Example for Structuring Your Summary

Here is an example of a well-structured LinkedIn summary following the steps provided:

Opening Statement: Captivating and Relevant

"As a financial analyst with 7+ years of experience, I specialize in uncovering insights from complex datasets to drive strategic business decisions."

Career Highlights: Showcasing Experience and Achievements

"Currently, I work at ABC Corp., where I lead a team of analysts in developing forecasting models that have improved the company's financial planning accuracy by 25%. Previously, I

worked at XYZ Bank, where I managed investment portfolios worth over $20 million and achieved an average return on investment (ROI) of 12% annually.

My expertise includes financial modeling, data visualization, and corporate budgeting. I am proficient in using tools such as Excel, Tableau, and Python to deliver actionable insights. I thrive in high-pressure environments and am committed to delivering results that exceed expectations."

Personality and Passion: Adding a Human Touch

"Beyond the numbers, I am passionate about mentoring junior analysts and fostering a collaborative team culture. I believe that clear communication and continuous learning are key to success in the financial sector. I take pride in helping businesses not only meet but exceed their financial goals."

Call to Action: Encouraging Engagement

"Let's connect! If you're looking for a dedicated financial professional to support your organization's growth, or if you'd like to discuss the latest trends in financial analytics, feel free to reach out. You can also view my portfolio at [insert portfolio link]."

Why This Example Works:

1. **The opening sentence grabs attention** by immediately highlighting the professional's expertise and unique value.

2. **The career highlights are detailed and quantified,** providing specific achievements and skills that demonstrate value.

3. **Personality shines through** in the section about mentoring and passion, making the summary feel relatable and authentic.

4. **The call to action is clear and inviting,** encouraging others to connect or explore the professional's work.

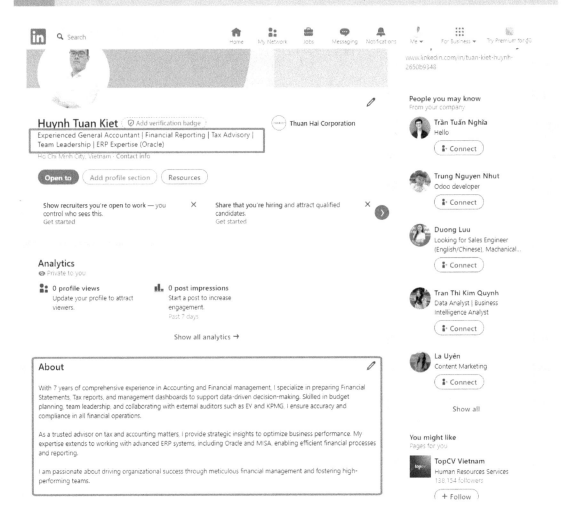

2.2.2 Highlighting Your Skills and Achievements

Your LinkedIn summary is one of the most important sections of your profile. It's a powerful tool to showcase your unique skills, accomplishments, and professional personality in a concise yet compelling manner. This section serves as your personal pitch to potential employers, clients, or professional connections. In this guide, we'll explore step-by-step how to effectively highlight your skills and achievements in your LinkedIn summary to maximize its impact.

1. Understand the Purpose of Your Summary

Before diving into writing, it's crucial to understand the purpose of this section:

- **Tell Your Story:** The summary is your opportunity to introduce yourself in your own words. It provides a narrative about who you are and what you bring to the table.

- **Showcase Your Value:** Employers and recruiters want to know how you can solve their problems or meet their needs. Use this space to explain the unique value you offer.

- **Encourage Action:** A well-written summary inspires readers to connect with you, learn more about your profile, or reach out with opportunities.

2. Identify Key Skills and Achievements to Highlight

Start by brainstorming your key skills and achievements. These should align with your career goals and the expectations of your target audience. Here's how to identify them:

- **Review Job Descriptions:** Look at job listings in your field and identify common skills or qualifications that employers seek. Highlight the ones you possess.

- **List Your Strengths:** Make a list of hard skills (technical abilities) and soft skills (interpersonal abilities) that you excel in. Examples might include data analysis, project management, leadership, or communication.

- **Consider Your Accomplishments:** Think about measurable achievements from your career. Examples include exceeding sales targets, leading successful projects, or earning industry certifications.

Pro Tip: Use the STAR method (Situation, Task, Action, Result) to frame your achievements. This ensures you provide context and show results. For instance: *"Increased sales revenue by 25% in six months by redesigning the customer acquisition strategy and training the sales team."*

3. Craft a Captivating Opening Statement

The first few lines of your summary are critical. These lines appear as a preview before someone clicks "See more," so they need to grab attention.

- **Use a Hook:** Start with a compelling statement, a powerful question, or an engaging fact about yourself. For example:

  "As a digital marketing strategist, I thrive on creating campaigns that drive measurable results and connect brands with their audiences."

- **Highlight Your Expertise:** Immediately mention your profession, expertise, or unique selling point.

4. Showcase Your Skills

To highlight your skills effectively, follow these tips:

- **Prioritize Relevant Skills:** Focus on the skills that are most relevant to your current career goals or target audience.

- **Incorporate Keywords:** Use industry-specific keywords throughout your summary to improve your profile's visibility in LinkedIn search results.

- **Provide Examples:** Don't just list your skills—showcase how you've applied them. For example:

  "My expertise in financial analysis and forecasting has enabled me to help organizations reduce costs by 20% through data-driven decision-making."

5. Highlight Your Achievements

Achievements are critical to demonstrating your value. Here's how to make them stand out:

- **Quantify Your Accomplishments:** Use numbers, percentages, or specific metrics whenever possible. For example:

  "Successfully led a cross-functional team of 15 members to complete a product launch 30% ahead of schedule, resulting in $2 million in additional revenue."

- **Showcase Leadership and Initiative:** Mention instances where you took the lead, solved a challenging problem, or implemented innovative solutions.

- **Include Recognitions or Awards:** Highlight any awards, certifications, or recognitions that set you apart. For example:

"Recipient of the XYZ Award for Excellence in Project Management, 2023."

6. Use a Professional Yet Personal Tone

Your summary should reflect your personality while maintaining professionalism.

- **Write in the First Person:** Use "I" statements to make the summary feel personal and authentic.

- **Balance Professionalism and Friendliness:** Avoid overly formal language but maintain a professional tone. For example:

  "I'm passionate about leveraging technology to create impactful business solutions."

7. Structure Your Summary for Readability

Recruiters and professionals skim profiles, so structure your summary to make it easy to read:

- **Use Short Paragraphs:** Break up text into paragraphs of 2-3 sentences.

- **Include Bullet Points:** Use bullet points to highlight key skills or achievements. For example:

  Key Highlights:

  - *Increased client retention by 40% through improved customer service initiatives.*

  - *Developed and implemented a marketing strategy that resulted in a 30% boost in website traffic.*

- **Incorporate Headings or Subheadings:** Use simple headings like *"Key Skills"* or *"Notable Achievements"* to organize content.

8. Tailor Your Summary to Your Audience

Customize your summary based on your target audience:

- **Job Seekers:** Focus on how your skills and achievements align with the roles you're pursuing.

- **Entrepreneurs or Freelancers:** Highlight your services, expertise, and the value you provide to clients.

- **Students or Recent Graduates:** Emphasize transferable skills, academic achievements, and your enthusiasm for learning.

9. Include a Call to Action

Conclude your summary with a clear call to action. Encourage readers to connect with you, visit your website, or send you a message. Examples include:

- *"Feel free to connect with me if you're looking for a results-driven marketing professional."*

- *"I'm always excited to discuss new opportunities and collaborations. Let's connect!"*

10. Example of a Complete LinkedIn Summary

Here's an example of a strong LinkedIn summary:

"As a results-oriented project manager with over 8 years of experience in the technology sector, I specialize in leading cross-functional teams to deliver complex projects on time and within budget. My expertise in agile methodologies, resource planning, and risk management has allowed me to drive a 25% improvement in team efficiency across multiple projects.

Key Highlights:

- *Led a $5 million software development project, achieving a 20% cost reduction through efficient resource allocation.*

- *Developed and implemented a new onboarding process, reducing employee turnover by 15% in the first year.*

I'm passionate about leveraging technology to solve business challenges and would love to connect with professionals who share my enthusiasm for innovation and growth. Let's collaborate!"

By following these steps, you can craft a LinkedIn summary that effectively showcases your skills and achievements while leaving a lasting impression on your audience. Would you like to expand further on any section?

Example Summaries for "Highlighting Your Skills and Achievements"

Here are a few examples of LinkedIn summaries tailored to different professions and career stages. Each example effectively highlights skills, achievements, and professional value:

1. Example for a Marketing Professional

"As a passionate digital marketer with over 5 years of experience, I specialize in creating data-driven campaigns that drive results. My expertise lies in SEO strategy, social media management, and content marketing. Over the years, I've helped businesses increase website traffic by up to 60% and achieve a 40% growth in lead generation through optimized campaigns.

Key Highlights:

- *Developed a content marketing strategy for a SaaS company that boosted blog traffic by 200% in six months.*

- *Managed a $100,000 annual advertising budget, achieving a 25% reduction in cost per lead.*

- *Launched a social media campaign that generated 1 million organic impressions in 30 days.*

I thrive on using analytics to inform strategy and am always seeking innovative ways to engage audiences and build brand loyalty. Let's connect to discuss how I can help your business grow!"

2. Example for an IT Professional

"As an experienced IT specialist with over 8 years of expertise in network infrastructure and cybersecurity, I am committed to delivering reliable, secure, and efficient IT solutions. I have

successfully led projects ranging from enterprise-level network upgrades to implementing advanced security protocols for global organizations.

Key Highlights:

- *Designed and deployed a company-wide network infrastructure upgrade, reducing downtime by 50%.*

- *Conducted cybersecurity training for 200+ employees, reducing phishing incidents by 30%.*

- *Led the integration of cloud-based systems, increasing operational efficiency by 40%.*

With a passion for problem-solving and staying ahead of the latest technology trends, I'm eager to connect with IT leaders and businesses looking to enhance their tech capabilities."

3. Example for a Recent Graduate

"As a recent graduate with a degree in Business Administration from XYZ University, I am eager to apply my academic knowledge and internship experiences to the corporate world. During my studies, I honed my skills in financial analysis, market research, and project management through coursework and real-world projects.

Key Highlights:

- *Completed a six-month internship at ABC Corporation, where I assisted in preparing financial reports and identifying cost-saving opportunities, resulting in a 10% expense reduction.*

- *Led a team of five students in a business simulation project, achieving first place by increasing simulated revenue by 25%.*

- *Conducted market research for a local startup, helping refine its target audience strategy and increasing sales by 15%.*

I am excited to bring my analytical mindset and collaborative spirit to a dynamic organization. Let's connect to explore opportunities!"

4. Example for a Healthcare Professional

"With over 10 years of experience as a registered nurse, I have dedicated my career to providing compassionate, patient-centered care in fast-paced medical environments. My strengths include acute care management, team leadership, and patient education.

Key Highlights:

- *Managed a 12-bed ICU unit, leading a team of 15 nurses and improving patient recovery rates by 20%.*

- *Developed a patient education program for chronic illness management, which increased patient compliance by 30%.*

- *Received the XYZ Healthcare Excellence Award for outstanding patient care in 2022.*

I am passionate about improving healthcare outcomes through education and innovation. If you're looking to connect with a dedicated healthcare professional, feel free to reach out!"

5. Example for a Freelance Graphic Designer

"As a freelance graphic designer with over 6 years of experience, I specialize in creating compelling visual content that tells a story and captivates audiences. My portfolio includes projects for startups, non-profits, and established brands across a variety of industries.

Key Highlights:

- *Designed a branding package for a tech startup that increased customer engagement by 50%.*

- *Created marketing collateral for a non-profit fundraising campaign that raised $500,000 in donations.*

- *Delivered 100+ successful projects on tight deadlines with a 99% client satisfaction rate.*

With a keen eye for detail and a passion for creative storytelling, I'm always excited to collaborate on new projects. Let's connect and create something amazing!"

6. Example for an Entrepreneur

"As the founder and CEO of ABC Startup, I am passionate about leveraging technology to solve real-world problems. With a background in software engineering and business strategy, I

have led our company from a small idea to a venture-backed enterprise serving thousands of users globally.

Key Highlights:

- *Secured $2 million in seed funding within 12 months of launching the business.*

- *Launched a SaaS product that increased productivity for small businesses by 35%.*

- *Built and led a diverse team of 20 professionals across 3 continents.*

I'm committed to fostering innovation and collaboration in the tech space. Let's connect to discuss opportunities to partner or share insights!"

Tips for Writing Your Own Summary

- **Tailor the Tone and Content:** Adjust the language and focus of your summary to match your industry and target audience.

- **Be Honest and Authentic:** Avoid exaggeration; instead, focus on genuine strengths and accomplishments.

- **Edit and Revise:** Keep your summary concise (200–300 words), proofread for grammar, and ensure clarity.

2.3 Adding Professional Experience

2.3.1 Detailing Your Work History

Your LinkedIn profile's **Experience section** is one of the most critical areas for showcasing your professional background, skills, and achievements. A well-detailed work history not only demonstrates your qualifications but also helps recruiters and potential collaborators understand your journey, strengths, and potential. Here's a detailed guide on how to effectively document your work history:

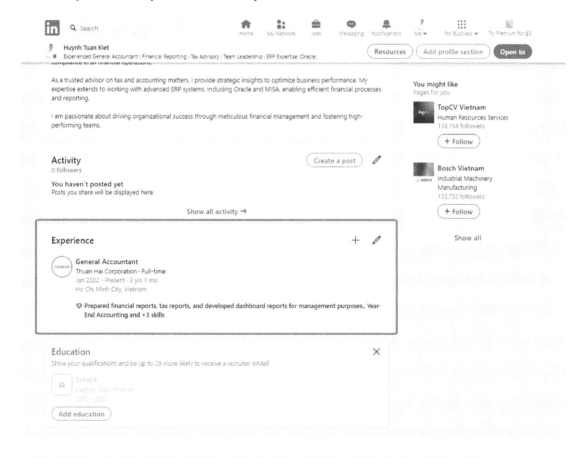

1. Understanding the Importance of Work History on LinkedIn

Your work history is more than just a chronological list of jobs—it's a marketing tool that communicates your value to employers and industry peers. When detailing your work history, keep in mind the following:

- **Showcase Your Career Path:** Highlight your growth, skills, and contributions over time.

- **Optimize for Recruiters:** Include keywords relevant to your industry to ensure your profile appears in recruiter searches.

- **Demonstrate Credibility:** Provide concrete examples of your achievements to establish trust and authority in your field.

2. Structuring Your Work Experience Entries

Each position in your work history should include the following key elements:

- **Job Title:** Be specific and accurate, reflecting your responsibilities.

  o Example: Instead of "Manager," use "Digital Marketing Manager" or "Project Manager – IT Infrastructure."

- **Company Name:** Include the official name of the organization.

- **Location:** Add the city and country where the role was based. If the role was remote, indicate it with "Remote."

- **Employment Dates:** Use the format "Month, Year – Month, Year" to specify the timeline. If you are still in the role, write "Present."

- **Responsibilities and Achievements:** This is the most critical part of each entry. Use bullet points to organize information, making it easy to read.

3. Writing Clear and Impactful Descriptions

When describing your roles and responsibilities, focus on clarity, relevance, and impact. Here's how to write strong descriptions:

a. Use Action-Oriented Language

Start each bullet point with a strong action verb to highlight what you accomplished. Examples include:

- "Led," "Implemented," "Developed," "Designed," "Managed," "Optimized."

b. Quantify Your Achievements

Whenever possible, include metrics and data to demonstrate the impact of your work. For example:

- Instead of: "Increased sales through marketing campaigns."

- Use: "Increased sales by 25% within six months by designing and implementing targeted email campaigns."

c. Highlight Skills and Tools

Incorporate relevant skills, software, and tools you used in your role. This not only highlights your technical abilities but also improves your profile's searchability. For example:

- "Utilized Salesforce to manage a client database of over 2,000 accounts, increasing retention rates by 15%."

d. Balance Responsibilities and Achievements

Provide a mix of your day-to-day tasks and the significant accomplishments you achieved in the role. Avoid listing every single responsibility and instead focus on the most impactful.

- Example of balance:
  - **Responsibility:** "Managed a team of five customer support specialists to ensure timely issue resolution."
  - **Achievement:** "Reduced average response time by 30% through workflow optimization and training programs."

4. Tailoring Your Experience for Your Career Goals

Your LinkedIn profile should reflect your current career goals. Here's how to tailor your work history to align with your aspirations:

a. Prioritize Relevant Roles

If you've had a long career with multiple roles, highlight the ones most relevant to your target industry or role. You can briefly summarize less relevant positions in one line (e.g., "Earlier roles include administrative positions at XYZ Corporation and ABC Inc.").

b. Use Industry-Specific Keywords

Incorporate terminology commonly used in your desired field. Research job descriptions for roles you are interested in and integrate those keywords into your experience descriptions.

c. Emphasize Transferable Skills

If you're transitioning into a new industry or role, focus on transferable skills such as leadership, problem-solving, or project management.

5. Common Mistakes to Avoid

Even a well-crafted experience section can lose its effectiveness if it includes common errors. Here are some pitfalls to watch out for:

a. Being Too Vague

Avoid generic descriptions like "Handled daily tasks" or "Responsible for managing a team." These statements don't provide value or insight into your contributions.

b. Including Irrelevant Information

Don't overload your profile with irrelevant details. Focus on roles, responsibilities, and achievements that align with your career goals.

c. Leaving Gaps Unexplained

If you have gaps in your work history, briefly explain them in your profile summary or descriptions. For instance:

- "Took a six-month career break to pursue professional certifications in digital marketing."

d. Using Unprofessional Language

Maintain a professional tone throughout your descriptions. Avoid slang, informal phrases, or excessive use of jargon.

6. Example of a Strong Work History Entry

Here's an example of how to structure and write a compelling work history entry:

Digital Marketing Specialist: XYZ Marketing Agency, New York, NY January 2020 – Present

- Developed and executed digital marketing campaigns across Google Ads, Facebook Ads, and LinkedIn, resulting in a 35% increase in client ROI over two years.

- Conducted SEO audits and implemented keyword optimization strategies, leading to a 50% growth in organic web traffic.

- Managed a $500,000 annual marketing budget, ensuring all campaigns were delivered on time and within budget constraints.

- Analyzed performance metrics using Google Analytics and Tableau, providing actionable insights to improve campaign effectiveness.

- Collaborated with cross-functional teams, including design, sales, and content, to ensure cohesive brand messaging.

7. Updating and Maintaining Your Work History

LinkedIn is a dynamic platform, and your profile should evolve with your career. Follow these tips to keep your work history up-to-date:

- **Regular Updates:** Add new roles, achievements, or responsibilities as they happen.

- **Refine Your Descriptions:** Periodically review and optimize your entries for clarity and relevance.

- **Stay Consistent:** Ensure that your LinkedIn profile aligns with your resume and other professional documents.

By following these steps, you'll create a compelling and polished work history section that showcases your expertise and positions you as a top candidate in your field. This section is your chance to tell your professional story—make it count!

Example: Work History Entry

Digital Marketing Manager
ABC Digital Solutions, New York, NY
March 2019 – Present

- **Developed and executed integrated marketing campaigns** across multiple channels (Google Ads, Facebook Ads, and LinkedIn) that resulted in a **30% increase in customer acquisition** within the first 6 months of the campaign launch.

- **Led a team of 6 marketers** in the successful execution of digital campaigns for high-profile clients in the tech industry, driving an average ROI of **250%**.

- **Optimized SEO strategy** by conducting a comprehensive audit of client websites and improving their rankings on Google, resulting in a **40% increase in organic traffic**.

- **Managed a monthly budget of $100,000** for paid ads, ensuring all campaigns were executed on time, within budget, and aligned with business goals.

- **Monitored and analyzed key performance indicators (KPIs)** such as conversion rates, click-through rates (CTR), and cost-per-click (CPC) using tools like **Google Analytics** and **Tableau**, providing actionable insights to improve campaign performance.

- **Collaborated with cross-functional teams** (including design, content, and product) to ensure marketing messages were consistent and on-brand.

- **Mentored junior marketing team members**, providing guidance on campaign strategy, performance analysis, and industry best practices.

Example of a Prior Role

Social Media Coordinator
XYZ Creative Agency, Chicago, IL
June 2016 – February 2019

- **Created and managed content** for social media platforms (Instagram, Twitter, and Facebook) that grew follower engagement by **50%** year-over-year.

- **Planned and executed social media campaigns** to increase brand awareness, contributing to a **20% increase in customer inquiries** within the first 3 months.

- **Analyzed social media performance** using tools like **Hootsuite** and **Sprout Social**, regularly presenting reports to senior management.

- **Worked closely with the design team** to create visually appealing social media posts and advertisements that aligned with the company's brand identity.

- **Led social media contests and giveaways**, boosting engagement and brand visibility, with one campaign increasing Instagram followers by **10,000** in a month.

- **Developed social media content calendars** to streamline posting schedules, ensuring consistent brand messaging across platforms.

- **Collaborated with influencers** to expand the brand's reach, resulting in a **15% increase in sales** from social media channels.

How This Example Demonstrates Key Principles:

1. **Action-Oriented Language:** Every bullet point begins with a strong action verb such as "Developed," "Led," "Optimized," "Managed," and "Analyzed." This draws attention to your achievements and paints a clear picture of your active involvement in each task.

2. **Quantifiable Results:** Metrics like "30% increase in customer acquisition," "40% increase in organic traffic," and "50% growth in follower engagement" give concrete evidence of the impact you've made in previous roles. These numbers not only demonstrate success but also help recruiters and potential employers understand the scale of your accomplishments.

3. **Relevant Skills and Tools:** The use of specific tools such as "Google Analytics," "Tableau," "Hootsuite," and "Sprout Social" shows that you're not only knowledgeable but also comfortable working with industry-standard software. This increases the likelihood of appearing in recruiter searches for those specific skills.

4. **Balance of Responsibilities and Achievements:** The descriptions are a mix of day-to-day tasks and key accomplishments. For example, leading a team and managing campaigns are important responsibilities, but showcasing the

measurable outcomes (e.g., "250% ROI," "40% increase in organic traffic") is where the impact is clearly demonstrated.

5. **Industry-Specific Keywords:** Phrases like "digital marketing," "SEO strategy," "paid ads," "KPI monitoring," and "social media campaigns" are terms that will resonate with hiring managers in the marketing industry and help optimize your profile for keyword searches.

Additional Tips for Tailoring Your Own Experience Entries:

- If your role includes a wide range of responsibilities, prioritize the tasks and achievements that are most relevant to your current career objectives or the job you're applying for.

- Use precise metrics whenever possible. For example, instead of simply saying you "increased sales," say you "boosted sales by 20% through targeted marketing efforts."

- Don't be afraid to showcase the soft skills that played a role in your success, such as leadership, communication, or time management.

By applying these strategies, you'll create a LinkedIn profile that stands out to recruiters and employers, demonstrating both your experience and the tangible value you can bring to an organization.

2.3.2 Using Action Words and Metrics

Crafting a professional LinkedIn profile requires more than just listing job titles and responsibilities; it demands a strategic approach to showcase your achievements and impact. This section will guide you in using action words and metrics effectively to make your LinkedIn experience section stand out to potential employers, clients, or collaborators.

1. Why Action Words Matter

Action words (also known as power verbs) are critical in demonstrating your impact and conveying a sense of energy and professionalism. They transform bland descriptions into dynamic narratives that grab the attention of readers.

- **Avoid passive phrases:** Instead of saying, "Was responsible for managing a team," use an action-oriented statement like, "Led a high-performing team of 10 to achieve a 20% increase in sales."

- **Show initiative and results:** Action words emphasize what you actively did rather than what happened under your watch.

Here are some examples of action words categorized by their purpose:

- **Leadership:** Directed, Led, Managed, Supervised, Orchestrated

- **Problem-solving:** Resolved, Improved, Streamlined, Optimized

- **Innovation:** Developed, Designed, Created, Implemented, Initiated

- **Collaboration:** Coordinated, Partnered, Facilitated, Engaged

- **Achievement:** Achieved, Exceeded, Delivered, Surpassed

When choosing action words, ensure they align with your actual contributions. Overuse or misuse of these words can come across as insincere.

2. The Power of Metrics

Metrics provide measurable proof of your accomplishments. They help quantify your contributions, making them more credible and easier to understand. For example, instead of saying, "Improved customer satisfaction," you could say, "Improved customer satisfaction scores by 25% over six months."

Why Metrics Are Important

- **They add context:** Metrics show the scale of your work and the impact of your efforts.

- **They build credibility:** Numbers give substance to your claims, distinguishing you from others with similar job titles.

- **They show results:** Employers and recruiters are more interested in what you achieved than what you were tasked with.

3. How to Incorporate Action Words and Metrics

Here's a step-by-step guide to incorporating action words and metrics effectively into your LinkedIn profile:

Step 1: Start with an Action Word

Begin each bullet point or sentence with a strong action word. This immediately captures attention and sets a professional tone.

Example:

- Weak: Responsible for organizing team meetings.

- Strong: Coordinated weekly team meetings to enhance communication and productivity.

Step 2: Specify Your Contributions

After the action word, provide details about your role or the task you completed. Focus on your specific contributions rather than generic responsibilities.

Example:

- Weak: Worked on marketing campaigns.

- Strong: Designed and executed targeted marketing campaigns for product launches.

Step 3: Quantify Your Results

Whenever possible, use numbers to showcase the impact of your work. Metrics can include percentages, dollar amounts, timeframes, or other quantifiable outcomes.

Examples:

- Increased sales revenue by 15% within the first quarter.

- Reduced operational costs by $50,000 annually through process optimization.

- Delivered a project two weeks ahead of schedule, saving 10% of the allocated budget.

Step 4: Focus on Outcomes and Impact

Employers value outcomes over activities. Highlight how your actions contributed to the organization's success.

Example:

- Weak: Managed a team of customer service representatives.

- Strong: Led a team of 15 customer service representatives, improving customer satisfaction scores from 78% to 92% in 12 months.

4. Examples of Using Action Words and Metrics by Industry

Marketing

- Developed a digital marketing strategy that increased website traffic by 40% within six months.

- Spearheaded a social media campaign that generated $200,000 in sales revenue.

Sales

- Exceeded annual sales targets by 25%, achieving $1.5 million in total revenue.

- Negotiated contracts with key clients, resulting in a 30% increase in repeat business.

Human Resources

- Designed and implemented a new onboarding process, reducing new hire turnover by 15%.

- Facilitated training sessions for 200+ employees, improving workplace productivity by 20%.

Operations

- Streamlined supply chain processes, cutting delivery times by 10%.

- Managed inventory worth $2 million with a 98% accuracy rate.

IT/Tech

- Implemented a cybersecurity protocol that reduced system downtime by 50%.

- Automated repetitive tasks, saving 500+ employee hours annually.

5. Common Mistakes to Avoid

- **Vagueness:** Avoid phrases like "helped with" or "worked on." Be specific about what you did.

- **Overloading with metrics:** Don't add numbers just for the sake of it. Metrics should support your claims, not overshadow them.

- **Repetitiveness:** Don't repeat the same action words across multiple roles. Use a variety of power verbs.

- **Overstating your role:** Be honest about your contributions. Exaggeration can backfire during interviews.

6. Tips for Beginners

- **Reflect on your accomplishments:** Take time to think about the projects you've completed and the results you achieved.

- **Ask for feedback:** Colleagues or supervisors may provide insights into your impact that you might overlook.

- **Use LinkedIn's analytics:** Review the profile views and recruiter engagement to refine your experience section.

- **Stay concise:** While it's important to be specific, keep your descriptions concise and easy to read.

By using action words and metrics effectively, you can elevate your LinkedIn profile from a simple list of responsibilities to a compelling showcase of your professional journey. This approach not only helps you stand out but also communicates your value to employers in a clear, impactful way.

Examples of Using Action Words and Metrics on LinkedIn

To help you better understand how to use **action words** and **metrics**, here are detailed examples for different job roles and industries. These can serve as templates or inspiration for crafting your own LinkedIn experience section.

1. Marketing Professional

Original (Generic and Weak):

- Responsible for running social media campaigns.

- Increased website traffic.

Improved (With Action Words and Metrics):

- **Developed and executed** a social media strategy across five platforms, increasing follower engagement by 35% within six months.

- **Spearheaded** a content marketing campaign that generated **$250,000 in revenue** from organic traffic in one quarter.

- **Optimized** email marketing workflows, resulting in a **15% increase** in open rates and a **25% boost** in click-through rates.

2. Sales Representative

Original (Generic and Weak):

- Worked with clients to achieve sales targets.

- Closed deals regularly.

Improved (With Action Words and Metrics):

- **Exceeded** quarterly sales quotas by **20%** on average, achieving **$1.2 million** in revenue annually.

- **Negotiated and secured** contracts with five high-value clients, contributing to a **30% increase in repeat business**.

- **Collaborated** with the product team to design customized solutions, increasing client retention rates by **15% year-over-year**.

3. Human Resources Specialist

Original (Generic and Weak):

- Managed the recruitment process for new hires.

- Improved the onboarding process.

Improved (With Action Words and Metrics):

- **Led** the end-to-end recruitment process, successfully hiring **50 employees** across three departments in one year.

- **Designed and implemented** a new onboarding program, reducing new hire turnover by **20%** and increasing time-to-productivity by **15%**.

- **Facilitated** company-wide training sessions for **200+ employees**, improving overall employee satisfaction scores by **10%** in annual surveys.

4. Software Developer

Original (Generic and Weak):

- Worked on developing software for clients.

- Fixed bugs in applications.

Improved (With Action Words and Metrics):

- **Designed and developed** a client-facing mobile application, resulting in **50,000 downloads** within the first three months of launch.

- **Optimized** back-end systems, reducing server response time by **40%** and improving user experience.

- **Resolved** over **300 software bugs** by collaborating closely with QA testers, achieving a **98% defect-free release rate**.

---

5. Supply Chain Manager

Original (Generic and Weak):

- Managed supply chain operations.

- Reduced costs for logistics.

Improved (With Action Words and Metrics):

- **Streamlined** supply chain operations, reducing delivery times by **15%** and cutting costs by **$500,000 annually**.

- **Orchestrated** the transition to a new logistics provider, resulting in a **20% improvement** in on-time delivery rates.

- **Implemented** an inventory tracking system, achieving a **99% accuracy rate** and reducing waste by **12%**.

---

6. Customer Service Representative

Original (Generic and Weak):

- Helped customers resolve complaints.

- Provided support via email and phone.

Improved (With Action Words and Metrics):

- **Resolved** customer complaints with a **95% satisfaction rate**, consistently exceeding monthly targets.

- **Managed** an average of **50+ customer inquiries daily**, achieving a **response time of under 2 hours**.

- **Developed** a new FAQ system, reducing support tickets by **30%** and improving self-service rates.

7. Project Manager

Original (Generic and Weak):

- Oversaw projects and ensured they were completed on time.

- Managed a team of employees.

Improved (With Action Words and Metrics):

- **Led** cross-functional teams of **20+ members** to deliver projects ahead of schedule, saving **$200,000** in costs annually.

- **Created and executed** a risk mitigation strategy, reducing project delays by **25%**.

- **Managed budgets** totaling **$5 million**, ensuring projects were completed under budget by an average of **10%**.

8. Graphic Designer

Original (Generic and Weak):

- Designed graphics for clients.

- Worked on branding projects.

Improved (With Action Words and Metrics):

- **Designed and delivered** branding packages for **15 clients**, increasing their brand recognition by **20%** through cohesive visual storytelling.

- **Created** a series of digital advertisements that drove a **30% increase** in online engagement for a major campaign.

- **Collaborated** with the marketing team to produce visuals that contributed to a **15% boost** in lead conversions.

9. Operations Manager

Original (Generic and Weak):

- Managed daily operations.

- Oversaw scheduling and logistics.

Improved (With Action Words and Metrics):

- **Optimized** operational workflows, reducing processing times by **20%** and saving **200+ hours** annually.

- **Implemented** a new scheduling system that increased employee efficiency by **15%** and reduced absenteeism by **10%**.

- **Supervised** logistics for **$10 million worth of goods**, ensuring **98% on-time delivery** across 50+ locations.

10. Teacher/Educator

Original (Generic and Weak):

- Taught classes to high school students.

- Helped improve students' performance.

Improved (With Action Words and Metrics):

- **Developed and delivered** engaging lesson plans that increased student engagement scores by **25%** in standardized surveys.

- **Mentored** over **50 students**, with **90% achieving above-average grades** in final exams.

- **Implemented** a new interactive teaching approach, leading to a **15% improvement** in subject comprehension.

These examples illustrate how to make your LinkedIn profile more dynamic and results-oriented by incorporating **action words** and **metrics**. Whether you're in marketing, IT, HR, or any other field, focus on your achievements, quantify your results, and start with strong action verbs to leave a lasting impression!

2.4 Skills, Endorsements, and Recommendations

2.4.1 Selecting Relevant Skills

Your LinkedIn profile's "Skills" section plays a crucial role in showcasing your expertise and signaling to others — including potential employers, recruiters, and colleagues — what you bring to the table. This section is more than just a list; it serves as a searchable database that aligns with your personal brand, helps your profile appear in search results, and strengthens your professional credibility. In this section, we'll guide you step-by-step to strategically select and manage relevant skills for maximum impact.

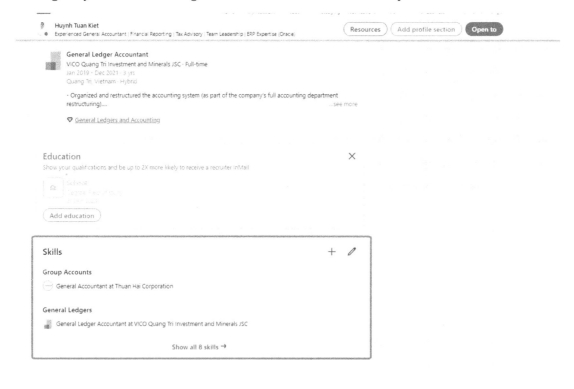

Understanding the Purpose of the Skills Section

The skills you choose to feature on your LinkedIn profile aren't just for show — they help tell a compelling story about your professional abilities and accomplishments. Here are the main purposes of the Skills section:

1. **Showcasing Your Expertise:** Adding skills communicates to others what you're good at, helping to clarify your unique value.

2. **Appearing in Recruiter Searches:** LinkedIn uses your listed skills to rank your profile in search results. Recruiters often search for candidates based on specific keywords, and having the right skills ensures your profile is more likely to be found.

3. **Earning Social Proof:** Endorsements for your skills serve as social proof, adding credibility to your claims of expertise. They show that colleagues, clients, and peers recognize your abilities.

4. **Aligning with Career Goals:** The skills you highlight signal to others (and LinkedIn's algorithms) the areas where you want to grow or seek opportunities.

Step-by-Step Guide to Selecting Relevant Skills

1. **Start with a Self-Assessment:** Before you begin adding skills, take some time to reflect on your professional experience, strengths, and goals. Ask yourself:

   o   What are my core competencies?

   o   What skills do I use most often in my current role?

   o   What skills are critical for the jobs or industries I'm targeting?

Create a list of your top skills and organize them into categories, such as technical skills (e.g., data analysis, programming), soft skills (e.g., communication, teamwork), and industry-specific skills (e.g., digital marketing, supply chain management).

---

2. **Research Industry and Role-Specific Skills:** To ensure your profile aligns with your career goals, research the most in-demand skills for your desired field or role. You can do this by:

   o   **Analyzing Job Descriptions:** Review job postings for roles you're interested in and look for recurring skills or qualifications mentioned.

   o   **Exploring LinkedIn Skills Insights:** LinkedIn offers tools like the "Skills and Endorsements" section to see what skills are trending for your industry.

- o **Checking Profiles of Successful Professionals:** Look at the profiles of people in roles similar to your target position and note the skills they've listed.

3. **Prioritize Quality Over Quantity:** While LinkedIn allows you to list up to 50 skills, it's better to focus on the most relevant and impactful ones. Prioritize skills that:

   - o Directly relate to your current or desired job.

   - o Highlight your unique strengths or niche expertise.

   - o Reflect emerging trends in your field to show you're keeping up-to-date.

Aim to showcase around 10–15 core skills that represent your professional brand effectively.

4. **Organize Skills Strategically:** LinkedIn allows you to "pin" up to three skills to the top of your profile. These featured skills should be:

   - o The most relevant to your career goals.

   - o Frequently searched keywords in your industry.

   - o Supported by endorsements from colleagues or peers.

For example, if you're a digital marketer, you might feature "Search Engine Optimization (SEO)," "Content Marketing," and "Google Ads" as your top three skills.

5. **Focus on Specificity:** Avoid adding vague or overly broad skills like "Microsoft Office" or "Communication." Instead, be specific to increase the value of your profile. For example:

   - o Replace "Microsoft Office" with "Advanced Excel" or "PowerPoint Design."

   - o Replace "Communication" with "Public Speaking" or "Business Writing."

Specific skills not only sound more professional but also make your profile more searchable.

6. **Highlight Transferable Skills:** If you're changing careers or industries, include skills that are transferable across roles. For example:

   o A teacher transitioning to corporate training might highlight skills like "Curriculum Development" and "Instructional Design."

   o A retail manager moving to operations might showcase skills like "Inventory Management" and "Customer Service."

Tips for Managing the Skills Section

1. **Keep Your Skills List Updated:** Regularly review and update your skills to reflect your current expertise and career goals. Remove outdated or irrelevant skills to maintain a polished profile.

2. **Use LinkedIn's Suggestions:** When adding skills, LinkedIn provides suggestions based on your profile and job title. Review these suggestions for ideas but only include those that are relevant.

3. **Validate Your Skills with Endorsements:** Encourage colleagues, peers, or clients to endorse your skills. Endorsements act as social proof, making your profile more credible.

4. **Align Skills with Certifications:** If you have certifications or training in specific areas, make sure the associated skills are listed on your profile. For example, if you're certified in Google Analytics, ensure "Google Analytics" is one of your skills.

5. **Leverage Assessments to Prove Expertise:** LinkedIn offers skill assessments in areas like programming, marketing, and design. Passing these assessments adds a badge to your profile, enhancing your credibility.

Examples of Skills for Different Professions

Here are some skill ideas to inspire you based on various fields:

- **Digital Marketing:** SEO, Google Ads, Social Media Strategy, Content Creation.

- **Data Science:** Python, Machine Learning, Data Visualization, SQL.

- **Human Resources:** Talent Acquisition, Employee Engagement, HR Analytics.

- **Finance:** Financial Analysis, Budgeting, Risk Management, Tax Planning.

- **Customer Service:** Conflict Resolution, CRM Software, Problem-Solving.

Common Mistakes to Avoid When Selecting Skills

1. **Adding Too Many Skills:** Listing irrelevant or excessive skills can dilute your profile's impact. Focus on quality and relevance instead.

2. **Being Too Generic:** Broad skills don't add value. Use specific keywords and industry terms.

3. **Neglecting to Update Skills:** Outdated skills can make you appear disconnected from current trends in your field.

By carefully selecting and managing your LinkedIn skills, you can significantly enhance your profile's visibility, credibility, and alignment with your career aspirations. This step is crucial in building a winning profile that stands out in the competitive professional world.

2.4.2 How to Request Endorsements

Endorsements on LinkedIn are a powerful way to showcase your skills and validate your expertise. They add credibility to your profile and demonstrate that others recognize your abilities in specific areas. In this section, we will explore how to effectively request endorsements, from identifying the right people to approach to crafting polite and professional messages. By following these detailed steps, you'll be able to grow your profile's credibility and attract more opportunities.

Why Endorsements Matter on LinkedIn

Endorsements act as a form of social proof. When others endorse your skills, it signals to potential employers, clients, or collaborators that your skills are not just self-proclaimed but also validated by others. Here are the key reasons endorsements are important:

- **Credibility:** A profile with numerous endorsements appears more credible than one without.

- **Searchability:** LinkedIn's algorithm prioritizes profiles with endorsed skills, making it easier for recruiters to find you.

- **First Impressions:** A strong list of endorsed skills immediately signals your expertise to anyone viewing your profile.

To maximize these benefits, it's essential to request endorsements strategically and professionally.

Step 1: Identify the Right People to Request Endorsements From

Before sending out requests, consider who would be most appropriate to endorse your skills. Focus on individuals who can provide genuine and meaningful endorsements. Here's how to identify them:

1. **Current and Former Colleagues:** People who have worked alongside you are the most qualified to endorse your skills, as they've seen your abilities in action.

2. **Managers and Supervisors:** A recommendation or endorsement from a supervisor carries significant weight. If you've delivered results under their leadership, they're likely to endorse you positively.

3. **Clients and Partners:** If you've worked on projects with external clients or partners, they can vouch for your skills, especially in areas like communication, project management, or technical expertise.

4. **Classmates or Professors (for Students):** If you're new to the workforce, consider asking classmates or professors who can validate your academic skills or collaborative abilities.

5. **Connections in Your Network:** Connections who frequently interact with your content or know you through professional circles can also provide endorsements, though these may be less impactful than those from direct collaborators.

Step 2: Prepare Before You Request

Requesting endorsements isn't just about asking; it's about ensuring your profile is set up to make it easy for people to endorse you.

1. **List Relevant Skills on Your Profile:** Make sure the skills you want endorsed are already visible on your profile. To do this:

   o   Go to your LinkedIn profile.

   o   Scroll down to the "Skills & Endorsements" section.

   o   Add or edit skills to ensure they align with your career goals.

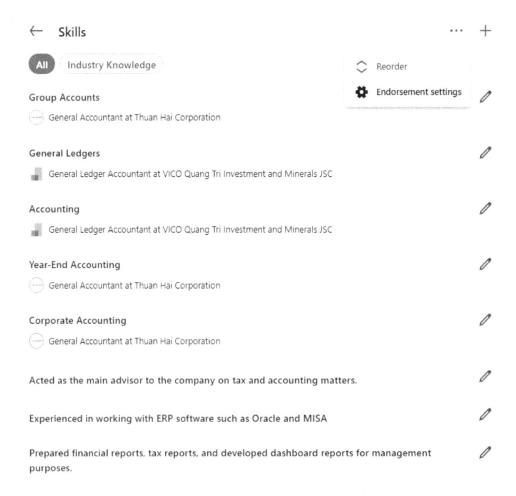

2. **Prioritize Your Top Skills:** LinkedIn allows you to pin up to three skills at the top of your profile. These are the skills most visible to others and are more likely to be endorsed.

3. **Optimize Your Profile:** Before requesting endorsements, ensure your profile is up-to-date and professional. A polished profile increases the likelihood of receiving endorsements when you ask.

Step 3: Craft a Professional and Polite Message

When reaching out to someone for an endorsement, always personalize your message. Avoid generic or impersonal requests. Below are some examples of how to ask for endorsements professionally:

Template 1: Requesting an Endorsement from a Colleague

Hi [Name],

I hope this message finds you well! I really enjoyed working with you on [specific project/team]. Your insights and collaboration were invaluable.

I'm currently updating my LinkedIn profile and would greatly appreciate it if you could endorse me for [specific skill(s)] that you've seen me demonstrate during our time together. Of course, I'd be happy to do the same for you if there's anything you'd like me to highlight.

Thank you so much for considering this, and let me know if there's anything I can do to support you as well!

Best regards,
[Your Name]

Template 2: Requesting an Endorsement from a Manager

Hi [Name],

I hope you're doing well! I really appreciated the opportunity to work under your leadership during [specific role/project]. Your guidance helped me grow in so many ways.

I'm enhancing my LinkedIn profile to reflect my skills and achievements, and I was wondering if you could endorse me for [specific skill(s)], as you've seen me utilize them firsthand. Your endorsement would mean a lot to me and would add significant value to my profile.

Thank you so much for your time, and please don't hesitate to let me know if there's anything I can assist you with!

Best regards,
[Your Name]

Step 4: Follow Up Politely

Not everyone will respond to your request immediately. If you don't hear back after a week or two, it's okay to follow up gently. Here's an example of a polite follow-up message:

Hi [Name],

I hope you're doing well! I wanted to follow up on my previous message about endorsing me for [specific skill(s)]. I completely understand if you're busy, but I thought I'd check in just in case my message got buried.

Please let me know if there's anything I can do to return the favor—I'd be happy to endorse you or help in any other way!

Thank you so much for considering my request. I truly appreciate your time and support.

Best regards,
[Your Name]

Step 5: Show Gratitude and Offer to Reciprocate

After someone endorses you, always thank them. Acknowledge their support publicly or privately, and offer to endorse them in return.

1. **Send a Thank-You Message:**

Hi [Name],

Thank you so much for endorsing me for [specific skill(s)]! Your support means a lot to me, and I truly appreciate it.

If there's any way I can return the favor, please don't hesitate to let me know—I'd be more than happy to endorse you as well!

Best regards,
[Your Name]

2. **Endorse Them in Return:** Go to their profile and endorse the skills you know they excel in. Reciprocity strengthens your professional relationship and encourages future collaboration.

Step 6: Maintain Professional Relationships

Building your network is not a one-time activity. Stay engaged with the people who have endorsed you by:

- Interacting with their posts or articles.

- Congratulating them on achievements or work anniversaries.

- Reaching out periodically to maintain your connection.

These small gestures help keep your relationships active and make it more likely they'll support you in the future.

Common Mistakes to Avoid When Requesting Endorsements

1. **Requesting Endorsements from Strangers:** Only ask people who know you professionally. Requests from strangers may seem inappropriate.

2. **Requesting Too Many Endorsements at Once:** Limit your requests to a few targeted individuals to avoid overwhelming your network.

3. **Being Impersonal:** Always personalize your messages to show genuine intent.

4. **Ignoring Reciprocity:** Endorse others as well to foster mutual support.

By following these steps, you'll be able to effectively request endorsements, enhance your LinkedIn profile, and boost your professional credibility. Remember, endorsements are not just about skills—they're about relationships. Nurturing those relationships is key to long-term LinkedIn success.

2.4.3 Writing and Requesting Recommendations

Recommendations on LinkedIn play a critical role in building your credibility and enhancing your professional reputation. They act as endorsements from colleagues, supervisors, clients, or business partners, giving potential employers or collaborators a better sense of your skills, work ethic, and professional achievements. This section will guide you step by step on how to write effective recommendations for others, how to request recommendations for yourself, and best practices to ensure that these endorsements align with your professional goals.

Why Recommendations Matter on LinkedIn

Before diving into the process, it's important to understand why recommendations are valuable:

1. **Validation of Skills**: Recommendations provide evidence of your skills and accomplishments from a trusted source.

2. **Improved Credibility**: A profile with thoughtful recommendations shows that others respect your work, adding to your credibility.

3. **Stronger Network Connections**: Writing recommendations for others can strengthen your relationships and lead to reciprocal endorsements.

4. **Visibility to Recruiters**: Recruiters often read recommendations to gain insights into a candidate's capabilities and character beyond the resume.

Writing Recommendations for Others

Writing recommendations is not just about being polite; it's an opportunity to highlight someone's strengths genuinely and meaningfully. Here's how to craft a strong LinkedIn recommendation:

Step 1: Understand Their Goals

Before writing, ask the person what they'd like you to emphasize. For example:

- Are they looking for a new job?

- Do they want to showcase leadership, teamwork, or technical expertise? This ensures your recommendation aligns with their career objectives.

Step 2: Follow a Structure

A clear structure makes your recommendation impactful and easy to read. Follow this outline:

1. **Start with Context**: Describe how you know the person, your professional relationship, and the context in which you worked together. Example: *"I had the pleasure of working with Jane Doe for three years at ABC Company, where we collaborated on multiple high-impact marketing campaigns."*

2. **Highlight Their Strengths**: Focus on specific skills or attributes that make the person stand out. Provide examples to back up your statements. Example: *"Jane's creativity and attention to detail were evident when she led the development of a campaign that increased engagement by 30%. Her ability to think strategically and execute flawlessly sets her apart."*

3. **Include a Memorable Anecdote**: A short story about a successful project or a challenging situation they handled well makes the recommendation more personal and credible. Example:

   "One instance that stands out was when Jane successfully managed a product launch under tight deadlines, ensuring every detail was executed perfectly. Her calm demeanor under pressure inspired the entire team."

4. **End with a Strong Closing**: Conclude by summarizing their qualities and recommending them wholeheartedly. Example:

   "I highly recommend Jane for any leadership role in marketing. She is not only an exceptional professional but also a great mentor and team player."

Step 3: Use Positive, Professional Language

Keep your tone positive and professional. Avoid vague or overly casual language, and focus on qualities that add value to their profile.

Step 4: Keep It Concise

While it's important to be detailed, a LinkedIn recommendation should ideally be 3–5 short paragraphs. This length is enough to be meaningful without overwhelming the reader.

Requesting Recommendations for Yourself

Requesting recommendations can feel daunting, but with the right approach, it's straightforward and effective. Here's how to do it:

Step 1: Identify the Right People

The best recommendations come from individuals who have worked closely with you and can provide specific examples of your skills and contributions. Consider these groups:

- **Managers and Supervisors**: They can speak to your work ethic, leadership, and ability to deliver results.

- **Colleagues and Peers**: They can highlight your teamwork, communication, and problem-solving skills.

- **Clients or Partners**: They can validate your ability to deliver value and build strong relationships.

Step 2: Personalize Your Request

When asking for a recommendation, avoid sending generic messages. Instead, craft a personalized request:

- **Start with Gratitude**: Acknowledge your relationship and express appreciation for their time.

- **Be Specific**: Let them know what aspects of your work you'd like them to highlight. For example:

  "Hi [Name], I hope you're doing well! I'm currently working on enhancing my LinkedIn profile, and I was wondering if you'd be willing to write a recommendation for me. Specifically, it would be great if you could highlight our collaboration on [Project/Task] and my [specific skills, e.g., leadership, problem-solving]."

Step 3: Make It Easy for Them

Some people may not know where to start or what to write. Offer to provide a brief outline or examples of key points they could mention. This makes their task easier and ensures the recommendation aligns with your goals.

Step 4: Follow Up and Thank Them

If they agree to write a recommendation, follow up politely if you don't hear back after a week or two. Once they've written it, express your gratitude with a thank-you message.

Best Practices for LinkedIn Recommendations

1. Quality Over Quantity

It's better to have a few thoughtful and detailed recommendations than a large number of generic ones. Each recommendation should add unique value to your profile.

2. Keep Your Recommendations Relevant

Over time, you may outgrow certain roles or industries. Periodically review your recommendations and archive those that no longer align with your current career goals.

3. Write and Receive Recommendations Proactively

Don't wait until you're job hunting to start requesting or writing recommendations. Building this part of your profile over time will make it more authentic and robust.

4. Be Reciprocal

If someone writes a recommendation for you, consider writing one for them in return. However, ensure your recommendation is genuine and not written out of obligation.

5. Edit and Proofread

If you're writing a recommendation or reviewing one written for you, check for spelling and grammar errors. A well-written recommendation reflects professionalism.

Examples of Strong LinkedIn Recommendations

Here are two sample recommendations to illustrate what a well-crafted one looks like:

Example 1: Manager's Perspective *"I had the privilege of managing John Smith for two years at XYZ Corporation. John consistently demonstrated exceptional problem-solving skills and a deep understanding of data analytics. One of his most impressive achievements was developing a predictive model that improved our forecasting accuracy by 20%. John's ability to explain complex data in a way that was easy to understand made him a go-to resource for our team. I wholeheartedly recommend John for any data-driven role—he's a true professional and a joy to work with."*

Example 2: Peer's Perspective *"Working alongside Sarah Johnson on several marketing campaigns has been a highlight of my career. Sarah's creativity and innovative thinking are unmatched. During our time at ABC Company, Sarah spearheaded a social media strategy that increased engagement by 35%. Beyond her technical expertise, Sarah is an excellent collaborator who always fosters a positive team dynamic. I can't recommend her enough to anyone looking for a skilled and dedicated marketer."*

By writing and requesting thoughtful recommendations, you'll elevate your LinkedIn profile, making it stand out to recruiters and colleagues alike. These endorsements are a testament to your professional journey and the positive impact you've had on others.

CHAPTER III
Building Your Network

3.1 Understanding Connections on LinkedIn

Connections are the cornerstone of LinkedIn. They represent the relationships you form with professionals in your industry, mentors, colleagues, and even friends. Unlike other social networks, LinkedIn focuses on professional connections, which can help you grow your career, explore opportunities, and build your personal brand. To truly leverage LinkedIn, you must understand how connections work and why they are vital.

3.1.1 Types of Connections (1st, 2nd, and 3rd Degree)

LinkedIn categorizes connections into three main degrees—1st, 2nd, and 3rd degree—based on how closely you are linked to another user. Each type of connection represents a different level of accessibility and opportunity for networking. Below is a breakdown of these connection types and how to navigate them effectively.

1st Degree Connections: Your Direct Network

What Are 1st Degree Connections? 1st degree connections are the people you are directly connected to on LinkedIn. These are individuals who have accepted your connection request or those whose requests you have accepted. They form the foundation of your LinkedIn network.

Why Are 1st Degree Connections Important? Your 1st degree connections are your immediate professional circle. They are most likely to engage with your posts, endorse your skills, and provide recommendations. These individuals can offer guidance, career advice, and even referrals for job opportunities.

How to Build Your 1st Degree Network

1. **Start with People You Know**: Begin by connecting with colleagues, classmates, mentors, and friends.

2. **Leverage Your Email Contacts**: LinkedIn allows you to import your email contacts to find people already on the platform.

3. **Focus on Quality, Not Quantity**: Aim to connect with individuals who are relevant to your career goals or industry.

Maintaining Relationships with 1st Degree Connections

- **Engage Regularly**: Comment on their posts, congratulate them on milestones, and stay active in your communication.

- **Offer Value**: Share helpful resources, insights, or advice that may benefit them.

2nd Degree Connections: The Gateway to Expansion

What Are 2nd Degree Connections? 2nd degree connections are people who are connected to your 1st degree connections. While you do not have a direct relationship with them, you can see their profiles, mutual connections, and engage with them by sending connection requests or InMail messages (depending on your LinkedIn membership).

Why Are 2nd Degree Connections Important? This group significantly expands your reach and networking opportunities. By leveraging mutual connections, you can establish trust and credibility with 2nd degree connections, making it easier to grow your network.

How to Connect with 2nd Degree Connections

1. **Leverage Mutual Connections**: Use the "Mutual Connections" section on a person's profile to identify shared acquaintances.

2. **Personalize Your Invitations**: When reaching out to a 2nd degree connection, always include a personalized note explaining why you'd like to connect.

   o Example:
   "Hi [Name], I noticed we both know [Mutual Connection's Name]. I admire your work in [specific field] and would love to connect to learn more about your expertise."

3. **Engage Before Connecting**: Interact with their posts or articles to increase your visibility and show genuine interest before sending a connection request.

Using 2nd Degree Connections to Your Advantage

- **Get Introductions**: Ask your 1st degree connections to introduce you to someone in their network.

- **Explore Their Activity**: Review their posts, comments, and shared content to identify common interests or opportunities for collaboration.

3rd Degree Connections: Expanding Beyond Your Network

What Are 3rd Degree Connections? 3rd degree connections are people connected to your 2nd degree connections. They are the farthest level of connection within your visible LinkedIn network. In most cases, you cannot directly interact with them unless you send a connection request or have a Premium account to message them through InMail.

Why Are 3rd Degree Connections Important? Although they are the most distant connections, this group represents untapped opportunities. Many professionals and potential collaborators are in this category, making it a valuable resource for expanding your network.

Challenges with 3rd Degree Connections

1. **Limited Accessibility**: You may not always have full access to their profiles, depending on their privacy settings.

2. **Higher Risk of Ignored Requests**: Without mutual connections, they may be less likely to accept your invitation.

How to Connect with 3rd Degree Connections

1. **Find Common Interests or Affiliations**: If you share an industry, group, or alma mater, mention it in your invitation.

2. **Be Clear About Your Intentions**: Briefly explain why you want to connect.

   o Example:
   "Hi [Name], I came across your profile while researching [specific topic]. Your experience in [specific area] is impressive, and I'd love to connect to learn more about your journey."

3. **Utilize LinkedIn Groups**: If they are part of the same group as you, interact with them through group discussions before sending a connection request.

Understanding the Ripple Effect of Connections

LinkedIn's connection structure operates like a web. Building a strong 1st degree network can dramatically increase your 2nd and 3rd degree connections. For example, adding one well-connected individual in your industry could potentially link you to hundreds or thousands of 2nd and 3rd degree professionals.

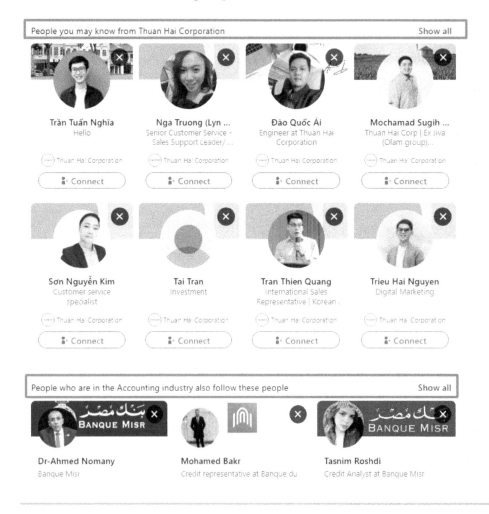

Best Practices for Managing Connections

1. **Avoid Random Connections**: Quality is better than quantity. Focus on building meaningful professional relationships.

2. **Be Strategic**: Connect with people in your industry, alumni from your university, and professionals who inspire you.

3. **Regularly Clean Your Network**: Remove outdated or irrelevant connections that no longer align with your career goals.

Conclusion: Building Strong Foundations

Understanding the types of connections on LinkedIn—1st, 2nd, and 3rd degree—is essential for making the most of this platform. Each degree offers unique opportunities to network, learn, and grow professionally. By focusing on authentic and strategic relationship-building, you can create a powerful network that supports your career ambitions.

3.1.2 The Importance of a Strong Network

Building a strong network on LinkedIn is not just about accumulating connections; it's about fostering meaningful relationships that can enhance your career and professional growth. In this section, we will dive into why a strong LinkedIn network is essential and how it can create opportunities that extend far beyond the platform. Let's explore the key benefits of building a strong LinkedIn network and the strategies to make the most out of it.

The Benefits of a Strong LinkedIn Network

1. Access to Opportunities

One of the primary reasons to invest in a strong LinkedIn network is the access it provides to career and business opportunities. A well-connected profile opens the door to:

- **Job Opportunities**: Many recruiters use LinkedIn to find candidates. Having connections with professionals in your industry increases the likelihood of recruiters noticing your profile.

- **Partnerships and Collaborations**: Entrepreneurs and business owners often use LinkedIn to identify potential partners or collaborators. A broad network ensures you're visible to these individuals.

- **Freelance Gigs and Projects**: For freelancers, LinkedIn can serve as a platform to showcase skills and connect with clients who are actively searching for services.

2. Professional Learning and Development

A strong network enables you to learn from others, stay informed about industry trends, and expand your knowledge. Here's how:

- **Sharing Knowledge**: Professionals frequently share insights, articles, and case studies. Your network becomes a valuable source of information.

- **Learning from Mentors**: By connecting with experienced individuals, you gain access to mentorship opportunities and career advice.

- **Joining Discussions**: Networking with thought leaders allows you to participate in meaningful discussions that enhance your understanding of complex topics.

3. Career Visibility

The more connections you have, the more visible your profile becomes. This improved visibility can lead to:

- **Endorsements**: Your connections can endorse your skills, which strengthens your credibility.

- **Recommendations**: A larger network increases the chances of receiving recommendations from colleagues, clients, or mentors.

- **Increased Profile Views**: When your network interacts with your content, it appears on their feed, attracting even more people to your profile.

4. Emotional Support and Motivation

A strong network isn't just about professional benefits; it can also provide emotional support during challenging times. Whether you're navigating a career transition or seeking feedback on a project, your LinkedIn network can offer encouragement and advice.

5. Building Your Personal Brand

Your LinkedIn network plays a significant role in shaping how others perceive you. A strong network allows you to:

- Share your achievements and milestones.
- Establish yourself as an authority in your niche by engaging with your audience.
- Amplify your reach when your connections share or engage with your content.

How to Build a Strong LinkedIn Network

Building a strong LinkedIn network isn't about adding random people; it requires a strategic approach. Here are some steps to help you grow a robust and meaningful network:

1. Identify Key Connections

Start by identifying the types of people you want in your network:

- **Industry Leaders**: Follow and connect with influential figures in your industry to gain insights.
- **Colleagues and Classmates**: People you've worked with or studied alongside are excellent additions to your network.
- **Recruiters and Hiring Managers**: Connecting with these professionals increases your chances of being considered for job opportunities.
- **Peers and Fellow Enthusiasts**: Networking with people who share similar interests fosters collaboration and learning.

2. Focus on Quality, Not Quantity

While it's tempting to add as many connections as possible, quality trumps quantity. A smaller, engaged network of relevant professionals is far more valuable than thousands of random connections.

3. Engage Consistently

Building a strong network requires ongoing interaction:

- **Comment on Posts**: Share thoughtful comments to add value to discussions.

- **Share Content**: Regularly post updates, articles, or ideas to keep your network engaged.

- **Congratulate and Acknowledge Achievements**: Celebrate your connections' successes by congratulating them on promotions, new roles, or accomplishments.

4. Attend Networking Events (Online and Offline)

LinkedIn often highlights events in your industry. Attending these events helps you meet people and expand your network beyond the platform.

5. Be Genuine and Authentic

Avoid sending generic messages or connection requests. A personalized approach shows that you're genuinely interested in building a relationship.

Avoiding Common Mistakes When Building a Network

As you build your LinkedIn network, it's important to avoid certain pitfalls that can harm your professional image.

1. Randomly Adding Connections

Sending connection requests to people you don't know or share any relevance with can dilute the quality of your network. Instead, focus on individuals who align with your career goals or interests.

2. Ignoring Your Network

Building a network isn't a one-time task. Neglecting to engage with your connections can cause your relationships to stagnate.

3. Over-Promoting Yourself

While LinkedIn is a platform to showcase your skills, overly promotional behavior can come across as insincere. Balance self-promotion with sharing insights and engaging with others' content.

4. Spamming with Messages

Avoid sending irrelevant or excessive messages to your connections. This behavior can damage relationships and lead to people removing you from their network.

Maximizing the Value of Your Network

1. Be a Giver, Not Just a Taker

A strong network is built on mutual value. Look for ways to help your connections, whether it's by:

- Offering advice.

- Sharing job opportunities.

- Introducing them to relevant contacts.

2. Stay Active and Visible

Consistent activity keeps you on your connections' radar. Post updates, share content, and engage with others regularly to maintain an active presence.

3. Leverage Your Second and Third-Degree Connections

Your network isn't limited to direct connections. Utilize LinkedIn's tools to reach out to second and third-degree connections who may be relevant to your goals.

4. Strengthen Relationships Offline

Whenever possible, take your LinkedIn relationships offline. Schedule coffee meetings, phone calls, or virtual meetups to deepen your connections.

Conclusion

A strong LinkedIn network is a powerful asset for career development, business growth, and personal branding. By strategically building and engaging with your connections, you'll unlock a wealth of opportunities and ensure your professional presence stands out. Remember, networking is about creating value, so approach it with authenticity and consistency to maximize the benefits.

To fully understand how a strong LinkedIn network can benefit you, let's explore some specific examples and scenarios. These real-world illustrations demonstrate how professionals have successfully leveraged their LinkedIn connections to achieve career growth, secure opportunities, and build meaningful relationships.

Example 1: Landing a Job Through Connections

Scenario:
Emma, a recent graduate in marketing, wanted to break into the industry but struggled to get responses to her job applications. She decided to actively grow her LinkedIn network by connecting with alumni from her university who worked in marketing roles.

Steps Emma Took:

1. **Personalized Connection Requests:** Emma sent a connection request to Sarah, a marketing manager at a top advertising agency and a fellow alumna. Her message read:

Hi Sarah, I noticed you're an alum of [University Name], and I'm inspired by your work in digital marketing. I'm just starting my career in marketing and would love to connect and learn from your experience!

2. **Engaging with Content:** After connecting, Emma regularly interacted with Sarah's posts by liking, commenting, and sharing valuable insights. For instance, when Sarah posted an article about the latest trends in social media marketing, Emma commented:

Great insights, Sarah! I found the point about short-form video content particularly interesting. Do you think this trend will continue in 2025?

3. **Seeking Guidance:** After building rapport, Emma messaged Sarah to ask for advice on entering the marketing field. Sarah responded with practical tips and even offered to review Emma's resume.

Outcome:
When a junior marketing position opened at Sarah's company, Sarah referred Emma for the role. Emma's LinkedIn activity and their interaction made her stand out as a motivated candidate. She got the job, thanks to her proactive networking efforts on LinkedIn.

Example 2: Securing a Freelance Client

Scenario:
James, a freelance graphic designer, wanted to expand his client base. He decided to use LinkedIn to connect with professionals in industries that frequently require design services, such as startups and marketing agencies.

Steps James Took:

1. **Posting Portfolio Content:** James started sharing examples of his work on LinkedIn, such as a carousel post showcasing logos he had designed. In the post, he added a compelling caption:

From bold to minimalistic, logos tell a brand's story. Here are a few designs I've created recently. If you're looking for custom design work, feel free to reach out!

2. **Joining Groups:** James joined LinkedIn groups related to startup growth and marketing, where he actively participated in discussions. When someone asked for tips on rebranding, James replied:

As a graphic designer, I recommend starting with a mood board to align your brand's vision. Let me know if you'd like a free consultation.

3. **Personalized Outreach:** James noticed a startup founder in his network posting about their upcoming product launch. He sent the founder a message:

Hi [Name], I saw your post about the product launch and wanted to say congratulations! If you need help with branding or promotional materials, I'd love to collaborate. I specialize in creating visuals that capture attention.

Outcome:
The startup founder hired James to design their promotional materials. This led to a long-term relationship, with James working on several projects for the startup.

Example 3: Gaining Mentorship Through Networking

Scenario:
Priya, a mid-level software engineer, aspired to move into a leadership role but wasn't sure how to develop the necessary skills. She decided to use LinkedIn to find mentors who had successfully transitioned into tech leadership positions.

Steps Priya Took:

1. **Targeted Search:** Priya searched for "engineering managers" and filtered by her city. She reviewed profiles to find professionals with inspiring career paths.

2. **Crafting Thoughtful Messages:** Priya sent a message to David, an engineering manager at a leading tech firm, saying:

Hi David, I admire your career progression from software engineer to engineering manager. I'm aspiring to move into a similar role and would love to hear about the skills and steps that helped you in your journey. Would you be open to a quick chat or sharing advice?

3. **Following Up:** After their conversation, Priya thanked David for his time and stayed connected by engaging with his posts. She also shared updates on her own progress, such as completing a leadership course he recommended.

Outcome:
David became a mentor to Priya, guiding her through the transition to a leadership role. He also introduced her to other professionals in his network, further expanding her opportunities.

Example 4: Enhancing Personal Branding

Scenario:
Sophia, a content writer, wanted to establish herself as an expert in her niche: writing for healthcare companies. She used LinkedIn to showcase her knowledge and connect with potential clients.

Steps Sophia Took:

1. **Creating Original Content:** Sophia wrote LinkedIn articles on topics like "5 Tips for Writing Compelling Healthcare Blog Posts." She also shared shorter posts with actionable tips, using relevant hashtags like #HealthcareContent and #WritingTips.

2. **Showcasing Expertise:** When someone in her network asked for recommendations on healthcare writing, Sophia responded with a thoughtful comment:

As a content writer specializing in healthcare, I've found that patient-centered language is key to engagement. If you'd like, I can share some examples from my portfolio.

3. **Connecting with Decision-Makers:** Sophia sent connection requests to marketing managers in healthcare companies, accompanied by personalized messages:

Hi [Name], I see you manage marketing for [Company Name]. I specialize in healthcare content and would love to connect and learn more about your work.

Outcome:
Over time, Sophia became known as an expert in healthcare writing. Her strong LinkedIn presence led to inbound inquiries from companies seeking content writers in her niche.

Lessons Learned from These Examples

1. **Be Strategic and Proactive**: Each example shows the importance of taking intentional steps to connect with the right people. Whether it's alumni, potential clients, or industry leaders, focus on building meaningful relationships.

2. **Engage Authentically**: Personalized messages, thoughtful comments, and genuine interactions stand out in the LinkedIn ecosystem.

3. **Provide Value**: Whether through sharing content, offering advice, or participating in discussions, always aim to contribute value to your network.

4. **Stay Consistent**: Building a strong network doesn't happen overnight. Regular activity and engagement are essential to maintaining and growing your connections.

By applying these strategies and learning from these examples, you can harness the full potential of your LinkedIn network and unlock opportunities that drive your career forward.

3.2 Sending Connection Requests

3.2.1 Crafting a Personalized Invitation

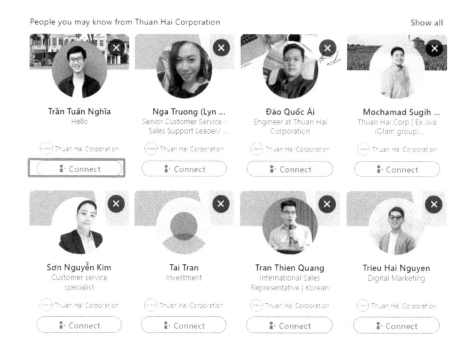

When building your professional network on LinkedIn, one of the most important steps is sending thoughtful, personalized connection requests. Unlike other social platforms where adding someone is often a casual action, LinkedIn emphasizes building meaningful and professional relationships. Crafting a personalized invitation significantly increases the likelihood that your request will be accepted while also setting a positive tone for the connection. Below is a detailed guide on how to craft an effective and professional LinkedIn invitation.

Why Personalization Matters

Sending the default LinkedIn connection request message, which simply states, "I'd like to connect with you on LinkedIn," can often come across as impersonal and, in some cases, unprofessional. Personalization demonstrates effort, respect, and genuine interest in the person you are reaching out to. This small touch can make a significant difference in how you are perceived by potential connections.

A personalized message:

- **Establishes Credibility:** It shows that you are intentional about building the connection and not just randomly adding people.

- **Encourages Engagement:** A tailored message often prompts the recipient to respond, potentially sparking a conversation.

- **Builds Trust:** When someone feels that you've taken the time to write a thoughtful message, they're more likely to trust and connect with you.

Steps to Crafting a Personalized Invitation

1. Start with a Polite Greeting

Begin your message by addressing the person by their name. Using their name makes the invitation feel more personal and respectful. Avoid generic greetings like "Hi there" or "Dear Sir/Madam." For example:

- **Good Example:** "Hi John,"

- **Avoid:** "Dear LinkedIn User,"

2. Mention How You Found Them

If you're reaching out to someone you don't know personally, briefly explain how you came across their profile. This could be through a mutual connection, a LinkedIn group, a shared professional interest, or even a post they published. For instance:

- "I came across your profile while browsing the [group name] and found your insights on [specific topic] fascinating."

- "I noticed your recent post about [topic] and thought it was very insightful."

3. State Your Intent Clearly

Explain why you want to connect with the person. Be honest and specific about your reasons, whether it's to learn from their expertise, collaborate on a project, explore job opportunities, or simply network within your industry. Examples include:

- "I'm currently exploring career opportunities in [industry], and I would love to learn more about your experience working at [company]."

- "I'm expanding my network in [field], and your profile caught my attention because of your impressive background in [specific area]."

4. Highlight Common Ground

Finding and referencing shared interests, experiences, or goals can create an instant sense of connection. This could include:

- Mutual connections: "I noticed we're both connected to [name]."

- Shared alma mater: "I see you also studied at [university]."

- Similar industries: "We both work in [industry], and I admire your expertise in [specific skill]."

5. End with a Polite Closing

Wrap up your invitation with a polite and professional closing. This reinforces your intention to build a meaningful connection and leaves a positive impression. For example:

- "Looking forward to connecting with you!"

- "Thank you for considering my request, and I hope to stay in touch."

Template Examples of Personalized Invitations

Below are a few sample messages tailored to different scenarios:

1. Reaching Out to a Thought Leader
"Hi Sarah,
I've been following your posts on supply chain management, and I found your recent article on sustainable logistics incredibly insightful. As someone who is transitioning into this field, I'd love to connect with you to learn more from your expertise. Looking forward to staying in touch!"

2. Connecting with a Colleague You Met at an Event
"Hi David,
It was great meeting you at the [event name] last week. I really enjoyed our discussion

about digital marketing trends. I'd like to connect here on LinkedIn and continue sharing ideas on this topic. Hope to hear from you soon!"

3. Connecting with Someone in the Same Industry

"Hi Emma,

I noticed that we both work in the renewable energy sector and share several mutual connections. Your work at [company] is inspiring, and I'd love to connect and exchange insights. Thank you!"

4. Networking as a Job Seeker

"Hi Michael,

I'm currently seeking opportunities in software development and came across your profile through [mutual connection or group]. Your experience at [company] is impressive, and I'd appreciate the chance to connect and learn from your career journey. Thank you!"

Best Practices for Sending Connection Requests

1. **Keep It Short and Clear:** While it's essential to personalize your message, avoid making it too lengthy. Aim for 2-3 concise sentences that convey your intent clearly.

2. **Be Professional:** Use proper grammar and avoid informal language or slang.

3. **Avoid Overly Generic Messages:** Avoid using phrases like "I'd like to add you to my professional network," unless followed by specific details.

4. **Follow Up if Needed:** If someone accepts your request but doesn't respond to your message, consider sending a polite follow-up to start a conversation.

Common Mistakes to Avoid

- **Using the Default Message:** This gives the impression that you're not genuinely interested in connecting.

- **Being Too Salesy:** Avoid pitching products or services in your connection request. Focus on building a relationship first.

- **Ignoring Context:** Don't send requests without a clear reason, especially if you have no mutual connections or shared interests.

Final Thoughts

Crafting a personalized LinkedIn invitation is more than just a courtesy—it's an opportunity to make a memorable first impression and set the stage for a meaningful professional relationship. By taking the time to personalize your connection requests, you demonstrate respect and genuine interest, which can go a long way in building a robust LinkedIn network.

3.2.2 Common Etiquette for Connecting

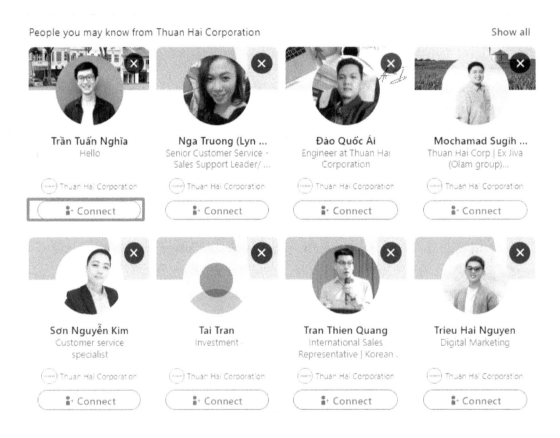

Sending connection requests on LinkedIn is not just about clicking the "Connect" button. It's an opportunity to make a professional first impression and build a meaningful relationship with someone in your industry. Following proper etiquette when sending connection requests is crucial to ensure you come across as professional, respectful, and genuine. This section will guide you through the essential dos and don'ts of LinkedIn connection requests, providing practical tips and examples.

The Importance of Connection Request Etiquette

When you send a connection request on LinkedIn, you are essentially introducing yourself to someone in a professional capacity. Your approach can determine whether the recipient accepts your request or ignores it. Proper etiquette not only increases your chances of building your network but also establishes trust and credibility. A poorly thought-out or generic request can leave a negative impression, while a well-crafted and polite request can open doors to new opportunities.

Do's of Sending Connection Requests

1. Always Personalize Your Invitation

One of the most important rules of LinkedIn etiquette is to personalize your connection request. Instead of using the default "I'd like to add you to my professional network on LinkedIn," take a moment to write a customized message. A personalized invitation shows that you've put thought into your request and that you're genuinely interested in connecting.

- **How to Personalize**: Mention how you know the person, why you're reaching out, or what you admire about their work.

- **Example**:

Hi [Name],
I came across your profile while researching [topic/industry], and I'm impressed by your work at [company/organization]. I'd love to connect and learn more about your expertise in [specific area].

2. Be Clear About Your Intentions

Be upfront about why you want to connect. Whether you're reaching out to learn, collaborate, or explore potential opportunities, stating your intentions helps the recipient understand your purpose. Avoid vague or overly broad statements.

- **Example**:

Hi [Name],
I'm currently exploring career opportunities in [industry] and noticed your extensive experience in [specific role]. I'd greatly appreciate the opportunity to connect and learn from your insights.

3. Mention a Common Connection or Context

If you have a mutual connection, attended the same event, or share a similar interest, highlight it in your message. This creates an immediate point of familiarity and makes the recipient more likely to accept your request.

- **Example**:

Hi [Name],
I noticed we both attended [event] last week. Your comments during the panel discussion on [topic] really resonated with me. I'd love to connect and continue the conversation.

4. Be Professional and Polite

Maintain a professional tone in your message, even if the recipient is someone you know personally. LinkedIn is a professional platform, so treat your connection requests as professional interactions. Use polite language and avoid slang or overly casual expressions.

- **Example**:

Hi [Name],
I recently read your article on [topic], and I found it very insightful. I'd like to connect and follow your updates on [specific subject].

5. Keep It Brief

While it's important to personalize your message, it's equally crucial to keep it concise. Aim for 2-3 sentences that get straight to the point. A lengthy message may discourage the recipient from reading it.

Don'ts of Sending Connection Requests

1. Don't Send Generic Requests

The default LinkedIn invitation message is generic and impersonal. While it may work for some people, it's less likely to result in meaningful connections. Avoid sending the default message unless you're connecting with someone you know very well.

2. Don't Be Pushy or Sales-Oriented

Avoid making your connection request feel like a sales pitch. LinkedIn is a platform for building relationships, not for immediately trying to sell a product or service. Overly aggressive or pushy messages can come across as spammy.

- **Example to Avoid**:

Hi [Name],
I noticed you work in [industry]. I'd love to show you how my product can help your business. Let's connect!

3. Don't Use Overly Casual Language

LinkedIn is not a social media platform like Facebook or Instagram. Avoid using overly casual language, emojis, or slang. This can make your request seem unprofessional.

- **Example to Avoid**:

Hey [Name],
Wanna connect? I'm trying to grow my network.

4. Don't Send Too Many Requests at Once

LinkedIn has limits on the number of connection requests you can send, and sending too many in a short period can flag your account for spam-like behavior. Additionally, it can overwhelm your potential connections and decrease your acceptance rate.

Tips for Sending Connection Requests

1. Timing Matters

Consider the timing of your connection request. If you're reaching out after meeting someone at an event, send your request within 24-48 hours while the interaction is still fresh in their mind. Similarly, if you reference a specific project or post, send your request shortly after engaging with it.

2. Follow Up if Necessary

If someone doesn't accept your request immediately, don't panic. People may take time to review and respond. If it's been more than two weeks, consider sending a polite follow-up message to reiterate your interest in connecting.

- **Example Follow-Up**:

Hi [Name],
I hope this message finds you well. I wanted to follow up on my connection request and see if you'd be open to connecting. I'd love to learn more about your work in [specific area].

3. Review Your Profile Before Sending Requests

Ensure your profile is up-to-date and professional before sending connection requests. A well-crafted profile increases the likelihood that your request will be accepted. Double-check your profile photo, headline, and summary to ensure they reflect your current professional goals.

Common Scenarios and Examples

Reaching Out to Someone You Admire

- Example:

Hi [Name],
I've been following your work in [field/industry] for a while, and I'm inspired by your achievements. I'd be honored to connect and learn more about your journey.

Connecting with a Colleague or Peer

- Example:

Hi [Name],
We both work in [industry/field], and I'd love to connect and exchange insights. I noticed your recent post on [topic] and found it very interesting.

Following Up After an Event

- Example:

Hi [Name],
It was great meeting you at [event]. I enjoyed our conversation about [topic] and would love to stay in touch and continue exchanging ideas.

By following these guidelines and maintaining a professional, thoughtful approach, you can build a strong and meaningful network on LinkedIn. Connection requests are more than just a formality—they're the first step in forming valuable professional relationships.

3.3 Joining Groups and Communities

3.3.1 Finding Relevant Groups

One of the most powerful features of LinkedIn is its ability to connect professionals through groups and communities. Whether you're seeking industry insights, networking opportunities, or advice from experts, joining LinkedIn groups provides an excellent platform for professional growth and engagement. However, the key to maximizing the benefits of LinkedIn groups is finding those that are most relevant to your career goals and areas of interest.

In this section, we will walk through how to find the most relevant LinkedIn groups and ensure they align with your professional aspirations. This step-by-step guide will help you use LinkedIn's search tools, evaluate group quality, and strategically engage with communities that offer value.

Step 1: Understanding the Types of Groups on LinkedIn

Before diving into the search process, it's important to recognize the different types of LinkedIn groups you may encounter. Knowing what you're looking for will help narrow down the search and guide you toward the best options.

1. **Industry-Specific Groups**: These groups focus on specific sectors, industries, or job functions, such as marketing, finance, healthcare, or technology. Joining industry-related groups allows you to connect with peers, stay up-to-date with trends, and gain access to industry-specific job opportunities.

2. **Professional Development Groups**: These groups are centered around skill-building, career advancement, and professional development. Examples include groups for leadership, public speaking, project management, or other certifications and credentials.

3. **Job Search and Career Groups**: Some groups specialize in helping members with job searches. These may feature job postings, interview advice, and tips for career growth. If you're seeking to transition to a new role or industry, these groups are highly beneficial.

4. **Alumni Groups**: Many universities, colleges, and professional organizations have LinkedIn groups for alumni. These groups can be valuable for building connections with former classmates and staying updated on alumni-related events or career opportunities.

5. **Interest-Based Groups**: These groups are based on personal or professional interests outside of specific industries. For example, groups related to tech innovations, sustainability, entrepreneurship, or any niche topic where like-minded professionals gather to discuss ideas and trends.

6. **Company or Organizational Groups**: Some companies create LinkedIn groups for their employees, prospects, or customers. These groups are often focused on networking within a company or industry-related updates, product discussions, or events.

Step 2: Using LinkedIn's Search Function to Find Groups

Now that you know the types of groups available, the next step is to use LinkedIn's search bar to locate relevant groups.

1. **Using the LinkedIn Search Bar**: At the top of your LinkedIn homepage, you'll find a search bar. This is where you will begin your search for groups. The most effective way to search is by using keywords that match your professional interests, job titles, or industries.

   o **Search by Keywords**: Enter terms like "marketing professionals," "software engineers," "leadership development," or any other specific area you're interested in. You can also use more niche terms for a more refined search.

   o **Search for Companies or Universities**: If you're looking for alumni groups or industry-specific company groups, type the name of the company or university into the search bar.

   o **Use Filters**: Once you've entered a keyword, click the "Groups" filter at the top of the search results. This will narrow the search results to only groups related to your search term.

2. **Refining Your Search with Boolean Operators**: If you want to refine your search further, consider using Boolean operators to combine multiple keywords. For example:

   o **AND**: Use "AND" to include multiple terms, such as "Marketing AND Social Media." This will find groups that mention both keywords.

   o **OR**: Use "OR" if you want to search for either of two terms, such as "Marketing OR Sales." This will broaden your search.

   o **NOT**: Use "NOT" to exclude terms, like "Leadership NOT Management," if you want to focus on a specific niche.

   o **Quotation Marks**: Enclose phrases in quotation marks to search for exact terms, such as "Digital Marketing Strategy."

3. **LinkedIn Group Categories**: When you search, LinkedIn categorizes the results. The main categories are:

   o **Groups**: Shows you LinkedIn groups relevant to your search terms.

   o **Posts**: Displays recent posts or discussions related to the search term.

   o **People**: This category helps you find professionals in the field you are exploring.

o **Jobs**: If you search for a specific job title, LinkedIn will also show you relevant job listings.

Focusing specifically on "Groups" will provide you with a curated list of communities that you can explore further.

Step 3: Evaluate the Relevance of a Group

Once you have found a list of potential groups, it's time to evaluate their relevance and quality. Simply joining any group isn't always beneficial—being selective and ensuring that the group aligns with your professional goals will provide more value. Here's what to look for when assessing groups:

1. **Group Size and Activity Level**

   o **Large Groups**: While large groups (thousands of members) offer great visibility, they can sometimes be overwhelming, and it might be harder to stand out. Consider whether you prefer larger groups with more potential connections or smaller, more niche communities where conversations are more focused.

   o **Active Discussions**: A relevant group will have a consistent flow of active discussions. Look at the number of posts, comments, and interactions in the group. If there are no new posts or little engagement, it might not be the best group to join.

2. **Quality of Content**

   o **Educational and Professional Content**: Check if the content being shared is aligned with your professional goals. Are members sharing industry updates, job opportunities, tips for skill development, or knowledge-sharing posts? The quality of content should match your objectives for joining the group.

   o **No Spam or Irrelevant Posts**: A quality group will limit spam and irrelevant content. If you see a lot of promotional material or off-topic posts, it may not be the best place to engage meaningfully.

3. **Moderation and Rules**

- ○ **Group Rules and Guidelines**: Each group typically has a set of rules or guidelines that dictate how members should behave. These can help you understand the group's expectations and ensure that you follow proper etiquette when engaging with others. Read these rules before joining and participating.

- ○ **Moderators**: Look for groups that have active moderators who ensure that the conversations stay on topic and maintain a professional environment.

4. **Members' Background**

- ○ **Targeted Professionals**: Check the profiles of members within the group to see if their experience, job titles, and industries align with your interests. Are they from similar or related fields? Are they decision-makers, recruiters, or influencers in your industry? This can give you an idea of the group's relevance to your professional network.

Step 4: Join Groups and Start Engaging

After you've found a relevant group, it's time to hit the "Join" button. However, simply joining the group is not enough—you need to engage actively. Here's how to get started:

1. **Read Group Content First**: Before jumping into conversations, take some time to read through existing posts and discussions. This will give you an understanding of the group's tone, interests, and the types of conversations happening. This also helps you get a feel for whether the group is active and informative.

2. **Participate in Discussions**: Begin by commenting on posts and offering insights, ideas, or asking questions. Adding value to conversations is one of the best ways to connect with other members. Share your experiences, ask for advice, or contribute helpful information when applicable.

3. **Post Your Own Content**: If you have valuable content to share, such as an article, a blog post, or an industry update, post it to the group. Ensure that the content is relevant and adds value. Avoid overly promotional content unless the group explicitly allows it.

4. **Connect with Members**: After engaging in discussions, consider reaching out to group members individually through LinkedIn connection requests. When doing

this, always include a personalized message to explain why you're reaching out and how you found them through the group.

Conclusion

Finding and joining the right LinkedIn groups can significantly expand your professional network, provide insights into your industry, and offer valuable career opportunities. By using LinkedIn's search features, evaluating group quality, and actively engaging with members, you can make the most of this valuable resource. Take the time to find groups that align with your professional goals, and you'll soon find yourself connected with a community of like-minded professionals who can help propel your career forward.

3.3.2 Participating in Discussions

Participating in discussions within LinkedIn groups is an effective way to demonstrate thought leadership, network with peers, and expand your visibility. However, it's crucial to engage strategically to ensure your involvement benefits both you and the group.

Why Participate in Discussions?

Participating in LinkedIn discussions offers several benefits:

- **Builds Authority and Credibility:** By offering helpful advice, sharing experiences, and responding thoughtfully to questions, you can position yourself as a knowledgeable and reliable professional in your field.

- **Expands Your Network:** Active participation increases your visibility, helping you connect with other members who may be valuable additions to your network.

- **Shows Engagement:** Active engagement demonstrates that you're not just passively consuming content but actively contributing to the community's growth.

- **Facilitates Learning:** Discussions are a great way to stay updated with industry trends, gain fresh perspectives, and learn from others' experiences.

Steps to Participate Effectively in LinkedIn Group Discussions

1. Find the Right Groups to Join

Before you can actively participate in discussions, you need to ensure you are part of the right LinkedIn groups. These groups should align with your professional interests, industry, or career goals.

- **Search for Groups:** LinkedIn has a built-in search feature that allows you to search for groups using relevant keywords (e.g., "Digital Marketing Professionals," "HR Experts," "Project Management Network"). You can also browse groups suggested by LinkedIn based on your profile information and interests.

- **Review Group Details:** Look at the group description, rules, and discussions happening in the group. This will give you an understanding of the topics discussed and whether it aligns with your expertise and interests.

- **Join the Groups:** Once you've found relevant groups, click "Join" to request access. Some groups may require you to answer a couple of questions to confirm your eligibility and purpose for joining.

2. Introduce Yourself and Establish Presence

Once you're accepted into a group, the first step is to introduce yourself to the community. A strong introduction helps you connect with other members and shows you're there to actively participate.

- **Craft a Professional Introduction Post:** Share a brief introduction about who you are, your professional background, and what you hope to gain from the group. Keep it concise but informative.

- **Offer Value:** In your introduction, mention specific ways you can contribute, such as sharing your expertise or discussing certain topics. Offering value from the outset will help set you up for success.

- **Personalize Your Tone:** Keep your introduction professional but friendly. Remember, the goal is to foster genuine connections.

3. Contribute Meaningfully to Discussions

Active participation involves more than just liking posts or occasionally commenting. To be truly engaged, you must contribute valuable insights and respond to other members thoughtfully.

- **Listen First, Speak Second:** Before you jump into a discussion, take time to understand the conversation. Read through previous comments and responses to gain context, so your contributions are relevant and thoughtful.

- **Add Value to Conversations:** When you comment on a post or discussion, aim to add something valuable. This could include sharing personal experiences, offering solutions, or providing resources like articles, blogs, or whitepapers. Your goal is to enhance the discussion, not merely echo existing comments.

- **Ask Thought-Provoking Questions:** One way to deepen discussions is by asking insightful questions. Open-ended questions that spark further conversations can demonstrate your leadership and engagement in the topic. For example, "How do you see AI impacting marketing strategies over the next five years?"

- **Be Respectful:** It's important to maintain professionalism in all interactions, even when discussing differing viewpoints. Respectful debate is encouraged, but avoid confrontation or overly critical comments. Always strive to contribute constructively.

4. Share Your Knowledge and Resources

LinkedIn Groups are the perfect place to share resources that will benefit others. Sharing valuable content not only adds value to the community but also positions you as someone who's generous with their knowledge.

- **Post Articles, Case Studies, or Blogs:** If you come across a relevant article, blog post, or research paper, feel free to share it in the group, particularly if it aligns with the group's interests. Make sure to add your perspective or a brief description of why the resource is valuable.

- **Share Industry News and Updates:** If you come across breaking news or industry updates, share it in a timely manner. Your participation in sharing important news showcases your active engagement in your field.

- **Post Your Own Content:** If you have a blog, podcast, or YouTube channel, you can occasionally share your own content that's relevant to the group's interests. Always ensure your content is insightful, well-researched, and adds value to the group.

5. Respond to Others' Questions and Requests for Help

Another great way to engage is by answering questions and helping others. LinkedIn Groups often have members who ask for advice, recommendations, or feedback, and this is where you can really make an impact.

- **Answer Questions Professionally:** When someone posts a question in the group, take the time to answer it based on your expertise. Even if you're not an expert in the specific area, offering your insights or pointing them to relevant resources can be incredibly helpful.

- **Be Timely:** Respond to posts and questions in a timely manner to ensure the group remains active and engaged. If you take too long to respond, the conversation may already have moved on.

6. Keep Your Interactions Positive and Professional

Maintaining a positive and professional tone in all group discussions is paramount. This helps in building rapport with other members and ensuring a supportive and respectful atmosphere.

- **Avoid Negative Comments:** Keep your comments polite and constructive. If you disagree with someone, express your viewpoint respectfully without personal attacks. Always focus on the facts and the topic rather than attacking individuals.

- **Use Proper Grammar and Spelling:** In professional communities, it's important to maintain a certain level of communication etiquette. Ensure your posts are well-written, error-free, and easy to understand.

7. Follow Up and Stay Engaged

Engagement doesn't end after you post or comment once. To build meaningful relationships within LinkedIn groups, follow up on discussions and keep contributing regularly.

- **Stay Active:** Set aside time each week to check in on your LinkedIn groups and contribute to ongoing discussions. Consistency is key to building your reputation as an active and valuable group member.

- **Follow Up on Conversations:** If someone replies to your comment or question, follow up with additional thoughts or clarifications. This keeps the conversation alive and shows you're engaged.

8. Leverage LinkedIn's Features for Advanced Participation

As you become more comfortable with group discussions, take advantage of advanced LinkedIn features to maximize your engagement.

- **Use LinkedIn Events:** Many LinkedIn groups host live events, webinars, and virtual meetings. Participate in these events to deepen your involvement in the group and connect with members in real-time.

- **Host Discussions or Webinars:** As a trusted and engaged member of a group, you may be invited to host your own discussion or webinar. If this opportunity arises, don't hesitate to take it. Hosting an event helps position you as an expert and builds your visibility.

- **Tag Relevant Members:** When sharing resources or answering questions, tag relevant members in your posts to engage them directly. This helps ensure your posts reach the right people and increases engagement.

Conclusion: Building Meaningful Relationships through Group Participation

Participating in LinkedIn group discussions is not just about building a reputation online; it's about forming meaningful relationships with others in your industry. By contributing thoughtfully, sharing your expertise, and being active in the community, you can grow your professional network and establish yourself as a leader in your field. So, start engaging with your LinkedIn groups today—every interaction is an opportunity to connect, learn, and grow!

Example of Participating in a LinkedIn Group Discussion

Let's assume you are a marketing professional, and you have joined a LinkedIn group for Digital Marketing Professionals. One day, a post appears in the group with the following question:

Post in Group: *"I'm struggling with generating leads through Facebook ads. Can anyone share their experience with effective ad strategies or tips on targeting the right audience?"*

Your Response:

Comment:

_*"Hi [Name], I understand your struggle with Facebook Ads—it's definitely a learning curve at first! In my experience, targeting the right audience is key. One strategy I recommend is starting with a broad audience and then narrowing it down using Facebook's 'Lookalike Audiences' feature. This allows you to target people who are similar to your existing customers.*

Additionally, it's important to experiment with different ad formats. For instance, carousel ads work well for showcasing multiple products, and video ads tend to drive higher engagement. Don't forget to A/B test your ads regularly to see what resonates with your audience.

Finally, I always recommend setting up conversion tracking to measure the ROI of your campaigns. Facebook's pixel is a great tool for this!

Hope this helps, and I'd love to hear how it works for you!"

Analysis of the Example

1. Addressing the Question Thoughtfully

The first key element is that the response is directly addressing the person's query. Instead of providing generic advice, the response offers a targeted strategy based on personal experience, which adds value to the discussion. By explaining how the "Lookalike Audiences" feature works and why it's effective, you've added actionable insights, helping the individual improve their Facebook ads strategy.

Why this works:

- **Personal Experience:** Sharing your experience makes your advice credible and real-world relevant, which builds trust with other group members.

- **Specificity:** The response is not vague. It gives a clear and specific approach to solving the problem, which is exactly what the original poster was asking for.

2. Offering Value Beyond the Question

In addition to answering the question, you've shared additional tips on ad formats, A/B testing, and conversion tracking. This not only shows that you're engaged with the topic but also that you're going above and beyond to help the person.

Why this works:

- **Value-Added Insights:** By giving more than just an answer to the question, you are positioning yourself as an expert who has a deeper understanding of the subject.

- **Wider Discussion:** You've expanded the discussion by introducing new concepts, such as A/B testing and conversion tracking, that the group can learn from.

3. Being Friendly and Approachable

The tone of the response is friendly and encouraging. You've said "Hope this helps," and expressed your interest in hearing about the poster's results. This invites further engagement and keeps the conversation open.

Why this works:

- **Engagement and Follow-Up:** Showing genuine interest in the outcome of your advice invites ongoing dialogue. It encourages the original poster to come back and continue the discussion, which can lead to deeper connections within the group.

- **Tone:** The response is polite and helpful without being condescending. This ensures that the person feels supported rather than criticized for asking for help.

4. Demonstrating Expertise

By using industry-specific tools like "Lookalike Audiences" and "Facebook Pixel," you are demonstrating your knowledge of Facebook Ads. You've shown that you are knowledgeable without overwhelming the poster with too much technical jargon. This strikes the right balance and positions you as someone who understands the subject matter.

Why this works:

- **Authority Building:** Mentioning well-known tools and strategies relevant to the industry shows that you are experienced. Over time, this helps you establish credibility within the group.

- **Clarity and Simplicity:** While you're showcasing your expertise, you've made sure your advice is accessible and easy to understand, ensuring that others in the group can follow your suggestions.

5. Invitation for Further Interaction

Lastly, by ending with "I'd love to hear how it works for you," you've extended an invitation for the original poster to share their results, which opens the door for further conversation.

Why this works:

- **Encouraging Interaction:** By asking for feedback, you show that you are interested in a two-way conversation, not just a one-time response. This could lead to further exchanges and an ongoing professional relationship.

- **Building Relationships:** This invitation for feedback makes your engagement more personal. It shows that you're invested in their success, rather than just providing generic advice.

How This Example Contributes to Building Your LinkedIn Presence

- **Building Relationships:** By offering genuine and thoughtful help, you build rapport with group members and the person who asked the question. This leads to networking opportunities and future collaborations.

- **Boosting Visibility:** Offering helpful responses increases your visibility in the group. When others see that you're a valuable member, they're more likely to connect with you and engage with your future posts or comments.

- **Establishing Thought Leadership:** Over time, consistent, high-quality contributions like this help establish you as a thought leader in your industry. This strengthens your professional reputation and increases the likelihood of others seeking out your advice or services.

- **Creating Opportunities for Engagement:** By keeping the conversation going and encouraging feedback, you create opportunities for further engagement, which helps to build a more robust and active professional network.

Conclusion

This example illustrates how effective participation in LinkedIn group discussions can foster engagement, build relationships, and establish you as a credible professional in your field. Remember that the key to successful participation is to provide meaningful, specific, and thoughtful contributions that add value to the community. Keep your interactions friendly, professional, and approachable, and you'll create opportunities to expand your network and grow your LinkedIn presence.

CHAPTER IV
Engaging with Content

4.1 Creating and Sharing Posts

4.1.1 Writing Professional Updates

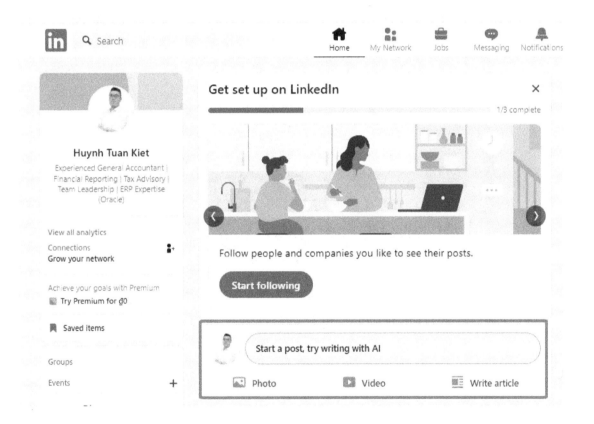

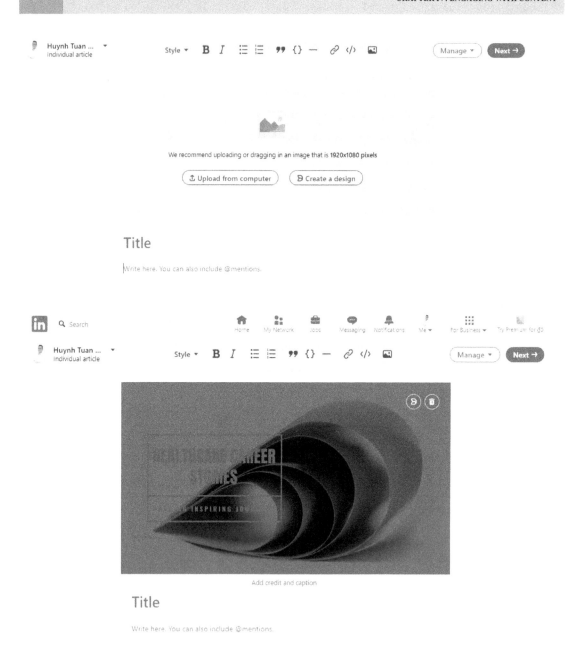

LinkedIn is a dynamic platform designed to connect professionals, showcase expertise, and build a personal brand. One of the most effective ways to engage with your network and stay top-of-mind is by writing and sharing professional updates. These updates can help you connect with peers, attract new opportunities, and reinforce your professional image.

In this section, we will walk you through the process of writing professional updates on LinkedIn that grab attention, drive engagement, and reflect your expertise.

Why Professional Updates Matter

Professional updates on LinkedIn serve a multitude of purposes. They allow you to:

- Share valuable insights, industry trends, or personal achievements.

- Establish your expertise in your field.

- Increase your visibility to potential employers, recruiters, clients, or business partners.

- Build stronger relationships with your network.

- Showcase your unique perspective on relevant topics.

The way you craft your updates can make a significant impact on how your professional network perceives you. Crafting engaging posts that reflect your expertise while maintaining professionalism is key to successfully using LinkedIn.

Step-by-Step Guide to Writing Professional Updates

To craft effective LinkedIn updates, consider the following essential steps:

1. Define the Purpose of Your Update

Before you begin writing, it's important to define the purpose of your update. This will help you stay focused and ensure your message is clear. Some potential purposes for a LinkedIn update include:

- **Sharing Industry News**: Provide commentary on recent developments in your industry or profession. This establishes you as someone who is knowledgeable and up-to-date.

- **Announcing Personal Milestones**: Share personal achievements, such as a promotion, a new certification, or the completion of a major project. This helps humanize your professional brand.

- **Offering Insights**: Share your thoughts or lessons learned from experiences in your career. This type of content can be particularly valuable to your network, as it helps others learn from your experiences.

- **Engaging in Conversations**: Initiate discussions by asking thought-provoking questions or sharing opinions on a hot topic. This encourages interaction and can help you establish deeper connections.

Once you've identified the purpose of your update, keep it in mind throughout the writing process to ensure that your content aligns with your overall objective.

2. Start with an Attention-Grabbing Hook

Your first sentence or two is the most important part of your update. It's your hook—the part that will determine whether someone continues reading or scrolls past. A great hook:

- **Creates curiosity**: Pose a question or make a bold statement that makes people want to learn more.

- **Tells a compelling story**: Share an anecdote or a brief personal story that draws readers in.

- **Shares a shocking statistic or fact**: Use numbers to highlight an important trend or issue in your industry.

For example, if you're sharing insights on a recent marketing trend, your hook might look like   this:
"Did you know that 75% of consumers are more likely to engage with brands they find on LinkedIn?"
This kind of statement sparks curiosity and encourages the reader to continue.

3. Be Clear and Concise

LinkedIn users are busy professionals, so it's important to get to the point quickly. Keep your update clear, concise, and easy to read:

- **Use short paragraphs**: Break up large blocks of text into smaller, digestible pieces. This makes it easier for your audience to read, especially on mobile devices.

- **Use bullet points**: If you are sharing a list of tips, insights, or statistics, use bullet points to make it easier to digest.

- **Avoid jargon**: Write in a way that your target audience will easily understand, avoiding industry jargon unless it's appropriate for the specific context.

If you're sharing a tip or insight, try something like this:
"Here are three ways you can improve your LinkedIn profile for better visibility:"

- **Complete your profile**

- **Use a professional headline**

- **Engage with relevant content**

This style of writing makes it easy for your audience to scan your post and extract key points quickly.

4. Add Value to Your Audience

Every update you post should offer value to your audience. Whether you're sharing advice, insights, or a link to a resource, ensure that your update has something useful for your network. Here are a few ideas on how to add value:

- **Share helpful tips**: Offering actionable advice can position you as a helpful and knowledgeable connection. For example, "Here's a quick tip to improve your email marketing strategy."

- **Provide resources**: If you've found an interesting article, report, or tool, share it with your network. Add your own commentary to explain why it's worth reading.

- **Offer industry insights**: Your opinion on a recent development or trend in your field can give your audience something to think about, establishing you as a thought leader in your area.

For instance, instead of just sharing an article about digital marketing trends, you could write:
"I found this article on the future of digital marketing fascinating. Here are my takeaways:"

- **Personalized marketing is on the rise.**

- **Video content will continue to dominate.**

- **Social commerce is the next big thing.**

By doing this, you provide both the original article and your own insights, adding more value to the content you're sharing.

5. Include a Call-to-Action (CTA)

A good professional update should always end with a call-to-action (CTA). A CTA invites your audience to take a specific action, whether it's engaging with your post or continuing the conversation elsewhere. A few CTA examples include:

- **Asking a question**: "What do you think about this trend? Let me know in the comments below."

- **Encouraging sharing**: "If you found this helpful, share it with your network!"

- **Providing a link**: "Click here to read the full article and learn more."

By including a CTA, you create an opportunity for your audience to engage directly with your content, fostering deeper interactions and relationships.

6. Use Hashtags Wisely

Hashtags are an important way to increase the visibility of your posts and make them easier for others to find. By using relevant hashtags, you help your content reach people who are interested in specific topics. Here's how to use hashtags effectively:

- **Keep them relevant**: Use hashtags related to your industry, expertise, or the topic of your post. For example, if you're posting about digital marketing, you might use #DigitalMarketing, #SEO, or #ContentStrategy.

- **Don't overuse them**: Using too many hashtags can make your post look spammy. Stick to 3-5 relevant hashtags per update.

- **Experiment with trending hashtags**: If a hashtag is trending in your industry, try incorporating it into your post to increase visibility.

Example:
"Great tips for increasing your LinkedIn engagement! #SocialSelling #LinkedInTips #PersonalBranding"

7. Include Visuals to Enhance Your Post

Incorporating visuals, such as images, videos, or infographics, can significantly enhance the impact of your update. Posts with visuals tend to receive higher engagement than text-only updates. Here are some ways to use visuals:

- **Images**: Use a high-quality image relevant to your post, whether it's a personal photo, a stock image, or a graphic you've created.

- **Videos**: Short videos (under 1 minute) can effectively convey your message and make your update more engaging. Whether it's a quick tip, an industry announcement, or a personal reflection, videos capture attention.

- **Infographics**: If you're sharing data or statistics, an infographic can present this information in an engaging and easy-to-understand format.

For example, if you're sharing a blog post, you might accompany your post with an image of the blog's cover or a relevant screenshot.

8. Edit and Proofread Your Update

Before hitting the "Post" button, take a moment to review your update. Check for spelling and grammar errors, ensure the tone is appropriate, and verify that the message is clear. Mistakes in your LinkedIn posts can undermine your credibility. A quick edit ensures that your post maintains a professional appearance.

Conclusion

Writing professional updates on LinkedIn is a powerful way to engage with your network, share valuable content, and build your personal brand. By following the steps outlined in this section, you can craft updates that resonate with your audience, increase your visibility, and strengthen your professional reputation.

Remember that consistency is key. Keep posting regularly, engage with others' content, and stay true to your professional goals. Over time, these small efforts will build a strong, impactful presence on LinkedIn.

4.1.2 Using Images, Videos, and Documents

In today's digital age, visual content plays a pivotal role in engaging an audience, and LinkedIn is no exception. While text-based posts are important, incorporating images, videos, and documents into your LinkedIn content strategy can significantly boost engagement, increase reach, and leave a lasting impression. This section will guide you step-by-step on how to effectively use these elements in your posts to maximize their impact.

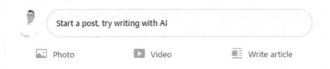

Why Use Visual Content on LinkedIn?

Visual content captures attention faster than text. Studies show that posts with visuals are more likely to be noticed, shared, and remembered. On LinkedIn, visual posts can help:

- **Increase Engagement:** Posts with images, videos, or documents receive higher engagement rates, including likes, comments, and shares.

- **Convey Complex Ideas:** Graphics, charts, and videos can simplify complicated concepts and make your content more digestible.

- **Enhance Professionalism:** High-quality visuals make your posts look polished and credible.

- **Build Your Brand:** Consistently branded images and videos help reinforce your professional or personal brand.

How to Add Images to LinkedIn Posts

Adding an image to your LinkedIn post can make it visually appealing and increase the likelihood of interaction. Here's how to use images effectively:

1. Selecting the Right Image

- **Professionalism is Key:** Always choose high-quality images that align with your professional goals. Avoid casual, blurry, or overly playful images unless they fit your branding.

- **Relevance Matters:** Your image should directly relate to the content of your post. For example, if you're sharing insights from an event, use photos of the event itself.

- **Brand Consistency:** If you represent a company, use branded templates or incorporate your logo and brand colors.

2. Optimal Image Formats and Sizes

- LinkedIn recommends an image size of **1200 x 627 pixels** for posts.

- Supported formats include JPEG, PNG, and GIF (but note that LinkedIn does not support animated GIFs in posts).

- Ensure your image is not pixelated or distorted by maintaining its aspect ratio.

3. Uploading Images to Your Post

1. On the LinkedIn home page, click the **"Start a post"** button.

2. Select the **"Photo"** option to upload an image from your computer or device.

3. Preview the image to ensure it appears as intended, then add your caption or text.

4. Enhancing Your Image

- Use editing tools to add text overlays, arrows, or highlights to draw attention to key details.

- Experiment with filters or contrast adjustments to make your image pop.

- Use tools like Canva or Adobe Express to create professional visuals.

Incorporating Videos in Your Posts

Videos are an excellent medium for storytelling and delivering complex messages in an engaging way. LinkedIn videos can be used to showcase expertise, share success stories, or even present tutorials.

1. Types of Videos to Post

- **Educational Videos:** Tutorials, how-tos, or case studies that provide value to your audience.

- **Behind-the-Scenes:** Showcase your workplace, team, or day-to-day activities to add a personal touch.

- **Event Highlights:** Share clips from conferences, workshops, or industry events.

- **Customer Testimonials:** Use video testimonials to build trust and credibility.

2. Best Practices for Video Content

- **Length:** Keep videos between **1 to 3 minutes** for optimal engagement. While LinkedIn supports videos up to 15 minutes, shorter videos perform better.

- **Captions:** Always include captions for accessibility. Many LinkedIn users watch videos without sound.

- **Quality:** Use a high-resolution camera or smartphone to ensure clear visuals and crisp audio.

- **Call-to-Action (CTA):** End your video with a clear CTA, such as asking viewers to visit your website, comment, or share the post.

3. Uploading and Posting Videos

1. Click the **"Start a post"** button on the LinkedIn home page.

2. Select the **"Video"** option and upload your file (MP4 is recommended).

3. Add a compelling caption to provide context for the video.

4. Use relevant hashtags to make your video discoverable.

4. Advanced Video Tips

- Use LinkedIn's **Native Video Feature** rather than linking to external platforms like YouTube. Native videos autoplay in the feed, which boosts engagement.

- Analyze video performance using LinkedIn's analytics to see metrics like views, clicks, and engagement.

- Experiment with live video via LinkedIn Live to interact with your audience in real-time.

Using Documents for Effective Storytelling

LinkedIn allows users to upload documents, such as PDFs, PowerPoint presentations, and Word files, directly to their posts. This feature is especially useful for sharing in-depth information in a visually appealing, easy-to-read format.

1. Types of Documents to Share

- **Case Studies:** Highlight successful projects or detailed reports.

- **Infographics:** Present data or statistics in a creative and concise way.

- **Guides and Tutorials:** Share step-by-step instructions or checklists.

- **Presentations:** Upload slides from webinars or workshops.

2. Formatting Your Document

- Ensure your document is **mobile-friendly**, as a large portion of LinkedIn users access the platform on their phones.

- Use clear headings, bullet points, and visuals to break up text and enhance readability.

- Include branding elements, such as your logo or color scheme, to reinforce your professional identity.

3. Uploading Documents to LinkedIn

1. Start a new post and select the **"Document"** option.

2. Upload your file (LinkedIn supports PDFs, DOCX, and PPTX formats).

3. Add a title to your document and a caption to your post.

4. Preview the document to ensure it displays correctly.

4. Tips for Maximizing Document Engagement

- Keep your documents concise—10 to 20 slides are ideal.

- Include a **clear cover page** with a title that grabs attention.

- Add a CTA at the end, such as encouraging readers to visit your website, contact you, or comment on your post.

Combining Images, Videos, and Documents

For maximum impact, consider combining different types of content in a single post. For example:

- Use an image as a thumbnail for your video.

- Create a post that includes a short video teaser and attach a detailed document for further reading.

- Combine photos and infographics to share highlights from an event.

Engaging Your Audience with Visual Content

Simply posting visuals isn't enough—you need to actively engage your audience. Here's how:

- **Ask Questions:** Encourage viewers to comment by asking for their opinions on the content.

- **Respond to Comments:** Acknowledge and reply to comments to foster a sense of community.

- **Use Hashtags:** Include 3–5 relevant hashtags to increase the visibility of your post.

By mastering the use of images, videos, and documents on LinkedIn, you can create posts that not only capture attention but also provide value to your audience. Experiment with different formats and track engagement metrics to refine your content strategy over time.

4.2 Interacting with Others' Content

Engaging with others' content on LinkedIn is one of the most effective ways to build your presence, establish relationships, and showcase your expertise. This section will guide you through the art of commenting and reacting to posts, providing detailed advice on how to maximize the value of your interactions.

4.2.1 Commenting and Reacting to Posts

LinkedIn is a platform built on meaningful professional interactions. Commenting on and reacting to posts is not only a way to engage with your network but also an opportunity to demonstrate your knowledge, contribute value, and foster connections. Here's how you can approach commenting and reacting effectively:

Why Commenting and Reacting Matter

Before diving into the "how," it's essential to understand *why* interacting with others' content is important:

1. **Visibility and Presence:** Each comment or reaction you leave becomes visible to your connections and the poster's network, increasing your exposure.

2. **Relationship Building:** Regularly engaging with someone's content shows interest and supports relationship-building over time.

3. **Thought Leadership:** Thoughtful comments can position you as an expert in your industry or area of interest.

4. **Engagement Algorithms:** LinkedIn favors active users, meaning your comments and reactions can lead to higher visibility of your own profile and posts.

The Basics of Commenting and Reacting

Reactions:

LinkedIn offers several reactions, each serving as a quick way to interact with content:

- 👍 **Like:** A simple way to acknowledge the post positively.

- 👏 **Celebrate:** Perfect for congratulatory or achievement-based posts.

- 💡 **Insightful:** Use this to highlight posts with valuable insights or unique perspectives.

- ☐ **Support:** Show encouragement or solidarity, particularly for challenges or personal stories.

- ❤☐ **Love:** Suitable for inspiring or heartfelt content.

Comments:

Unlike reactions, comments allow you to add your thoughts and contribute to the conversation. Comments can vary from simple acknowledgments to in-depth analyses.

How to Write Effective Comments

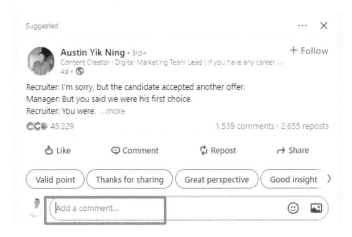

1. Be Genuine and Professional: Your comments reflect your personal brand. Avoid generic or insincere responses like "Great post!" Instead, share specific thoughts or ideas. For example:

- Instead of: "Great insights!"

- Say: "I found your point about XYZ particularly insightful because it aligns with a trend I've noticed in [specific field]. Thanks for sharing this!"

2. Add Value to the Conversation: The best comments go beyond acknowledgment and add value. Here's how you can do that:

- **Ask Questions:** Show curiosity and keep the conversation going. For example:

  o "You mentioned the importance of XYZ. How would you recommend someone new to the industry get started with this?"

- **Share Personal Experiences:** Relate the post to your own experiences.

  o "I encountered a similar challenge last year, and I found that [specific solution] worked well. What has your experience been?"

- **Offer Additional Resources:** Suggest tools, books, or articles related to the topic.

  o "This reminds me of the book 'ABC' by [author], which discusses this in detail. Highly recommend checking it out!"

3. Keep It Concise but Impactful: While it's tempting to write long comments, brevity often works best. Aim for 2-4 sentences that are clear and to the point.

4. Maintain a Positive Tone: Even if you disagree with the post, express your opinion respectfully. Constructive criticism can open a dialogue, but negativity can harm your reputation. For example:

- Instead of: "This idea won't work because it's flawed."

- Say: "This is an interesting perspective. I've seen different results in [specific context]. What are your thoughts on XYZ?"

5. Proofread Before Posting: Errors in grammar or spelling can harm your professional image. Take a moment to proofread before submitting your comment.

Tips for Specific Scenarios

1. Congratulatory Posts: When someone shares an achievement, go beyond "Congrats!"

- Example: "Congratulations on the promotion! Your hard work and dedication truly paid off. Looking forward to seeing the impact you'll make in your new role."

2. Industry Insights or News: When engaging with thought leadership posts, share your takeaways or perspectives.

- Example: "This is such an insightful take on the current market trends. I especially agree with your point about XYZ and have seen similar patterns in my industry."

3. Opinion-Based Posts: For posts where someone shares a personal opinion, acknowledge their perspective and add your thoughts.

- Example: "I appreciate your perspective on this topic. I've approached this differently by focusing on XYZ, but your strategy makes me think about other possibilities. Thanks for sharing!"

4. Personal Stories: When someone shares a personal or vulnerable story, offer support or encouragement.

- Example: "Thank you for sharing your story. It takes courage to open up, and I'm sure this will inspire others who are facing similar challenges."

5. Questions Posed by Others: If someone asks a question in their post, take the opportunity to provide a thoughtful response.

- Example: "Great question! In my experience, [specific solution or method] has worked well. Curious to hear what others think!"

Mistakes to Avoid

While commenting and reacting can be powerful tools, there are pitfalls to avoid:

1. **Generic Comments:** Avoid vague comments like "Interesting!" or "Good post!" that don't contribute anything meaningful.

2. **Over-Promotion:** Refrain from using comments as a platform to promote your services or products.

3. **Negativity:** Avoid arguments, sarcasm, or offensive language. These can damage your reputation.

4. **Hijacking the Conversation:** Don't steer the conversation toward unrelated topics or make it about yourself unnecessarily.

Reacting Strategically

While reactions are simpler than comments, using them strategically can still make a difference:

- React thoughtfully based on the content type. For example, use "Celebrate" for milestone posts, "Insightful" for industry analysis, and "Support" for personal stories.

- Don't overreact. Randomly reacting to every post in your feed can dilute the value of your engagement.

Tracking Your Engagement

Engagement is a two-way street. After commenting or reacting:

- Check back to see if the post creator or others have responded to your comment. Reply to their responses to keep the conversation going.

- Use LinkedIn's "My Network" and "Notifications" features to track posts where you've interacted.

By mastering the art of commenting and reacting to posts, you'll build stronger relationships, enhance your visibility, and establish yourself as a thoughtful and engaged professional on LinkedIn. It's not about the quantity of interactions—it's the quality that makes the difference.

4.2.2 Sharing Content with Your Network

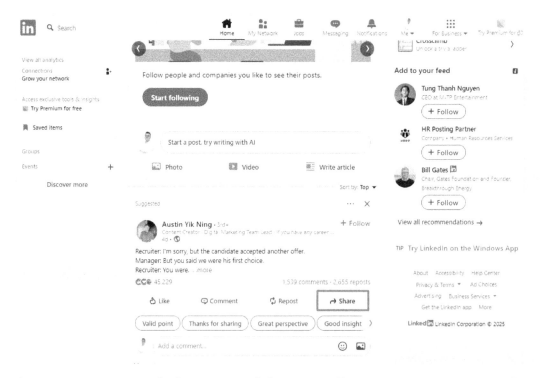

Sharing content on LinkedIn is one of the most effective ways to engage with your professional network, establish your expertise, and contribute to meaningful conversations. Whether you are sharing a news article, a company update, or a thought-provoking post, the act of sharing demonstrates that you are an active participant in your industry. In this section, we will explore the importance of sharing content, best practices for doing so, and step-by-step instructions for sharing different types of posts.

Why Sharing Content Matters

Sharing content on LinkedIn is more than just an act of posting—it is a way to build relationships, showcase your knowledge, and add value to your network. Here are a few reasons why sharing content is essential:

- **Positioning Yourself as a Thought Leader:** By sharing insightful and relevant content, you can demonstrate your expertise in a specific field and build credibility among your peers, recruiters, and potential employers.

- **Expanding Your Network's Knowledge:** Sharing content that is valuable, educational, or inspiring helps others stay informed and contributes to their professional growth.

- **Fostering Engagement:** Shared content often sparks discussions, which can lead to meaningful connections and opportunities.

- **Staying Visible:** Regularly sharing content ensures that your profile remains active and visible on your network's newsfeed, keeping you top of mind.

What to Share on LinkedIn

Before diving into how to share content, it's important to understand what types of content resonate well on LinkedIn. Here are some common types of content that perform well:

1. **Industry News and Insights:** Articles, reports, or studies that highlight trends or developments in your industry.

2. **Personal Achievements and Milestones:** Sharing updates about your professional accomplishments can inspire and connect with others.

3. **Company Updates:** Announcements, events, or achievements from your company help build brand awareness and loyalty.

4. **Tips and Advice:** Share your experiences, lessons learned, or actionable advice that others in your field can benefit from.

5. **Inspirational Content:** Stories of overcoming challenges or achieving success resonate well with LinkedIn's professional audience.

6. **Job Opportunities:** Sharing job postings or information about open positions can help those in your network find opportunities.

Best Practices for Sharing Content

To maximize the impact of the content you share, follow these best practices:

1. **Add Your Perspective:** Simply sharing a link without context can feel impersonal. Add a comment explaining why the content is valuable or how it relates to your professional experience.

2. **Keep It Professional:** Remember that LinkedIn is a professional platform. Avoid sharing overly personal, political, or controversial content unless it directly ties into your industry or professional goals.

3. **Engage With Your Audience:** When people comment on your shared content, take the time to respond. This creates dialogue and strengthens connections.

4. **Use Hashtags Strategically:** Adding relevant hashtags can help your post reach a wider audience beyond your direct network.

5. **Maintain Consistency:** Sharing content regularly helps establish your presence on LinkedIn. Aim for 1-3 posts per week.

6. **Proofread Before Posting:** Ensure that your shared content is free of typos and errors, as this reflects on your professionalism.

Step-by-Step Guide to Sharing Content

Below is a detailed guide on how to share content on LinkedIn:

1. **Log in to LinkedIn:** Begin by accessing your LinkedIn account on your desktop or mobile device.

2. **Locate the Content You Want to Share:** This could be an article, a post from another user, or content from your company's LinkedIn page.

3. **Click the Share Button:** Once you find the content, click on the "Share" button located below the post or article.

4. **Add a Personal Note:** A text box will appear where you can write your thoughts or add a caption. For example:

   o *"This article provides great insights into the future of digital marketing. Highly recommend it for anyone in the industry!"*

   o *"Proud to share this exciting new project my team has been working on at [Company Name]."*

5. **Include Hashtags:** Use relevant hashtags to increase visibility. For example:

   o *#Marketing #DigitalTransformation #Leadership*

6. **Tag People or Organizations:** If the content involves specific individuals or companies, tag them by typing "@" followed by their name. This notifies them and encourages engagement.

7. **Adjust Privacy Settings:** Choose who can see your post—whether it's your connections, the public, or a specific group.

8. **Click Post:** Once you're satisfied with your message, click "Post" to share it with your network.

How to Share Different Types of Content

1. **Sharing Links to Articles or Blog Posts:**

   o Copy the URL of the article you want to share.

   o Paste the link into the LinkedIn share box. LinkedIn will automatically generate a preview, including the article's title, image, and summary.

   o Add your personal comment and post.

2. **Reposting Content from Your Feed:**

   o If you see a post in your LinkedIn feed that resonates with you, click the "Share" button.

   o Add your thoughts on why the post is important or relevant to your audience.

   o Post it directly or schedule it for later using third-party tools if necessary.

3. **Sharing Multimedia Content:**

    o Upload videos, images, or PDFs directly to LinkedIn.

    o Use captions or descriptions to provide context. For example, if you're sharing a presentation, briefly explain its purpose.

4. **Sharing Job Postings:**

    o If your company is hiring, you can share the job posting from the company page or LinkedIn Jobs section.

    o Mention why it's a great opportunity and encourage your network to apply or share it further.

Analyzing the Performance of Shared Content

After sharing content, it's important to monitor its performance to understand what resonates with your audience. LinkedIn provides analytics for your posts, including:

1. **Views:** The number of people who saw your content.

2. **Engagements:** The number of likes, comments, and shares.

3. **Demographics:** Insights into who viewed your post (e.g., industries, job titles, or locations).

Regularly reviewing these metrics can help you refine your content strategy and focus on topics that generate the most engagement.

By consistently sharing thoughtful and relevant content on LinkedIn, you can actively contribute to your network while strengthening your professional presence. It's a small but powerful way to demonstrate your expertise, connect with others, and open the door to new opportunities.

4.3 Publishing Articles on LinkedIn

4.3.1 Benefits of Writing Articles

Writing articles on LinkedIn is one of the most impactful ways to showcase your expertise, build your professional brand, and engage meaningfully with your audience. Unlike short posts or status updates, articles allow you to dive deeper into topics, provide valuable insights, and establish your credibility in your field. This section will explore the benefits of writing articles on LinkedIn, guiding beginners on why it's worth investing their time and effort into this feature.

1. Establishing Yourself as an Expert

One of the primary benefits of writing articles is the opportunity to position yourself as a thought leader in your industry. By sharing your knowledge, insights, and unique perspectives on specific topics, you demonstrate your expertise to your network and beyond.

- **Build Authority:** Articles allow you to delve into complex topics that a simple post cannot cover. By providing in-depth analysis, tips, or solutions, you establish yourself as a go-to professional in your niche.

- **Showcase Problem-Solving Skills:** Writing articles about challenges in your industry and offering actionable solutions showcases your ability to think critically and solve real-world problems.

- **Increase Credibility:** Regularly publishing high-quality articles builds trust with your audience and helps you stand out as a credible professional.

For example, if you're an HR professional, you could write an article titled *"How AI is Changing Recruitment Practices in 2025"* to showcase your understanding of emerging trends in your field.

2. Enhancing Your Personal Brand

LinkedIn articles play a crucial role in shaping your professional brand. In today's competitive job market, your personal brand is what sets you apart. Articles allow you to control the narrative about who you are and what you stand for.

- **Consistency in Branding:** By consistently writing about topics aligned with your career goals or industry, you strengthen your professional identity. For instance, a digital marketer writing about social media trends reinforces their expertise in that area.

- **Visibility:** Well-written articles have the potential to be shared widely, increasing your visibility beyond your immediate connections. LinkedIn's algorithm often promotes long-form content, helping you reach a larger audience.

- **Professionalism:** Thoughtfully written articles demonstrate your ability to communicate effectively and professionally—skills highly valued by employers and collaborators.

3. Engaging with a Broader Audience

While LinkedIn posts primarily reach your immediate connections, articles have the potential to attract a much larger audience. This wider reach offers several advantages:

- **Appearing in Search Results:** LinkedIn articles are indexed by search engines like Google, making them discoverable to professionals searching for related topics outside of LinkedIn.

- **Attracting Like-Minded Professionals:** Your articles can act as a magnet for individuals who share similar interests or challenges, opening doors for networking and collaboration opportunities.

- **Engaging International Audiences:** Since LinkedIn is a global platform, writing articles on topics of broad relevance can attract readers from different parts of the world, helping you build a diverse network.

For example, an article titled *"The Future of Remote Work: Trends and Predictions"* might resonate with professionals in multiple industries and regions.

4. Driving Conversations and Building Relationships

Writing articles is an excellent way to spark meaningful discussions within your professional network. Thought-provoking content encourages readers to engage, comment, and share their perspectives.

- **Initiating Discussions:** When you write about emerging trends, challenges, or innovative ideas, you invite others to share their opinions, fostering professional dialogue.

- **Gaining Feedback:** Articles can be a great way to crowdsource ideas or gather feedback from industry peers. For instance, ending your article with a question like *"What strategies have worked for you in overcoming this challenge?"* can encourage responses.

- **Building Connections:** Engaging with readers who comment on your articles often leads to meaningful connections and collaborations.

5. Demonstrating Thoughtfulness and Creativity

An article is a creative outlet that allows you to present your ideas in a structured, thoughtful manner. Unlike quick posts, articles give you the space to refine your message and back it up with data, case studies, or personal experiences.

- **Structured Communication:** Writing an article forces you to organize your thoughts logically, improving your communication skills over time.

- **Creative Freedom:** You can experiment with storytelling, visuals, and formatting to make your content more engaging and memorable.

- **Showcasing Innovation:** Writing about new ideas or unconventional approaches demonstrates your ability to think outside the box, an essential skill in any profession.

6. Attracting Recruiters and Employers

For job seekers, LinkedIn articles can serve as an extended resume, showcasing not just what you've done but how you think. Articles highlight your expertise and passion, making you more attractive to recruiters and potential employers.

- **Highlighting Expertise:** If you're looking to pivot into a new industry or role, writing insightful articles in that field can demonstrate your understanding and commitment, even if your past experience doesn't align perfectly.

- **Demonstrating Passion:** Sharing your enthusiasm for a specific topic or industry through articles can make a strong impression on hiring managers.

For example, a software developer could write an article titled *"Why I'm Passionate About Open-Source Development and Its Future Impact"* to showcase both technical expertise and personal motivation.

7. Boosting Engagement Metrics

Articles often receive more engagement than regular posts because they offer more value to readers. This increased engagement can significantly impact your LinkedIn metrics:

- **Profile Views:** High-quality articles often lead readers to visit your profile to learn more about you.

- **Connection Requests:** Readers who find your content valuable may send you connection requests, expanding your network.

- **Endorsements and Recommendations:** Engaging articles can encourage others to endorse your skills or write recommendations.

8. Long-Term Value

Unlike short posts, which may lose visibility within days, LinkedIn articles have a much longer lifespan. They remain on your profile under the "Activity" section, providing ongoing value to new visitors.

- **Timeless Content:** Articles that tackle evergreen topics, such as *"5 Tips for Effective Time Management,"* continue to attract readers long after publication.

- **Portfolio of Work:** Over time, your collection of articles becomes a body of work that showcases your expertise to anyone viewing your profile.

9. Supporting Career Growth

Whether you're looking to land a new job, secure a promotion, or grow your business, articles can play a pivotal role in advancing your career:

- **Building Influence:** Regularly publishing articles helps you become a recognized voice in your field, opening up opportunities for speaking engagements, collaborations, or mentorship.

- **Impressing Employers:** Many recruiters and employers actively seek candidates who contribute thought leadership in their industries. Your articles can set you apart from other applicants.

- **Growing Your Business:** Entrepreneurs and freelancers can use LinkedIn articles to showcase their services, attract clients, and build trust.

10. Summary

Writing articles on LinkedIn is an investment in your professional development. It allows you to share your expertise, build your brand, connect with like-minded professionals, and grow your career. The platform's tools and features make it easy to publish high-quality, engaging content that can reach a global audience. Whether you're new to LinkedIn or an experienced user, taking the time to craft thoughtful articles can yield significant personal and professional benefits.

4.3.2 How to Structure a Professional Article

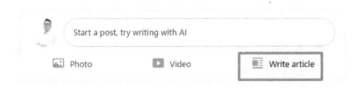

Publishing articles on LinkedIn is a powerful way to establish yourself as a thought leader, demonstrate your expertise, and engage with your network. Structuring your article effectively ensures your ideas are conveyed clearly and professionally, capturing your audience's attention and maintaining their interest throughout. This section provides a detailed step-by-step guide on how to structure a professional article on LinkedIn.

Step 1: Start with a Captivating Title

The title is the first thing people see, and it determines whether they'll click to read your article. A good title is clear, concise, and intriguing, making the value of your article immediately apparent.

- **Characteristics of a Strong Title**:
    - **Specific**: Avoid vague titles. Instead of "Tips for Success," use "5 Proven Strategies to Succeed in Digital Marketing."
    - **Actionable**: Use verbs that inspire action, such as "Master," "Discover," or "Learn."
    - **Relevant**: Ensure the title aligns with your target audience's interests and challenges.
    - **Engaging**: Consider adding numbers, questions, or intriguing adjectives. For example, "How to Build a Personal Brand That Stands Out."

- **Tips for Creating Titles**:
    - Write multiple options and choose the most compelling one.
    - Test different styles, such as "How-To," "Listicles," or "Case Studies."
    - Avoid clickbait – the title should reflect the content accurately.

Step 2: Write a Strong Introduction

Your introduction sets the tone for the article and should immediately capture the reader's attention. Use it to hook the audience, establish credibility, and preview what they'll gain by reading further.

- **Key Elements of an Introduction**:
    - **Hook**: Start with a question, a surprising fact, a relatable scenario, or a bold statement. For example, "Did you know that over 50% of LinkedIn users never optimize their profiles, missing out on career opportunities?"

- **Context**: Explain why the topic is important or relevant. Connect it to the reader's needs or challenges.

- **Purpose**: Clearly state what the article will cover. For instance, "In this article, we'll explore five actionable tips to improve your LinkedIn profile and attract recruiters."

Step 3: Structure the Main Body Clearly

The body of your article is where you deliver value. Break down your content into sections and use subheadings to organize ideas logically. This makes it easier for readers to skim and digest the information.

- **Divide Content into Clear Sections**:
  - Use headings and subheadings (H1, H2, H3) to segment your article.
  - Each section should focus on one main idea or point.

- **Include Examples and Case Studies**:
  - Support your points with real-life examples, statistics, or case studies.
  - For instance, if discussing personal branding, share a success story of someone who leveraged LinkedIn effectively.

- **Use Bullet Points and Lists**:
  - Break down complex ideas into simple, actionable steps.
  - For example:
    - Step 1: Update your headline.
    - Step 2: Add measurable achievements to your experience section.
    - Step 3: Publish regular content to engage your audience.

- **Maintain a Consistent Flow**:
  - Transition smoothly between sections.
  - Use linking phrases like "Next, let's explore..." or "Building on that point..."

Step 4: Add Visuals to Enhance Readability

Visual elements like images, graphs, or infographics can make your article more engaging and help readers understand complex ideas.

- **Tips for Using Visuals**:
    - Use relevant and high-quality images that complement your content.
    - Add charts or graphs to present data visually.
    - Embed videos, if applicable, to provide additional depth.
- **Placement of Visuals**:
    - Include at least one visual element in the introduction to catch attention.
    - Use visuals strategically in the body to break up text and highlight key points.

Step 5: Write a Powerful Conclusion

The conclusion ties everything together and leaves a lasting impression. It's also an opportunity to encourage engagement and action.

- **Summarize Key Points**:
    - Recap the main ideas discussed in the article.
    - Avoid introducing new information here.
- **Call to Action (CTA)**:
    - Encourage readers to take a specific action, such as leaving a comment, sharing the article, or connecting with you on LinkedIn. For example, "What strategies have worked for you in building your LinkedIn profile? Share your thoughts in the comments below!"
    - If applicable, provide links to related articles or resources for further reading.
- **End on an Inspiring Note**:

- Use a motivational statement or a thought-provoking question to leave readers with something to ponder.

Step 6: Optimize for LinkedIn's Audience

Before publishing your article, make sure it's optimized for LinkedIn's unique audience and platform.

- **Keep the Tone Professional Yet Approachable**:
  - Use language that reflects your expertise while remaining conversational.
  - Avoid overly technical jargon unless your audience is familiar with it.

- **Use Keywords for SEO**:
  - Identify relevant keywords related to your topic and naturally incorporate them into your title, headings, and content.
  - For example, if your article is about personal branding, include terms like "personal brand," "LinkedIn profile," and "networking."

- **Include a Professional Bio**:
  - At the end of your article, add a short bio introducing yourself. Mention your expertise and invite readers to connect or follow you on LinkedIn.

Step 7: Review, Edit, and Publish

Editing is a critical step in creating a professional article. A well-polished article reflects your attention to detail and credibility.

- **Proofread Your Content**:
  - Check for grammar, spelling, and punctuation errors.
  - Ensure your sentences are clear and concise.

- **Seek Feedback**:
  - Share your draft with a trusted colleague or mentor for their input.
  - Incorporate constructive suggestions to improve your article.

- **Use LinkedIn's Publishing Tools**:
    - Preview your article to check formatting, spacing, and visual alignment.
    - Ensure your title and images display correctly in the preview.
- **Publish and Promote**:
    - Share the article with your network and in relevant LinkedIn groups.
    - Engage with readers by responding to comments and messages.

Conclusion

Writing a professional article on LinkedIn is both an art and a science. By following this structured approach, you can create content that resonates with your audience, establishes your expertise, and helps you build meaningful connections. Whether you're sharing insights from your industry or offering practical advice, your article can become a valuable resource for your network while advancing your personal brand.

Example: A Professional LinkedIn Article

Title

"5 Simple Strategies to Build a Personal Brand on LinkedIn"

Introduction

Did you know that 85% of jobs are filled through networking? LinkedIn has become the go-to platform for professionals looking to grow their careers, connect with industry leaders, and showcase their expertise. Yet, many users struggle to stand out in this crowded space.

In this article, I'll share five simple and actionable strategies to help you build a strong personal brand on LinkedIn. Whether you're just starting your career or looking to grow professionally, these tips will help you establish credibility and attract the right opportunities.

Main Body

1. Optimize Your LinkedIn Profile

Your LinkedIn profile is your digital business card. It's often the first impression recruiters, potential clients, or collaborators will have of you.

- **Profile Photo**: Use a clear, professional photo with good lighting and a neutral background. Profiles with photos get 14 times more views than those without.

- **Headline**: Go beyond just your job title. For example, instead of "Marketing Specialist," try "Helping Businesses Grow with Data-Driven Marketing Strategies."

- **Summary**: Use this section to tell your story. Highlight your unique value proposition, your career goals, and what makes you different.

2. Share Relevant and Valuable Content

To position yourself as a thought leader, consistently share content that provides value to your network.

- **Post Your Insights**: Share your experiences, lessons learned, and tips related to your industry. For instance, "5 Lessons I Learned from Managing My First Marketing Campaign."

- **Curate Industry News**: Share articles or reports and add your personal thoughts. For example, "This report on digital marketing trends is a must-read for anyone in the field. I found the section on AI-driven strategies particularly insightful."

- **Use Visuals**: Posts with images or videos tend to get more engagement. Share infographics, slides, or even short video clips to convey your message more effectively.

3. Engage with Your Network

Building a personal brand isn't just about sharing content; it's also about meaningful interactions.

- **Comment Thoughtfully**: Engage with others' posts by leaving insightful comments. For example, "Great point! I've also noticed that leveraging data analytics can significantly improve campaign performance."

- **Celebrate Others**: Congratulate connections on their achievements, such as promotions, certifications, or anniversaries.

- **Respond to Messages**: Keep your interactions professional and timely. A simple "Thank you for reaching out! I'd love to discuss this further" goes a long way.

4. Publish Long-Form Articles

Long-form content allows you to dive deeper into your expertise and showcase your thought leadership. Here's how to structure a professional article:

- **Introduction**: Hook readers with a compelling opening. For example, "The marketing landscape has changed dramatically in the past decade. Are you keeping up with the trends?"

- **Body**: Break the article into sections with clear headings. Use examples, data, and visuals to support your points.

- **Conclusion**: Summarize key takeaways and include a call to action, such as "What strategies have worked for you in building your personal brand? Share your thoughts in the comments below."

5. Build and Maintain a Professional Network

Your connections are your greatest asset on LinkedIn. Focus on quality over quantity.

- **Personalize Connection Requests**: Instead of the generic "I'd like to connect," write a brief note explaining why you want to connect. For example, "Hi [Name], I enjoyed your recent post on leadership strategies. I'd love to connect and learn more from your insights."

- **Join Relevant Groups**: Participate in discussions to showcase your expertise. For example, if you're in marketing, join groups focused on digital marketing trends.

- **Follow Industry Leaders**: Engage with posts from influential figures in your field. This not only helps you learn but also increases your visibility.

Conclusion

Building a personal brand on LinkedIn doesn't happen overnight, but with consistent effort, you can create a profile and presence that sets you apart. Start by optimizing your profile, sharing valuable content, and engaging authentically with your network.

What are your favorite strategies for building your brand on LinkedIn? I'd love to hear your thoughts in the comments below!

Call to Action (CTA)

If you found this article helpful, feel free to share it with your network. For more tips and insights, follow me on LinkedIn or check out my other articles.

CHAPTER V
Job Searching on LinkedIn

5.1 Using the LinkedIn Job Board

5.1.1 Searching for Jobs Effectively

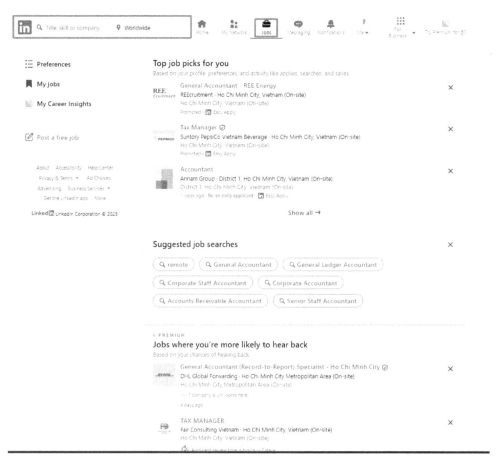

The LinkedIn Job Board is a powerful tool that connects job seekers with opportunities across industries and geographical locations. Whether you are searching for your first job, planning a career transition, or looking for a role to advance your professional journey, using LinkedIn's job board effectively can significantly improve your chances of success. Here, we'll explore how to optimize your job search and make the most of this feature.

1. Understand the Basics of LinkedIn's Job Board

The Job Board is located in the **"Jobs"** tab on LinkedIn's navigation bar. Once you click on it, you will find a wide range of features tailored to help you explore roles, save job listings, and monitor applications. The search interface includes fields for job titles, skills, or companies, as well as filters for location, experience level, and job type (e.g., full-time, part-time, remote, or contract). Familiarizing yourself with these elements is the first step in maximizing your experience.

Key Features of the LinkedIn Job Board:

- **Search Bar**: Allows you to search by job titles, keywords, or company names.

- **Filters**: Helps narrow down options by industry, job function, company size, and more.

- **Job Alerts**: Lets you save specific search criteria and receive notifications for matching opportunities.

- **Saved Jobs**: Enables you to bookmark listings for future reference.

- **Easy Apply**: Offers a streamlined application process for select roles.

- **Insights**: Displays additional data, such as company size, number of applicants, and connections within the organization.

2. Defining Your Job Search Goals

Before you dive into job postings, take a moment to outline your goals. A targeted approach will help you save time and focus on roles that align with your skills and interests. Here are some tips for defining your goals:

- **Identify Your Career Objectives**: What type of role are you seeking? Consider factors like job title, responsibilities, and industry.

- **Determine Your Priorities**: What matters most to you? Examples include location, salary, work-life balance, or opportunities for growth.

- **Know Your Skill Set**: Understand your strengths, technical skills, and areas where you may need improvement. This clarity will help you search for jobs that are a good match.

3. Using Keywords to Find the Right Roles

The search bar on LinkedIn's Job Board is your gateway to finding relevant positions, but its effectiveness depends on the keywords you use. Keywords are words or phrases related to job titles, skills, industries, or specific requirements.

Steps to Use Keywords Effectively:

1. **Research Common Job Titles**: Roles can have different titles depending on the company (e.g., "Marketing Specialist" vs. "Digital Marketing Coordinator"). Identify variations of titles in your field.

2. **Incorporate Relevant Skills**: Include key skills that align with the roles you want. For example, if you're looking for roles in data analysis, use terms like "data visualization," "SQL," or "Tableau."

3. **Use Boolean Search**: LinkedIn supports advanced search techniques such as Boolean operators:

   o **AND**: Combine multiple keywords (e.g., "Marketing AND Social Media").

   o **OR**: Broaden your search by including variations (e.g., "Content Marketing OR Copywriting").

   o **NOT**: Exclude specific terms (e.g., "Marketing NOT Sales").

   o **Quotation Marks**: Search for exact phrases (e.g., "Product Manager").

4. **Include Location Preferences**: Add city or country names to narrow your search to specific areas.

Example:

If you are looking for a remote marketing job, you could type: "Marketing Manager AND Remote" OR "Digital Marketing Specialist NOT Intern."

4. Refining Your Search with Filters

LinkedIn offers several filters to help you narrow down the vast pool of job postings. Here's how to use them:

- **Location**: Choose specific cities, regions, or countries where you want to work. You can also select "Remote" for work-from-home opportunities.

- **Experience Level**: Select from entry-level, mid-level, senior-level, or internships, depending on your qualifications.

- **Job Type**: Filter for full-time, part-time, contract, temporary, or freelance roles.

- **Company**: If you have specific companies in mind, use this filter to focus your search.

- **Posted Date**: Choose how recent the job posting should be (e.g., past 24 hours, past week).

- **Industry and Function**: Narrow results by the type of industry (e.g., finance, healthcare) or job function (e.g., human resources, engineering).

By applying multiple filters, you can significantly reduce irrelevant results and focus on roles that meet your preferences.

5. Analyzing Job Descriptions

When you find a job that looks appealing, take time to carefully read the job description. Pay attention to the following elements:

- **Responsibilities**: Ensure you fully understand the scope of the role and whether it matches your expectations.

- **Qualifications**: Check the required skills, certifications, and experience levels.

- **Keywords**: Identify recurring terms to better tailor your profile and application.

- **Company Information**: Review details about the company's mission, culture, and size. Use LinkedIn to explore their official page and employee reviews.

Pro Tip:

If you find recurring keywords or qualifications in job descriptions, incorporate them into your LinkedIn profile to increase visibility to recruiters.

6. Saving Jobs and Creating Alerts

If you come across jobs that interest you but aren't ready to apply yet, use the "Save" feature. Saved jobs can be accessed later, giving you time to research the company or prepare your application materials.

Creating Job Alerts:

LinkedIn allows you to save specific search criteria and receive notifications for new postings that match. Here's how to set up job alerts:

1. Perform a search using your desired keywords and filters.

2. Toggle the "Set Alert" switch at the top of the results page.

3. Customize the frequency of notifications (daily or weekly).

4. Monitor your email or LinkedIn notifications for updates.

7. Networking While Searching

LinkedIn is not just a job board—it's a networking platform. Leveraging your connections can give you an advantage in your job search.

Steps to Use Networking in Your Job Search:

1. **Research the Hiring Team**: Use LinkedIn to find recruiters or managers involved in the hiring process.

2. **Leverage Your Connections**: If someone in your network works at the company, reach out for insights or referrals.

3. **Join Relevant Groups**: Engage in discussions within LinkedIn groups related to your industry or job role.

4. **Follow Companies**: Stay updated on company news, job postings, and announcements.

8. Staying Organized

A well-organized job search is essential for tracking opportunities and ensuring timely applications. Use LinkedIn's features alongside personal tools like spreadsheets or productivity apps to:

- Keep track of jobs you've applied for.

- Note application deadlines.

- Monitor follow-ups and interview dates.

9. Common Mistakes to Avoid

- **Using Generic Keywords**: Be specific to find targeted roles.

- **Applying Without Reading the Description**: Ensure the role matches your qualifications.

- **Not Using Filters**: Filters can save time by narrowing down results.

- **Ignoring Analytics**: Pay attention to how your profile views correlate with your search activity.

Conclusion

Searching for jobs effectively on LinkedIn requires a combination of strategy, attention to detail, and consistent effort. By leveraging advanced search techniques, applying relevant filters, and optimizing your networking efforts, you can significantly enhance your job search experience and land a role that aligns with your career aspirations.

5.1.2 Setting Up Job Alerts

LinkedIn's Job Alerts feature is one of the most powerful tools for job seekers. It allows you to stay updated on new opportunities that match your criteria without manually searching every day. With the right setup, LinkedIn will do the heavy lifting for you, sending job postings directly to your inbox. This section will provide a detailed, step-by-step guide on how to set up, customize, and manage job alerts effectively.

What Are Job Alerts on LinkedIn?

Job Alerts are notifications generated by LinkedIn whenever a job posting matches your search criteria. These alerts help you stay ahead of the competition by letting you apply as soon as relevant jobs are posted. You can set alerts for specific roles, companies, locations, industries, or even a combination of filters.

LinkedIn delivers these alerts either through email or via notifications in the LinkedIn app or website, depending on your preferences.

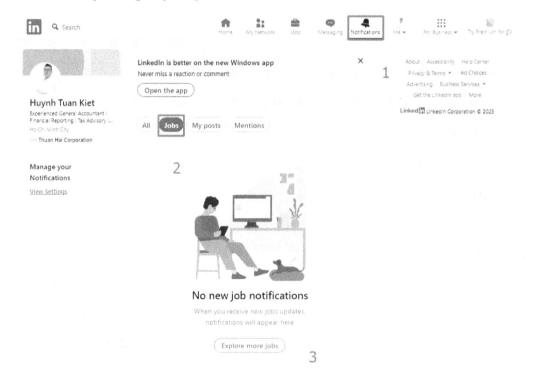

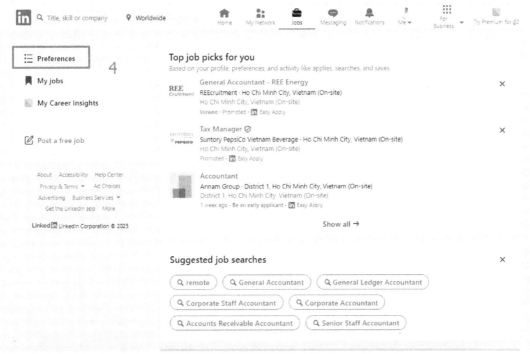

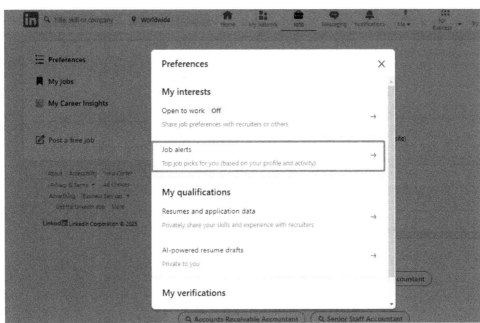

Benefits of Using Job Alerts

1. **Save Time:** Instead of repeatedly searching for jobs manually, you'll get updates as new positions are posted.

2. **Stay Competitive:** Applying early can increase your chances of catching a recruiter's attention.

3. **Personalized Results:** Job alerts ensure you only see postings relevant to your career goals and preferences.

4. **Track Hiring Trends:** By observing the frequency and type of jobs posted, you can better understand the market demand for your skills.

How to Set Up Job Alerts: A Step-by-Step Guide

Step 1: Navigate to the LinkedIn Jobs Tab

1. Log in to your LinkedIn account.

2. On the top menu bar (desktop) or bottom menu (mobile app), click on the "Jobs" tab. This will take you to the LinkedIn job board.

Step 2: Conduct a Job Search

1. In the search bar, enter the job title, keyword, or company name. For example: *"Marketing Manager," "Data Analyst,"* or *"Google."*

2. Add location details in the "Location" field. You can specify a city, region, or even opt for "Remote" if you're looking for work-from-home roles.

3. Click "Search" to see the job listings that match your criteria.

Step 3: Apply Filters for Precise Results

1. Use the filters at the top of the search results to refine your search. Filters include:

   o **Date Posted:** Filter jobs posted in the last 24 hours, past week, etc.

   o **Experience Level:** Select from options like Entry Level, Associate, Mid-Senior Level, etc.

   o **Job Type:** Full-time, Part-time, Contract, Temporary, Internship, etc.

- o **Industry:** Narrow down by industries such as Healthcare, Technology, Finance, etc.

- o **Company:** Focus on specific companies or industries you're targeting.

- o **Remote/On-site:** Choose between on-site, hybrid, or remote work.

2. Once the filters are applied, review the refined list to ensure it aligns with your preferences.

Step 4: Activate the Job Alert

1. On the search results page, look for the "Set Alert" toggle near the top of the results or in the upper right corner.

2. Turn on the toggle to activate job alerts for this search.

Customizing Your Job Alerts

Once you've set up your job alert, you can further customize it for better results.

Frequency of Alerts

- Decide how often you want to receive job alerts:

  - o **Daily Alerts:** Ideal if you're actively job hunting and want to apply quickly.

  - o **Weekly Alerts:** Suitable for passive job seekers or those casually exploring opportunities.

Notification Method

- Choose how you'd like to receive alerts:

  - o **Email Notifications:** Alerts will be sent directly to your registered email.

  - o **LinkedIn Notifications:** Alerts will appear as pop-up notifications on your LinkedIn homepage or app.

Modifying or Deleting Alerts

1. Go to the "Jobs" tab on LinkedIn.

2. Click on "Manage Alerts" or "Job Alerts" (varies by platform).

3. From here, you can:

- ○ **Edit Alert Settings:** Update the title, location, or filters.

- ○ **Delete Alerts:** Turn off alerts that are no longer relevant.

Tips for Maximizing Job Alerts

1. Create Multiple Alerts

- If you're exploring multiple career paths or industries, create separate alerts for each. For example:

  - ○ Alert 1: *Data Analyst roles in New York City.*

  - ○ Alert 2: *Remote Marketing Manager roles.*

2. Use Broad and Narrow Searches Strategically

- **Broad Searches:** Use general job titles or keywords to cast a wide net (e.g., "Marketing").

- **Narrow Searches:** Include specific job titles or requirements to target niche roles (e.g., "Digital Marketing Specialist with SEO experience").

3. Update Alerts as Your Goals Change

- Regularly revisit your alerts to ensure they align with your evolving career goals or geographic preferences.

4. Monitor Alert Frequency

- Avoid overwhelming your inbox by limiting the number of alerts to the most critical searches.

5. Combine Alerts with Networking

- Use job alerts as a starting point, but remember to engage with your LinkedIn network to increase visibility and gain referrals.

Troubleshooting Job Alerts

Issue 1: Not Receiving Alerts

- Check your email spam/junk folder to ensure LinkedIn emails aren't being flagged.

- Verify your LinkedIn notification settings to ensure alerts are enabled.

Issue 2: Alerts Are Too Broad or Irrelevant

- Refine your search criteria by adding more filters. For example, specify industries or job types.

- Review keywords in your job search to ensure they align with your goals.

Issue 3: Alerts Are Too Narrow

- Broaden your filters by removing restrictive criteria like specific company names or experience levels.

Real-Life Example: Setting Job Alerts for Success

Let's say Jane is a marketing professional looking for a remote role in content marketing. Here's how she sets up her job alerts:

1. **Search Criteria:**

   o Job Title: "Content Marketing Manager"

   o Location: "Remote"

   o Filters: Full-time, Marketing & Advertising Industry

2. **Alert Frequency:** Daily (to stay updated on new postings).

3. **Results:** Jane begins receiving tailored job postings within hours, allowing her to apply to high-quality roles before many other applicants.

Conclusion

Setting up job alerts on LinkedIn is an essential step for any job seeker. By leveraging this feature, you can stay proactive in your search while saving time and effort. Whether you're actively job hunting or just exploring opportunities, job alerts provide a personalized, efficient way to connect with the right opportunities.

With a properly configured alert system, you'll never miss a chance to apply for your dream job. So, start setting up your alerts today and let LinkedIn work for you!

5.2 Optimizing Your Profile for Recruiters

5.2.1 Enabling "Open to Work" Features

One of the most powerful tools LinkedIn offers to job seekers is the **"Open to Work" feature**, which lets recruiters know you are actively seeking opportunities. When enabled, this feature increases your visibility to hiring professionals and makes your job search more efficient. Here's a comprehensive guide on how to enable and optimize the "Open to Work" feature effectively.

What is the "Open to Work" Feature?

The "Open to Work" feature is a LinkedIn tool that allows you to discreetly or publicly signal your interest in new job opportunities. Depending on your preference, you can display the "Open to Work" badge on your profile photo for everyone to see, or you can share this information privately with recruiters only.

By enabling this feature, LinkedIn allows recruiters to match your skills, experience, and preferences with relevant job openings. This feature is particularly useful for passive job seekers who want to explore opportunities without committing to a full-fledged job search.

Benefits of Enabling "Open to Work"

Before diving into the steps, it's important to understand the benefits of this feature:

1. **Increased Visibility to Recruiters**: Recruiters actively search for candidates with the "Open to Work" status, giving you a better chance of being contacted.

2. **Personalized Job Suggestions**: Once enabled, LinkedIn's algorithm will recommend jobs tailored to your preferences, saving you time in your search.

3. **Showcasing Availability**: If you choose to display the badge, it makes your intentions clear to your network, potentially leading to referrals.

4. **Enhanced Profile Targeting**: Recruiters can view your location, preferred job titles, industries, and availability, helping them assess your fit for roles.

Step-by-Step Guide to Enabling "Open to Work"

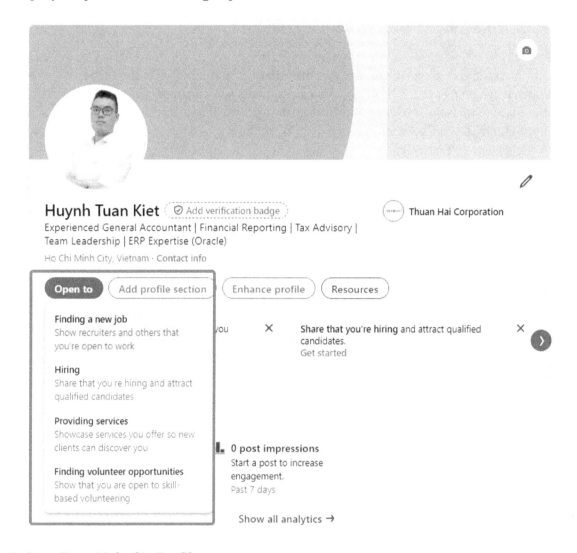

1. Go to Your LinkedIn Profile

- Log in to your LinkedIn account.

- Click on the **"Me"** icon at the top of your LinkedIn homepage and select **"View Profile."**

2. Locate the Open to Work Section

- Below your profile photo and headline, find the **"Open to Work"** or **"Show recruiters you're open"** prompt.

- If you don't see it, click the **"Add Profile Section"** button and select **"Intro"** followed by **"Looking for a new job."**

3. Set Up Your Preferences

- A pop-up window will appear asking for details about your job search. Fill in the following fields:

  - **Job Titles**: Enter specific roles you are targeting (e.g., Marketing Manager, Software Engineer).

  - **Job Locations**: Select your preferred work locations, such as cities or countries. If you're open to remote work, be sure to include that option.

  - **Start Date**: Indicate when you're available to start a new job. Options include "Immediately," "Flexible," or a future date.

  - **Job Types**: Specify whether you're looking for full-time, part-time, contract, freelance, or internship opportunities.

4. Choose Your Audience

You'll be given two audience options:

- **Recruiters Only**: Selecting this option ensures that only LinkedIn recruiters using the Recruiter tool can see your "Open to Work" status. This is ideal if you're currently employed and want to keep your job search private.

- **All LinkedIn Members**: This option displays the **"Open to Work" badge** on your profile photo, making your job search visible to your entire network. It's a great choice if you're open to more public exposure or want to signal your availability broadly.

5. Save Your Settings

- Once all the details are complete, click **"Save"** to activate the feature.

- Your profile will now reflect your "Open to Work" preferences, and recruiters can find you based on the criteria you've set.

Best Practices for Using "Open to Work"

1. Be Strategic with Your Job Titles

Include job titles that align with your skills and career goals. Avoid vague terms like "Manager" or "Specialist." Instead, use specific roles like **"Digital Marketing Specialist"** or **"Project Manager in IT."** This improves your chances of appearing in recruiter searches.

2. Include Remote Work Preferences

In today's job market, remote work is a highly sought-after option. If you're open to remote positions, make sure to include this preference when setting up the "Open to Work" feature. It signals flexibility and expands your job search beyond geographical boundaries.

3. Keep Your Profile Updated

Your "Open to Work" feature will only be effective if your LinkedIn profile is complete and up-to-date. Ensure your headline, experience, skills, and summary reflect your current career goals.

4. Use Relevant Keywords

When filling out your job titles and preferences, use industry-specific keywords to improve your visibility in recruiter searches. For example, instead of "Designer," specify **"UI/UX Designer"** or **"Graphic Designer."**

5. Be Mindful of Privacy Settings

If you're currently employed and don't want your job search to be public, choose the **"Recruiters Only"** option to avoid awkward conversations with your employer. LinkedIn takes precautions to prevent your employer's recruiters from seeing your status, but always exercise caution.

Troubleshooting Common Issues

1. Why Can't I Find the "Open to Work" Feature?

This feature might not appear if your profile isn't complete. Ensure your profile includes:

- A profile photo

- A headline

- At least one job experience

2. Recruiters Aren't Contacting Me. What Can I Do?

If you're not receiving recruiter messages, consider these adjustments:

- Refine your job titles and preferences.

- Add more relevant skills to your profile.

- Engage with LinkedIn by sharing posts or commenting on industry-related topics to increase visibility.

3. Can I Change My Preferences After Saving?

Yes, you can edit or update your "Open to Work" settings at any time. Simply return to the "Open to Work" section on your profile and click the pencil icon to make changes.

Advanced Tips for Maximizing "Open to Work"

1. Combine It with LinkedIn Premium

Upgrading to LinkedIn Premium offers additional benefits, such as seeing who has viewed your profile, accessing LinkedIn Learning, and sending InMails to recruiters. While not mandatory, it can enhance your job search.

2. Leverage Your Network

Reach out to connections in your industry and let them know you're exploring opportunities. Combine the "Open to Work" feature with active networking to increase your chances of referrals.

3. Monitor Profile Analytics

Regularly check your profile views and engagement metrics to see how effective your settings are. Adjust your preferences or profile content based on these insights.

By following this comprehensive guide, you'll be able to effectively set up and optimize the "Open to Work" feature on LinkedIn, increasing your chances of landing your next role.

This tool, when paired with an optimized profile and strategic networking, can significantly enhance your job search journey.

5.2.2 Keywords to Get Noticed

When recruiters search for potential candidates on LinkedIn, one of the primary tools they use is keywords. LinkedIn's search engine relies heavily on keywords to match job seekers with open positions, which means using the right keywords can significantly increase your chances of getting noticed. In this section, we'll break down how keywords work on LinkedIn, why they matter, and how you can strategically use them to optimize your profile and improve your chances of being discovered by recruiters.

Why Keywords Matter on LinkedIn

Keywords are specific terms or phrases that recruiters and hiring managers type into the LinkedIn search bar when they are looking for candidates with particular skills, experiences, or qualifications. These keywords can relate to job titles, skills, certifications, or even industries. Essentially, the right keywords ensure that your profile appears in the search results when recruiters are looking for someone with your expertise.

LinkedIn uses an algorithm to scan your profile for these keywords in key areas such as your headline, summary, work experience, skills, and endorsements. When your profile matches the keywords in the recruiter's search query, you are more likely to appear in the search results, making it easier for recruiters to find you.

Identifying the Right Keywords

The first step to keyword optimization is identifying the right keywords to use in your profile. There are several ways to find keywords that will make your profile stand out:

1. **Job Descriptions**: One of the best ways to find relevant keywords is to look at the job descriptions for positions you are interested in. Pay attention to the skills, qualifications, and job titles mentioned most frequently. These are often the keywords that recruiters are searching for.

2. **Industry Terms**: Certain industries have specific terminology that is commonly used to describe skills, processes, and certifications. Research your industry and understand the common terms that apply to your role.

3. **Competitor Profiles**: You can also analyze profiles of people in similar roles or industries who are successful in attracting recruiters. Take note of the keywords they use in their profile, such as their headline, skills, and summary.

4. **Job Titles**: If you're aiming for a specific job or career path, including the job titles in your profile will help make your profile more discoverable. For example, if you're looking for a role as a "Digital Marketing Manager," ensure that the title is used in your profile.

5. **LinkedIn Suggestions**: LinkedIn provides suggestions for skills that you might want to add to your profile. These suggestions are often based on popular searches in your industry and can help you identify key terms relevant to your field.

Where to Use Keywords on Your LinkedIn Profile

Now that you know which keywords to target, the next step is to strategically place them in your profile. Below are the most important sections where you should include keywords:

1. **Headline**: Your LinkedIn headline is one of the first things recruiters see, and it's also one of the first places LinkedIn looks when searching for candidates. Make sure to include your most important job title or industry-specific keyword in your headline. For example, instead of just "Marketing Professional," use something like "Digital Marketing Specialist | SEO Expert | Content Marketing Strategist." This not only includes your job title but also relevant skills and areas of expertise.

2. **Summary**: Your LinkedIn summary is a great place to expand on your experience, skills, and achievements, and it's a perfect place to add several of your chosen keywords. Try to naturally incorporate keywords into the narrative of your summary, rather than just listing them out. For instance, you might say something like, "With over 5 years of experience in digital marketing, I specialize in SEO, content marketing, and social media strategy to help businesses improve their online presence and grow their customer base."

3. **Work Experience**: In your work experience section, you should include job-specific keywords related to the positions you've held. List the specific skills, tools, and achievements associated with each role, making sure to include relevant keywords. For example, if you worked as a software developer, you might list skills like "JavaScript," "Python," and "Agile Methodologies."

4. **Skills Section**: The skills section is one of the most important areas to add keywords. LinkedIn allows you to list up to 50 skills, and many recruiters will use this section to search for candidates with specific skills. Be strategic and ensure that

the skills listed are tailored to the types of roles you want to pursue. Don't just add every skill you've ever used—focus on the key ones that matter for the roles you're targeting.

5. **Education and Certifications**: If you have relevant education or certifications, ensure that you list them with appropriate keywords. For example, if you completed a project management certification, use the full name of the certification, such as "Project Management Professional (PMP)." You might also want to include terms like "Certified ScrumMaster" or "Six Sigma Green Belt" if they are relevant to the positions you're targeting.

6. **Recommendations**: Recommendations are also a great place to get more keywords naturally included in your profile. When someone writes a recommendation for you, they might mention specific skills, achievements, or tools you used that will help reinforce the keywords in your profile.

How to Avoid Keyword Stuffing

While it's important to include relevant keywords, it's equally important to avoid keyword stuffing. Keyword stuffing is the practice of overloading your profile with keywords in an unnatural way, and it can make your profile sound robotic or spammy. This can also hurt your chances of being discovered by recruiters, as LinkedIn's algorithm is designed to penalize profiles that don't read naturally.

To avoid keyword stuffing, focus on writing a compelling, authentic profile. Keywords should be integrated in a way that makes sense for the narrative you're telling about your skills, experience, and career goals. Make sure the flow of your profile remains smooth and professional, and don't force keywords where they don't belong.

Additional Tips for Optimizing Your Profile with Keywords

- **Be Specific**: Instead of using broad terms like "Marketing," try using more specific keywords such as "SEO," "Email Marketing," or "Content Strategy." Specific keywords can help you stand out to recruiters searching for candidates with niche expertise.

- **Match the Job Requirements**: If you are actively applying for jobs, tailor your LinkedIn profile to match the key skills and qualifications listed in the job description. This can increase the likelihood of your profile appearing in relevant recruiter searches.

- **Use Synonyms**: Different recruiters might use different search terms, so include variations of your primary keywords. For example, if you're in the finance industry, use both "Financial Analyst" and "Finance Specialist" as keywords, depending on the job titles used in your field.

- **Keep Your Profile Updated**: Regularly updating your profile with new skills, certifications, or job experiences ensures that your profile stays relevant to recruiters and increases your chances of being discovered.

Conclusion

By strategically using keywords throughout your LinkedIn profile, you significantly improve your chances of getting noticed by recruiters and being matched with relevant job opportunities. Remember to focus on the most important skills, job titles, and certifications that are directly relevant to the roles you're interested in. Keep your profile natural and authentic, and avoid keyword stuffing to ensure that your profile stands out for all the right reasons.

With the right keywords in place, your LinkedIn profile will be better positioned to catch the attention of recruiters and increase your opportunities for career advancement.

5.3 Applying for Jobs on LinkedIn

5.3.1 How to Use the "Easy Apply" Feature

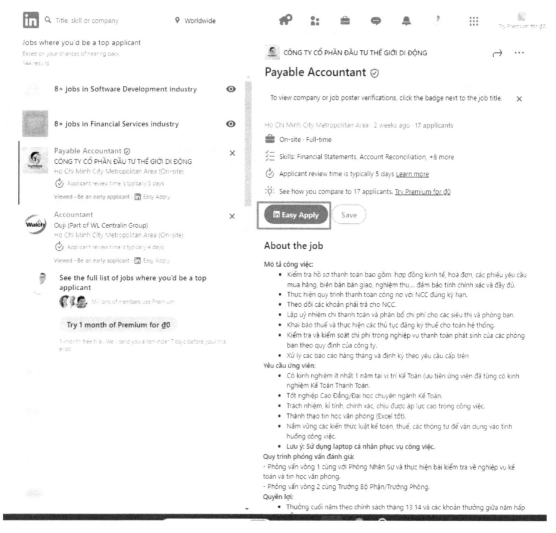

The **"Easy Apply"** feature on LinkedIn streamlines the job application process, making it faster and more convenient for both job seekers and employers. When you apply for a job via LinkedIn, the traditional process often involves uploading your resume, filling out additional forms, and answering questions. However, with **Easy Apply**, all of this is simplified to just a few clicks. This feature is designed to make applying for jobs as seamless and straightforward as possible, saving you time and effort.

What is the "Easy Apply" Feature?

The **"Easy Apply"** button is a simplified job application tool that allows you to apply for positions on LinkedIn without needing to leave the platform. When an employer posts a job listing, they can enable the **Easy Apply** option, which lets you submit your application by uploading your resume and completing a few fields. In many cases, your profile information will automatically be populated into the application, further streamlining the process.

The **Easy Apply** feature is typically available for job postings that require minimal additional information beyond your resume, such as entry-level positions, internships, and roles with fewer specific application requirements. This makes it particularly useful for candidates applying to multiple jobs or those who want to submit an application quickly.

How to Find Jobs with "Easy Apply"

Before diving into how to use the **Easy Apply** feature, let's go over how you can find jobs that have the **Easy Apply** option available.

1. **Search for Jobs on LinkedIn**: Start by navigating to the **Jobs** tab at the top of your LinkedIn homepage. From here, you can search for jobs using keywords, company names, locations, and filters like industry, experience level, and date posted.

Tip: Use relevant search terms to narrow down your results. You can also save job searches for future reference.

2. **Look for the "Easy Apply" Label**: Once you've filtered your search results, look for jobs with the **Easy Apply** label next to the job title. This is your signal that you can apply directly through LinkedIn without having to go through an external application portal.

Tip: To save time, filter your job search by using the **"Easy Apply"** option from the filters section to only show jobs with this feature enabled.

How to Use the "Easy Apply" Button

Applying for jobs using the **Easy Apply** feature is quick and easy. Here's a step-by-step guide on how to use it:

1. **Review the Job Description** Before applying, carefully read through the entire job description. Ensure that the position aligns with your skills, experience, and career goals. Pay special attention to the job requirements and responsibilities to determine if you're a good fit for the role.

2. **Click the "Easy Apply" Button** Once you've found a job you want to apply for, look for the **"Easy Apply"** button. This button is usually located near the top-right corner of the job posting page, just below the company's name and the job title. Simply click on the button to start your application process.

3. **Review Your Profile Information** After clicking **"Easy Apply"**, LinkedIn will automatically pre-fill certain sections of the application with information from your LinkedIn profile. This includes your name, contact details, work experience, education, and skills. Review this information carefully to ensure it's accurate and up to date.

Tip: Make sure that your LinkedIn profile is fully updated before applying. The more complete your profile, the more professional and accurate your application will appear.

4. **Upload Your Resume** Although LinkedIn pre-fills a lot of information for you, the next step is usually to upload your resume. LinkedIn allows you to either upload a new resume or use an existing one from your profile (if you've previously uploaded one). If you don't have a resume ready, you can quickly download it from your LinkedIn profile by clicking on the **"Upload Resume"** button.

Tip: Even though the process is simplified, make sure your resume is tailored to the specific job you're applying for. Customizing your resume for each job increases your chances of getting noticed by recruiters.

5. **Add Any Additional Information** Some employers may require additional information, such as a cover letter, answers to specific questions, or a brief message about your qualifications. While this is optional in many **Easy Apply** applications, it's always a good idea to include a customized cover letter or brief note to further highlight your suitability for the role. If prompted, attach a brief message or response to specific questions.

6. **Submit Your Application** Once everything is in place and you've double-checked your information, click the **"Submit Application"** button. Your application will be sent directly to the employer via LinkedIn's application system. Depending on the company, you might also receive a confirmation email or notification once your application has been received.

What Happens After You Apply Using Easy Apply?

Once your application is submitted, you'll be able to track its progress through your LinkedIn account. Here's what to expect:

1. **Application Status Updates** LinkedIn will notify you if your application has been reviewed, shortlisted, or passed over. You can check the status of your applications by visiting the **Jobs** section of your LinkedIn profile and selecting **"Applied"** to see your application history.

2. **Recruiter Engagement** If the employer is interested in your application, they may reach out to you through LinkedIn messages or via email. Keep an eye on your inbox for any follow-up communications from recruiters, as well as any interview invitations or requests for additional information.

3. **Job Recommendations** If your application is unsuccessful, LinkedIn may still offer you similar job recommendations based on your search history and the positions you've applied for. This can help you continue your job search and find new opportunities.

Tips for Maximizing the Effectiveness of Easy Apply

While the **Easy Apply** feature is convenient, it's important to use it strategically to get the best results. Here are some tips for making the most out of **Easy Apply**:

1. **Tailor Your Resume for Each Job** Even though **Easy Apply** makes applying faster, it's still essential to tailor your resume and profile to each job you apply for. Highlight the skills and experience that are most relevant to the position, and make sure your resume aligns with the keywords and qualifications in the job description.

2. **Keep Your Profile Updated** Your LinkedIn profile is often the first impression an employer has of you, so it's crucial to keep it current. Update your work experience, education, skills, and accomplishments regularly, and ensure your profile is professional and complete.

3. **Use Keywords for Better Visibility** Recruiters often search for candidates using specific keywords related to job roles. Make sure your profile contains the right keywords by referring to job descriptions that interest you. Use these keywords in your headline, summary, experience, and skills sections.

4. **Connect with Recruiters** After applying through **Easy Apply**, consider connecting with the recruiter or hiring manager on LinkedIn. Send a brief, polite message introducing yourself and expressing your enthusiasm for the position. This can help you stand out and create a more personal connection.

5. **Follow Companies of Interest** Many companies post jobs via LinkedIn. By following companies you're interested in, you'll receive updates about their job postings and company news, keeping you informed about new opportunities.

6. **Monitor Your Application Status** Don't just apply and forget about it. Keep track of your applications and check for updates. If you haven't heard back after a few weeks, consider following up with a polite LinkedIn message to inquire about your application status.

Conclusion

The **Easy Apply** feature is an incredibly valuable tool for job seekers on LinkedIn. By simplifying the application process and allowing you to apply directly on the platform, it saves you time and makes it easier to submit your resume for multiple job opportunities. However, it's important to ensure that your LinkedIn profile is fully optimized, and that you tailor each application to the specific job. By doing so, you can maximize your chances of being noticed by recruiters and increase your likelihood of landing the job you desire.

By leveraging the **Easy Apply** feature effectively, you can streamline your job search, save time, and create a professional, tailored application every time. Keep using LinkedIn strategically, and you'll be well on your way to success in your career journey.

5.3.2 Tracking Your Applications

Tracking your job applications on LinkedIn is a crucial step in staying organized, maintaining a professional approach, and ensuring follow-ups with potential employers. This section will provide you with a detailed guide to monitor your job applications effectively using LinkedIn's features and best practices.

Why Tracking Applications is Important

Applying for jobs online can become overwhelming, especially if you are applying to multiple positions at the same time. Without proper tracking, you risk losing track of key information, such as:

- **Which roles you applied for.**

- **When you applied.**

- **Which stage you are in during the hiring process.**

- **Employer responses or follow-up deadlines.**

Tracking your applications helps you to:

- Stay proactive and follow up appropriately.

- Keep your job search organized.

- Avoid applying to the same job multiple times.

- Understand which application strategies work best for you.

How to Track Applications Directly on LinkedIn

LinkedIn offers a built-in feature to help you manage and review your applications. Here's how you can utilize it effectively:

1. Accessing Your Job Applications

1. Navigate to the **Jobs** section by clicking the **"Jobs"** icon in the top menu bar.

2. On the Jobs page, locate the **"My Jobs"** tab, typically on the left-hand menu or at the top of the page.

3. Click on **"My Jobs"** to view a list of all the positions you've applied for or saved.

2. Reviewing Your Application Status

Once you're on the **"My Jobs"** page, you'll see a list of jobs categorized by application status:

- **Saved Jobs:** These are positions you have bookmarked but not applied to yet.

- **Applied Jobs:** These are roles where you've successfully submitted an application.

- **In Progress:** These might include jobs where the employer has started reviewing your application.

LinkedIn may also display additional statuses, such as **"Viewed"** (when the employer has viewed your application) or **"Not Selected"** (if you weren't chosen for the role).

3. Viewing Job Details

Click on a specific job title in your **My Jobs** list to:

- See the full job description.

- Review the date you applied.

- Access the employer's company page.

4. Adding Notes to Applications

LinkedIn allows you to add personal notes to track additional details for each job. For example:

- Date of application submission.

- Key contacts (e.g., the recruiter's name).

- Follow-up reminders.
  This feature is particularly helpful for tracking deadlines or interview schedules.

Creating a Personal Job Application Tracker

While LinkedIn provides built-in tools, creating a personal tracker can give you more flexibility. Here's how to create one:

1. Choose a Tool for Tracking

You can use various tools to build your tracker:

- **Spreadsheets** (e.g., Google Sheets, Microsoft Excel).

- **Note-taking apps** (e.g., Notion, OneNote, or Evernote).

- **Dedicated job application platforms** (e.g., JibberJobber or Huntr).

2. Structure Your Tracker

Include key columns to keep all relevant details in one place:

- **Company Name**: The name of the company you applied to.

- **Job Title**: The title of the position you applied for.

- **Date Applied**: When you submitted your application.

- **Application Status**: Examples: "Applied," "Under Review," "Interview Scheduled," "Rejected," etc.

- **Contact Person**: Name and email of the recruiter or hiring manager.

- **Follow-Up Date**: When to follow up with the employer.

- **Job Link**: Direct URL to the job posting (important in case you need to revisit it).

- **Additional Notes**: Any other relevant details (e.g., salary expectations, interview feedback, etc.).

3. Update Your Tracker Regularly

Make it a habit to update your tracker as soon as you apply for a job, receive a response, or move to the next stage of the hiring process. Consistency ensures you don't miss any important details.

Following Up on Applications

Proper follow-up is an integral part of the application process. Here's how you can approach it professionally:

1. When to Follow Up

- Wait **7–10 business days** after submitting your application.

- If a specific response date is mentioned in the job posting, follow up a few days after that date if you haven't heard back.

2. How to Follow Up

- Use LinkedIn to message the recruiter or hiring manager if their profile is available.

- Alternatively, send a professional follow-up email.

- Your message should be concise, polite, and express genuine interest in the role. Example:

Subject: Follow-Up on Application for [Job Title]

Body:
Dear [Recruiter's Name],

I hope this message finds you well. I recently applied for the [Job Title] position at [Company Name] on [Date], and I wanted to kindly follow up to inquire about the status of my application. I'm very enthusiastic about the opportunity to contribute to your team and would be happy to provide any additional information you may need.

Thank you for your time, and I look forward to hearing from you.
Best regards,
[Your Name]

Leveraging LinkedIn Insights to Refine Your Applications

LinkedIn offers tools to evaluate your application performance and make improvements:

1. Insights on Job Postings

Some job postings display the number of applicants and provide insights into the competition, such as:

- Skills most applicants possess.

- Average experience level of applicants.

Use these insights to tailor your profile or resume to match the employer's expectations.

2. Profile Analytics

Regularly check your LinkedIn analytics to see if recruiters are viewing your profile after you apply. If your profile views spike after submitting an application, it's a good sign that your application has drawn attention.

Common Mistakes to Avoid When Tracking Applications

1. **Applying Without Saving Job Details:** Always save the job posting or copy key information before it's removed.

2. **Forgetting to Follow Up:** Timely follow-ups can make a big difference.

3. **Mixing Up Applications:** Be organized to avoid confusing roles or companies.

4. **Overlooking Notes:** Always add details about your interactions and responses.

Final Thoughts

Tracking your applications on LinkedIn not only helps you stay organized but also positions you as a thoughtful and proactive candidate. By leveraging LinkedIn's tools, creating a personalized system, and maintaining a professional approach, you'll increase your chances of landing interviews and ultimately securing the job you want. Stay consistent, remain patient, and remember that every step you take moves you closer to your goal.

CHAPTER VI
Growing Your Personal Brand

6.1 Understanding Personal Branding

6.1.1 What is Personal Branding?

Personal branding is the process of crafting and managing the way others perceive you in a professional setting. It's about showcasing your skills, expertise, values, and unique qualities in a way that resonates with your target audience, whether that's potential employers, collaborators, or industry peers. Personal branding on LinkedIn is especially important because the platform serves as a global hub for networking, recruitment, and thought leadership.

In this section, we'll dive into the key concepts of personal branding, why it matters, and how to start creating a strong and authentic brand that works for you.

What is Personal Branding?

At its core, personal branding is the combination of your professional identity and your reputation. It's what people think of you when they see your LinkedIn profile or hear your name in a professional context. A strong personal brand communicates who you are, what you stand for, and why someone should want to connect or work with you.

On LinkedIn, your personal brand includes every detail of your profile: your photo, headline, summary, experience, skills, endorsements, recommendations, and the content you share or engage with. Each of these elements plays a role in shaping how others perceive you online.

Think of your personal brand as your professional fingerprint — it's uniquely yours, and no two are alike. The goal is to make your fingerprint as clear and impactful as possible, so it leaves a lasting impression.

The Importance of Defining Your Personal Brand

Your personal brand is not just about how you present yourself but also about how you differentiate yourself from others in your field. Defining your personal brand can benefit you in several key ways:

1. **Showcasing Your Unique Value**: Personal branding allows you to highlight your specific skills, strengths, and experiences that set you apart. By communicating your unique value proposition (UVP), you make it easier for potential employers, clients, or collaborators to understand why you are the right person for a job or partnership.

2. **Building Trust and Credibility**: A well-thought-out personal brand builds trust. When your LinkedIn profile reflects a consistent and professional image, others are more likely to see you as knowledgeable and credible in your field. This trust can open doors to job offers, new opportunities, and meaningful connections.

3. **Establishing Thought Leadership**: A strong personal brand positions you as a thought leader in your industry. By sharing your expertise through posts, articles, and comments, you demonstrate your authority on key topics, making you a go-to person for insights in your niche.

4. **Creating Opportunities**: A clear and compelling personal brand attracts opportunities. Recruiters, hiring managers, and business partners often search for professionals who stand out, and your brand ensures you're visible to them.

5. **Navigating Career Transitions**: Whether you're changing industries, looking for a promotion, or pivoting to entrepreneurship, a personal brand can help smooth the transition by showcasing your adaptability and the value you bring in different contexts.

Core Elements of Personal Branding on LinkedIn

To develop your personal brand, you need to focus on the following key elements:

1. **Authenticity**
   Your brand should reflect who you truly are. Avoid pretending to be someone you're not or exaggerating your abilities. Authenticity builds trust and ensures that the opportunities you attract align with your actual skills and values.

2. **Clarity**

   Your brand message should be simple and easy to understand. A recruiter or potential connection should be able to glance at your LinkedIn profile and immediately grasp what you do and what you stand for.

3. **Consistency**

   Consistency is crucial in personal branding. All aspects of your profile, from your photo to your posts, should align with the message you want to convey. Inconsistent branding can confuse your audience and dilute your impact.

4. **Value-Driven Content:** Sharing valuable insights, tips, and opinions demonstrates your expertise and builds your reputation. Regularly engaging with content that aligns with your brand strengthens your professional presence on LinkedIn.

5. **Adaptability**

   Your personal brand should evolve as you grow in your career. Updating your profile regularly to reflect new skills, achievements, and roles ensures your brand stays relevant and impactful.

Steps to Define Your Personal Brand

Creating a personal brand on LinkedIn involves several deliberate steps:

1. **Identify Your Goals**: Start by clarifying what you want to achieve with your LinkedIn presence. Are you looking to land a job, build a professional network, or establish yourself as an expert in your field? Your goals will shape how you approach your brand.

2. **Define Your Unique Value Proposition (UVP)**: Your UVP is what makes you stand out. Ask yourself:

   o   What skills or experiences do I bring to the table?

   o   How have I contributed to previous roles or projects?

   o   What problems can I solve for employers or clients?

3. **Understand Your Target Audience**: Who do you want to reach on LinkedIn? Whether it's recruiters, industry peers, or potential clients, understanding your audience will help you tailor your profile and content to their interests and needs.

4. **Audit Your Current LinkedIn Presence**: Take a critical look at your current profile. Does it reflect the professional image you want to project? Are there areas for improvement, such as updating your summary or removing outdated information?

5. **Craft Your Professional Narrative**: Use your headline, summary, and experience sections to tell your professional story. Your narrative should highlight your expertise, achievements, and future aspirations while staying concise and engaging.

6. **Optimize Your Profile for Visibility**: Incorporate relevant keywords throughout your profile to ensure it appears in LinkedIn searches. Focus on industry-specific terms that recruiters or peers are likely to search for.

7. **Develop a Content Strategy**: Regularly share content that aligns with your brand. This could include industry insights, tips, or updates on projects you're working on. Engaging with others' posts also helps you stay visible.

Common Pitfalls to Avoid in Personal Branding

While building your personal brand, be mindful of these common mistakes:

1. **Being Too Generic**: Avoid using vague or overused terms like "hardworking" or "detail-oriented." Instead, provide concrete examples of your skills and accomplishments.

2. **Neglecting Your Profile**: An incomplete or outdated profile can undermine your credibility. Make it a habit to review and update your LinkedIn profile regularly.

3. **Oversharing Personal Details**: While it's important to show personality, LinkedIn is a professional platform. Focus on sharing insights and achievements relevant to your career.

4. **Ignoring Engagement**: Simply having a strong profile isn't enough. Regularly engage with your network by commenting on posts, joining discussions, and sharing your own content.

By understanding what personal branding is and how it applies to LinkedIn, you lay the foundation for a strong professional presence. In the next section (*6.1.2 Why It's Important on LinkedIn*), we'll explore why personal branding matters specifically on this platform and how it can help you achieve your career goals.

6.1.2 Why It's Important on LinkedIn

In today's professional world, personal branding has become essential for career growth, and LinkedIn is one of the most powerful platforms for building and showcasing that brand. Whether you are a job seeker, a business owner, or a professional looking to grow your network, understanding why personal branding is important on LinkedIn will help you achieve your goals more effectively. This section explores the key reasons why cultivating a strong personal brand on LinkedIn matters and provides actionable insights for leveraging it to your advantage.

What is Personal Branding? A Quick Recap

Before diving into why personal branding is crucial on LinkedIn, let's recap the concept. Personal branding is the process of establishing and promoting what you stand for—your unique skills, values, and professional identity. It's the way you present yourself to the world, both online and offline. On LinkedIn, personal branding revolves around how you communicate your expertise, accomplishments, and career goals through your profile, content, and interactions.

The Importance of Personal Branding on LinkedIn

1. LinkedIn Is the Professional Network of Choice

LinkedIn is specifically designed for professionals. With over 900 million members worldwide, it is the go-to platform for recruiters, hiring managers, industry leaders, and peers. If someone wants to learn more about you professionally, your LinkedIn profile is often the first place they will look. A strong personal brand ensures that this first impression aligns with the story you want to tell about yourself.

A well-crafted personal brand on LinkedIn signals credibility, competence, and professionalism. It also ensures that you stand out in an increasingly crowded and competitive space. Whether someone is searching for a project manager, a software developer, or a creative designer, a polished profile with a clear brand identity will likely grab attention.

2. Personal Branding Helps You Stand Out

The job market and professional landscape are highly competitive. Thousands of professionals may share your job title, skills, or industry, but your personal brand is what makes you unique.

On LinkedIn, recruiters and potential clients often sift through countless profiles before making a decision. By presenting a cohesive and authentic brand, you give yourself an edge. For example:

- **Clear and concise messaging** in your profile headline and summary helps people understand what you bring to the table.

- **Tailored keywords** in your profile make you more discoverable in search results.

- **Engaging content** (such as articles or posts) positions you as a thought leader in your industry.

Your personal brand is the magnet that draws the right opportunities, connections, and recognition your way.

3. It Builds Trust and Credibility

People prefer to work with individuals they trust. LinkedIn allows you to showcase your expertise and establish yourself as a reliable professional through:

- **Endorsements and Recommendations:** These validate your skills and demonstrate your reliability from the perspective of others.

- **Sharing knowledge and insights:** By posting valuable content or engaging in discussions, you can showcase your expertise and gain the trust of your network.

For instance, if you're a marketing professional, sharing articles about SEO strategies or contributing to discussions about social media trends can highlight your expertise and make others view you as a trusted resource.

4. It Boosts Your Visibility

LinkedIn operates on search algorithms that prioritize profiles based on their completeness and relevance. By strategically branding yourself, you can appear higher in search results. A well-optimized personal brand means:

- Your **profile gets noticed** by recruiters and potential collaborators.

- Your **posts and activities gain traction** through likes, shares, and comments.

- Your **connections expand**, as people who resonate with your brand are more likely to send you connection requests.

For example, if your personal brand focuses on "data-driven marketing," including those keywords in your headline, summary, and posts will help you appear in search results for individuals or companies looking for expertise in that area.

5. It Attracts Opportunities

Your personal brand acts as a passive opportunity generator. When you present yourself clearly and professionally, recruiters, employers, or potential clients are more likely to reach out to you. Some opportunities you can attract with a strong LinkedIn brand include:

- **Job offers:** Companies actively scout talent on LinkedIn.

- **Partnerships:** Professionals looking for collaborators often search for those with a proven track record in their field.

- **Speaking engagements or freelance gigs:** Being active and visible can lead to invitations for consulting, speaking at events, or taking on exciting projects.

6. It Helps You Control Your Narrative

In the absence of a personal brand, people will create their own assumptions about you based on incomplete or outdated information. LinkedIn gives you the tools to tell your own story in your own words. By actively curating your profile, sharing content, and engaging with others, you ensure that your narrative is clear, consistent, and aligned with your goals.

For example, if you're transitioning from a corporate role to entrepreneurship, your LinkedIn profile and activity can reflect that shift through your headline, summary, and posts about your new business endeavors.

How to Build a Personal Brand on LinkedIn

Now that we've covered why personal branding is important on LinkedIn, here are actionable steps to start building one:

1. **Define Your Brand:**
   - What are your career goals?
   - What skills and experiences set you apart?
   - What value can you offer to others?

2. **Optimize Your Profile:**
   - Use a professional headshot and write a compelling headline.
   - Craft a strong summary that reflects your unique selling points.
   - Include relevant keywords for your industry.

3. **Showcase Your Expertise:**
   - Regularly post or share content relevant to your field.
   - Publish articles to establish thought leadership.
   - Participate in group discussions to engage with your peers.

4. **Engage Authentically:**
   - Comment on and share others' posts.
   - Celebrate your connections' successes.
   - Build meaningful relationships by sending personalized messages.

5. **Track Your Progress:**
   - Use LinkedIn Analytics to measure the impact of your profile and posts.

    o   Make adjustments based on what works and what doesn't.

Real-Life Success Stories

Here are a few examples of how personal branding has led to LinkedIn success:

- **Story 1:** A graphic designer gained freelance clients by regularly sharing their design work and posting about creative trends.

- **Story 2:** A sales professional received a job offer after optimizing their profile with industry-specific keywords.

- **Story 3:** An entrepreneur built a network of investors by engaging with relevant content and actively participating in groups.

Conclusion

In conclusion, personal branding on LinkedIn is not just important—it's essential. It allows you to stand out, build credibility, attract opportunities, and control your professional narrative. By investing time in creating a strong, authentic brand, you set yourself up for long-term success in the professional world. Take the first step today, and let your LinkedIn profile become the foundation of your personal brand.

6.2 Creating a Consistent Professional Presence

6.2.1 Aligning Your Profile with Your Career Goals

Creating a consistent and professional presence on LinkedIn is crucial for building your personal brand, and aligning your profile with your career goals is the first step toward achieving that goal. A LinkedIn profile that reflects your aspirations, skills, and values acts as your digital résumé, helping recruiters, potential employers, and industry peers understand who you are and what you aim to accomplish.

Below, we'll walk through a step-by-step guide to align your LinkedIn profile with your career goals.

Step 1: Define Your Career Goals

Before you can align your LinkedIn profile with your aspirations, you need a clear understanding of what your career goals are. Ask yourself:

- What type of role or position do I want to achieve?

- Which industry or niche am I targeting?

- What skills, experience, or accomplishments do I want to highlight?

- What kind of impression do I want others to have of my professional brand?

Clearly defining your career goals ensures that every element of your profile reflects and supports those objectives. For example:

- **Aspiring for a managerial role?** Highlight leadership skills and accomplishments.

- **Switching industries?** Focus on transferable skills.

- **Entering a creative field?** Emphasize portfolio links, projects, and creativity in your summary and experience sections.

Step 2: Optimize Your Headline

Your headline is one of the first things people see on your profile, making it a critical component of your professional branding. Instead of simply listing your current job title, use the headline to reflect your aspirations and expertise.

Tips for Writing a Powerful Headline

- **Be Specific**: Clearly state your role or field of expertise. For example:
    - "Aspiring Marketing Manager | SEO Specialist | Content Strategist"
    - "Software Engineer | Passionate About AI and Machine Learning"

- **Incorporate Keywords**: Use industry-relevant keywords to make your profile searchable.

- **Include Your Career Objective**: Showcase your value proposition. For example:
    - "Helping Companies Increase Revenue Through Data-Driven Marketing Strategies."

Examples for Different Career Goals

- **Goal: Transition into Data Science**
    - "Data Science Enthusiast | Skilled in Python, R, and Machine Learning | Exploring Opportunities in Analytics."

- **Goal: Advance in Human Resources**
    - "HR Professional | Talent Acquisition Specialist | Building Employee-Centric Workplaces."

Step 3: Write a Compelling Summary

Your LinkedIn summary (or "About" section) is your chance to tell your story and align your personal narrative with your career objectives. Think of it as your elevator pitch—concise yet impactful.

Structure of an Effective Summary

1. **Start with a Hook**: Begin with a strong opening that captures attention. For example:

   o "As a passionate digital marketer, I thrive at the intersection of creativity and data analysis."

2. **Highlight Your Key Skills and Accomplishments**: Focus on what makes you unique.

   o Mention key achievements that are relevant to your career goals.

3. **Connect with Your Audience**: Share what drives you professionally.

   o "I'm driven by a desire to help businesses connect with their audience through authentic storytelling."

4. **End with a Call to Action**: Encourage viewers to connect with you.

   o "Feel free to reach out if you'd like to discuss growth strategies or collaborative opportunities."

Example of a Summary for Career Alignment

Goal: Transition into Project Management

"As a results-driven professional with a background in operations, I'm passionate about delivering high-impact projects that streamline processes and drive organizational growth. I specialize in resource optimization, team collaboration, and leveraging technology to achieve business objectives. With a recent certification in Agile Project Management, I'm now seeking opportunities to transition into a project management role where I can bring my operational expertise to cross-functional teams."

Step 4: Highlight Relevant Experience

The Experience section is more than a record of your job history; it's a chance to showcase how your past roles align with your future goals.

Steps to Align Your Experience Section

1. **Focus on Relevant Roles**: If you're changing industries or roles, emphasize positions where you gained transferable skills.

2. **Use Action-Oriented Descriptions**: Write descriptions that highlight your impact and contributions. For example:

   o Instead of: "Managed social media accounts."

   o Write: "Increased social media engagement by 35% through data-driven content strategies."

3. **Show Progression**: Demonstrate growth in responsibilities over time.

4. **Add Career Milestones**: Include promotions, awards, or recognitions that reinforce your professional growth.

Tailoring for Career Goals

- **Goal: Leadership Role**

  o Focus on achievements like team management, decision-making, and successful project completions.

- **Goal: Creative Role**

  o Showcase projects, portfolios, and creative outputs that highlight your skills.

Step 5: Showcase Skills and Endorsements

The Skills section allows you to highlight the capabilities most relevant to your career goals.

Steps to Optimize Skills for Career Alignment

1. **Prioritize Relevant Skills**: List the top skills that align with your desired role.

2. **Get Endorsements**: Ask colleagues or peers to endorse key skills.

3. **Regularly Update Your Skills**: Remove outdated skills and add new ones as you gain expertise.

Example Skills for Different Career Goals

- **Marketing Career**: SEO, Content Marketing, Google Analytics, Social Media Strategy.

- **IT Career**: Python, Java, Cloud Computing, Database Management.

Step 6: Request Recommendations

Recommendations from colleagues, supervisors, or mentors add credibility to your profile.

How to Request Recommendations

1. **Be Specific**: Politely ask the recommender to highlight specific skills or projects.

2. **Target Relevant Contacts**: Choose people who can speak to your strengths in areas relevant to your career goals.

3. **Offer to Reciprocate**: Writing a recommendation for them can encourage mutual support.

Example Recommendation Request

"Hi [Name], I hope you're doing well! I'm currently refining my LinkedIn profile to align with my career goals in project management. Would you be open to writing a short recommendation that highlights our work together on [specific project]? It would mean a lot to me as I continue building my professional brand. I'd be happy to return the favor if you need!"

Step 7: Use Visual Media to Enhance Your Profile

Adding rich media to your profile helps demonstrate your expertise visually.

What to Include

- **Portfolio Samples**: Showcase your work if you're in a creative or technical field.

- **Certifications**: Upload images or PDFs of relevant certifications.

- **Presentations**: Include slides or reports that highlight your accomplishments.

- **Videos**: Share short videos introducing yourself or demonstrating your skills.

Conclusion

Aligning your LinkedIn profile with your career goals is about presenting a cohesive and compelling professional story. Each element of your profile—from the headline to the skills section—should reflect your aspirations and demonstrate how your experience and skills align with your target role.

By taking the time to optimize your profile, you're not only increasing your chances of being discovered by recruiters and employers but also positioning yourself as a professional who knows exactly where they're headed.

6.2.2 Engaging with Your Niche Audience

Engaging with your niche audience on LinkedIn is one of the most effective ways to build a meaningful professional presence and establish yourself as a trusted voice in your industry. This involves understanding your target audience, creating and sharing relevant content, and actively participating in discussions to foster relationships. Below is a step-by-step guide on how to effectively engage with your niche audience on LinkedIn.

1. Identify Your Niche Audience

To engage effectively, you first need to understand who your niche audience is. Your niche audience consists of individuals or groups who share specific professional interests, industries, or goals that align with your career or expertise. Here's how to define them:

- **Determine Your Industry Focus:** Decide which sector or industry you want to focus on (e.g., digital marketing, software engineering, healthcare management).

- **Define Your Target Demographics:** Consider who you want to reach based on factors such as job titles, career levels (entry, mid, or senior), geographic location, or company size.

- **Pinpoint Common Challenges:** Identify the pain points, challenges, or needs your niche audience faces. For example, if you are in marketing, your audience might seek insights into lead generation or SEO strategies.

Once you have a clear idea of your niche audience, you can tailor your LinkedIn activity to address their needs and interests.

2. Optimize Your Profile for Your Audience

Your LinkedIn profile is often the first impression people in your niche will have of you. Ensure that it resonates with your target audience by doing the following:

- **Headline:** Write a headline that clearly communicates your expertise and the value you bring to your audience. For example, "Helping Small Businesses Increase Revenue with Effective Digital Marketing Strategies."

- **Summary:** Use your summary to address the challenges your audience faces and explain how you can help. Be concise, use action-oriented language, and include keywords relevant to your niche.

- **Featured Section:** Showcase relevant content, such as articles, presentations, or case studies that demonstrate your expertise.

3. Share Relevant and High-Quality Content

Content is a powerful way to engage your audience and establish credibility. Here are some tips for creating and sharing content that resonates with your niche:

- **Understand What Your Audience Values:** Research what topics are trending or commonly discussed in your field. Use LinkedIn's search function or hashtags to find popular posts within your industry.

- **Types of Content to Share:**

  - **Original Posts:** Share your own insights, experiences, or tips in a professional yet relatable tone. For example, write about how you solved a specific problem in your role.

  - **Curated Content:** Share relevant articles, industry reports, or resources from others, adding your commentary to show your perspective.

- o **Visual Content:** Use images, infographics, or videos to make your posts more engaging. For instance, if you're in graphic design, showcase your work with visuals.

- **Consistency is Key:** Post regularly to stay visible. Aim for at least 2–3 posts per week, but ensure quality over quantity.

4. Engage with Content from Your Audience

Engaging with your audience's content is just as important as sharing your own. It shows that you're an active participant in your industry and helps build relationships. Here's how to do it effectively:

- **Like and React to Posts:** A simple "like" or reaction lets others know you're paying attention to their updates.

- **Comment Thoughtfully:** Add meaningful comments to posts that align with your expertise. Avoid generic comments like "Great post!" Instead, share a specific takeaway or opinion. For example:

  - o "This is an excellent take on the importance of email marketing! I've also found that A/B testing subject lines significantly improves open rates. Have you tried this approach?"

- **Ask Questions:** Engage in discussions by asking insightful questions. This not only encourages conversation but also positions you as someone curious and knowledgeable.

5. Participate in Groups and Communities

LinkedIn Groups are a great way to connect with like-minded professionals and contribute to discussions in your niche. Here's how to make the most of them:

- **Join Relevant Groups:** Search for groups that align with your industry or interests. Look for active groups with regular discussions and high engagement.

- **Be an Active Contributor:** Participate by sharing relevant insights, answering questions, or initiating discussions. For example, in a project management group, you could start a thread about effective time management techniques.

- **Avoid Over-Promotion:** Focus on adding value rather than promoting your services. Build trust first, and opportunities will follow naturally.

6. Build Relationships Through Direct Messaging

LinkedIn messages are a powerful tool for deepening connections and engaging with your audience on a more personal level. However, it's essential to approach messaging thoughtfully:

- **Personalize Your Messages:** Avoid sending generic messages. Instead, reference a recent post, mutual connection, or shared interest. For example:

  - "Hi [Name], I really enjoyed your recent post on remote work challenges. I've been exploring similar topics and would love to connect and share ideas."

- **Follow Up Strategically:** If someone responds positively, keep the conversation going by asking questions or offering insights.

7. Use Polls and Questions to Spark Engagement

Interactive posts like polls or open-ended questions can generate significant engagement from your audience. Here's how to use them effectively:

- **Create Polls:** Use LinkedIn's poll feature to ask questions relevant to your industry. For example:

  - "What's your biggest challenge when it comes to email marketing? A) Writing subject lines B) Designing templates C) Tracking results D) Other (comment below)."

- **Ask Open-Ended Questions:** Encourage thoughtful responses by asking your audience for their opinions or experiences. For example:

 ○ "What's the most valuable lesson you've learned from working in [industry]?"

8. Leverage LinkedIn Analytics to Understand Your Audience

LinkedIn provides analytics that can help you assess how well you're engaging your niche audience. Focus on these metrics:

- **Profile Views:** Monitor who's visiting your profile to see if your content is attracting the right audience.

- **Post Engagement:** Track likes, comments, and shares to understand which topics resonate most with your audience.

- **Follower Growth:** Assess whether your network is growing with individuals relevant to your niche.

9. Collaborate with Influencers or Industry Experts

Partnering with established professionals in your field can help you reach a broader audience. Here's how to collaborate effectively:

- **Engage with Their Content:** Regularly comment on and share posts from influencers in your niche.

- **Offer Value:** Reach out with a proposal to collaborate on a post, webinar, or article. For example:

 ○ "Hi [Name], I admire your work on [topic]. I'd love to collaborate on a LinkedIn Live session about [specific topic]. Let me know if this interests you!"

10. Stay Authentic and Consistent

Finally, always stay true to your voice and values. Authenticity is crucial to building trust and long-term engagement. Avoid trying to appeal to everyone—focus on your niche and deliver consistent value.

By following these strategies, you'll not only engage with your niche audience but also position yourself as a trusted and influential professional in your field. Consistency, authenticity, and a genuine desire to add value will set you apart on LinkedIn.

6.3 Leveraging LinkedIn Analytics

6.3.1 Tracking Profile Views and Engagement

LinkedIn Analytics is one of the most powerful tools available for understanding how your profile and content are performing. By leveraging these insights, you can learn who is viewing your profile, how your posts are engaging your audience, and how effectively your network-building efforts are paying off. This section will guide you through the process of tracking your profile views and engagement, interpreting the data, and using it to refine your personal branding strategy.

What Are LinkedIn Analytics?

LinkedIn Analytics provides you with valuable data to evaluate the performance of your LinkedIn presence. These insights are broken down into several key categories, such as:

- **Profile Views:** The number of people who have visited your profile and details about their job titles, industries, and companies.

- **Post Engagement:** Insights into how your posts, articles, and other content are performing, including likes, comments, shares, and impressions.

- **Search Appearances:** Data on how often your profile appears in LinkedIn searches and the keywords driving those searches.

Understanding these analytics helps you measure the effectiveness of your LinkedIn strategy and identify opportunities for improvement.

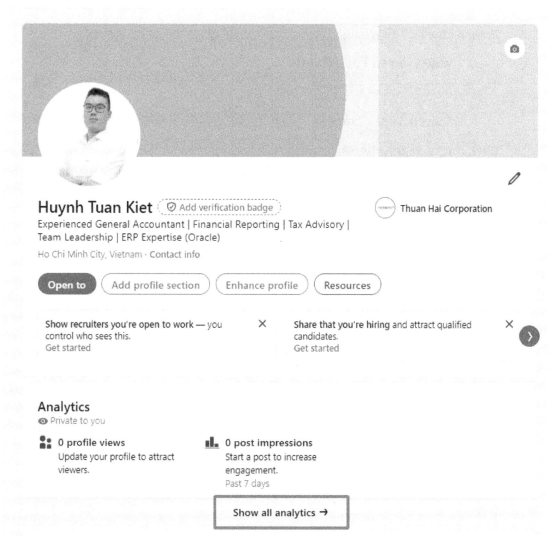

Accessing LinkedIn Analytics

To access your analytics, follow these steps:

1. **Go to Your Profile:** Log into LinkedIn and click on your profile picture or name to visit your profile page.

2. **Locate the Analytics Section:** Below your profile photo and headline, you'll see a section labeled **"Analytics."** This section displays three key metrics:

   o **Who Viewed Your Profile**

   o **Post Views**

   o **Search Appearances**

3. **Click for More Details:** Click on any of these metrics for a more in-depth view. For example, clicking **"Who Viewed Your Profile"** provides additional data about your visitors, while clicking **"Post Views"** shows how your recent content has performed.

Note: Some analytics features may be limited for free LinkedIn accounts. Upgrading to LinkedIn Premium unlocks advanced data, such as detailed viewer insights and historical trends.

Tracking Profile Views

Why Profile Views Matter

Profile views are a direct indicator of your visibility on LinkedIn. When someone views your profile, it means your profile caught their attention—whether through a post, a comment, a group interaction, or a search result. By analyzing profile views, you can:

- Identify the audience you're attracting.

- Determine whether your profile aligns with your personal branding goals.

- Measure the impact of your LinkedIn activity, such as posting content or sending connection requests.

How to Analyze Profile Views

When you click on the **"Who Viewed Your Profile"** section, you'll see insights like:

1. **Viewer Demographics:**

- ○ **Job Titles:** What roles do your viewers have? Are they recruiters, hiring managers, or peers in your industry?

- ○ **Industries:** Which sectors do your viewers come from? For instance, if you're targeting the tech industry but your viewers are mainly from education, you may need to refine your content or connections.

- ○ **Locations:** Where are your viewers located? This is particularly helpful if you're looking for opportunities in a specific region.

2. **Connections:**

   - ○ Are your profile viewers first-degree, second-degree, or third-degree connections?

   - ○ This information helps you identify whether your network is engaging with you or if you're reaching a broader audience.

3. **Profile Activity Trends:**

   - ○ LinkedIn displays how your profile views have changed over time (e.g., the past week or month). Look for patterns or spikes in views, and correlate them with your activity. For instance, did you post a new article or join a group discussion that led to increased visibility?

Actionable Steps to Improve Profile Views

If your profile views are low or stagnant, here are some strategies to improve them:

1. **Optimize Your Profile:**

   - ○ Use relevant keywords in your headline, summary, and experience sections to appear in more search results.

   - ○ Add a professional and approachable profile photo.

   - ○ Customize your URL to make your profile easier to share.

2. **Be Active:**

- Engage regularly by posting updates, liking and commenting on posts, and participating in group discussions.

- Share insights, articles, or achievements to keep your profile visible in your network's feed.

3. **Expand Your Network:**

- Send personalized connection requests to people in your industry.

- Attend webinars or events and connect with participants afterward.

4. **Leverage LinkedIn Premium:**

- Consider a LinkedIn Premium account to unlock more data about who views your profile and get tools to enhance your visibility.

Tracking Post and Content Engagement

Why Engagement Metrics Matter

Engagement metrics, such as likes, comments, shares, and impressions, help you understand how well your content resonates with your audience. High engagement indicates that your posts are relevant, valuable, and aligned with your audience's interests.

Analyzing Post Engagement

To view your post engagement data:

1. **Go to Your Activity Feed:** Scroll down on your profile to find the **"Activity"** section.

2. **View Specific Post Metrics:** Click on a specific post to see its performance metrics, including:

- **Impressions:** The number of times your post appeared in someone's feed.

- **Engagements:** The total number of likes, comments, and shares.

- o **Click-Throughs:** If you included a link, check how many people clicked on it.

3. **Audience Insights:**

    - o **Demographics of Viewers:** Similar to profile views, you can see who is engaging with your posts based on their job titles, industries, and locations.

    - o **Engagement Rate:** Calculate the percentage of people who engaged with your content out of the total impressions.

Improving Post Engagement

Here are actionable tips to boost your post engagement:

1. **Post High-Quality Content:**

    - o Share content that aligns with your expertise, such as industry trends, case studies, or personal insights.

    - o Include visuals like images, infographics, or videos to make your posts more engaging.

2. **Be Consistent:**

    - o Post regularly to keep your audience engaged. A good starting point is 2-3 posts per week.

    - o Experiment with different types of content to see what resonates best with your audience.

3. **Engage with Comments:**

    - o Respond to comments on your posts to foster conversations.

    - o Tag people when appropriate to draw more attention to your posts.

4. **Use Hashtags Strategically:**

    - o Add 3-5 relevant hashtags to your posts to increase discoverability.

5. **Post at Optimal Times:**

o   Experiment with different posting times to find when your audience is most active. Generally, mid-morning on weekdays works well for LinkedIn.

Key Takeaways

Tracking and analyzing your LinkedIn profile views and engagement metrics is essential for optimizing your personal brand. By understanding who is viewing your profile and how your content is performing, you can make data-driven adjustments to improve your visibility and relevance.

In the next section, **6.3.2 Improving Your Visibility**, we'll explore how to use the insights from your analytics to refine your strategy and further grow your LinkedIn presence.

6.3.2 Improving Your Visibility

LinkedIn Analytics is a powerful tool that offers insights into how your profile and content perform on the platform. By understanding and acting on these insights, you can strategically improve your visibility and attract the right audience, whether it's recruiters, potential clients, or industry peers. In this section, we will explore actionable steps to enhance your visibility on LinkedIn by leveraging analytics data effectively.

1. Understanding Key LinkedIn Analytics Metrics

To improve your visibility, you need to first understand the analytics metrics provided by LinkedIn and what they represent. Some of the most important metrics include:

1. **Profile Views:** This metric shows how many people have visited your profile over a given period. A higher number indicates increased interest in your professional presence.

2. **Search Appearances:** This shows how many times your profile appeared in search results on LinkedIn. It also provides details about the searchers' job titles and industries, which can help you understand your audience.

3. **Post and Article Performance:** For every piece of content you share, LinkedIn provides analytics such as views, likes, comments, shares, and engagement rates. These numbers indicate how well your content resonates with your audience.

4. **Follower Growth:** This tracks how many new followers you've gained over time, showing whether your content and networking efforts are attracting new people to your network.

2. Optimizing Your Profile Based on Analytics

Once you understand your analytics, use the data to optimize your profile to attract more views and engagements.

Step 1: Review Who's Viewing Your Profile

Analyze the industries, locations, and job titles of those viewing your profile. If the viewers align with your target audience, you're on the right track. If not, consider revising your profile to better reflect the keywords and skills relevant to your desired audience.

- **Example:** If you're targeting recruiters in the tech industry but most of your viewers are in unrelated fields, you may need to update your headline, skills, or summary to include tech-related keywords.

Step 2: Use Relevant Keywords

Search appearances analytics highlight the keywords people are using to find you. If these keywords align with your professional goals, continue incorporating them. If they don't, adjust your profile language to better reflect the skills and roles you aim to target.

- **Actionable Tip:** Add keywords to your headline, job titles, summary, and skills section to align with the terms recruiters or professionals in your niche might search for.

Step 3: Enhance Your Visual Appeal

A professional profile picture and a customized banner can make a significant difference in attracting attention. If your analytics show low engagement with your profile, consider refreshing these visuals to better reflect your brand.

3. Creating High-Quality Content to Boost Visibility

Regularly sharing content on LinkedIn significantly increases your profile visibility. Content shows your expertise and keeps you top of mind within your network.

Step 1: Focus on Value-Driven Content

Analytics can help you identify which types of posts your audience finds most engaging. Review the performance of previous posts and note what topics, formats, or styles received the highest engagement.

- **Examples of Content Ideas:**
    - Industry insights and trends
    - How-to guides or tutorials
    - Personal stories or career milestones
    - Thought-provoking questions or polls

Step 2: Leverage LinkedIn's Native Features

LinkedIn offers tools like polls, articles, and live videos to diversify your content. Analytics can show which format performs best for your audience. For instance, if polls receive the most engagement, incorporate more polls into your strategy.

Step 3: Post Consistently

Regular posting improves visibility as LinkedIn's algorithm prioritizes active users. Aim to post at least 2–3 times per week, balancing quality and consistency.

4. Engaging with Your Network for Increased Visibility

Visibility isn't just about creating content; it's also about engaging with others. Analytics can show how well your interactions are resonating with your network.

Step 1: Comment and Share Thoughtfully

Comment on posts from your connections or within your industry groups. Thoughtful comments often lead to profile visits and potential new connections.

Step 2: Tag Relevant People

When sharing content, tag people who might find it valuable or have expertise in the topic. Tagged individuals often engage with the post, extending its reach to their networks.

Step 3: Respond to Comments on Your Posts

Engaging with commenters not only boosts the visibility of the post but also builds relationships and trust within your network.

---

5. Expanding Your Network Strategically

Improving visibility involves increasing the size and relevance of your network.

Step 1: Connect with People in Your Industry

Analyze the job titles and industries of your profile viewers. If certain industries or roles align with your goals, proactively connect with individuals in those spaces.

Step 2: Join Active Groups

Participate in LinkedIn Groups that cater to your interests or profession. By sharing insights and engaging with members, you position yourself as a thought leader and drive profile visits.

---

6. Adjusting Your Strategy with Analytics Insights

LinkedIn Analytics isn't just a tool for measurement—it's a feedback mechanism to improve your strategy over time.

Step 1: Experiment and Measure

Try different strategies, such as posting at different times, using varied content formats, or targeting specific industries. Use analytics to measure the impact of these changes.

Step 2: Identify Trends Over Time

Monitor trends in your profile views, post engagement, and follower growth. A consistent upward trend indicates that your efforts are paying off, while stagnation or decline signals the need for adjustments.

Step 3: Set Achievable Goals

Use analytics to set measurable goals, such as increasing your profile views by 20% in a month or doubling your content engagement within a quarter. Track progress and refine your approach as needed.

7. Using Premium Analytics Tools

If you're serious about improving visibility, consider upgrading to LinkedIn Premium. Premium accounts provide advanced analytics, such as detailed insights into who viewed your profile and more robust job-related data.

- **Benefits of Premium Analytics:**
    - Access to viewer demographics for strategic targeting
    - Insights into how you compare to other professionals in your field
    - Advanced tools for improving job search visibility

Conclusion

Improving your visibility on LinkedIn is a continuous process that involves optimizing your profile, creating valuable content, engaging with your network, and using analytics to refine your strategy. By taking deliberate actions based on LinkedIn Analytics, you can enhance your professional presence, attract the right audience, and unlock new career opportunities.

Start small, track your progress, and remember: consistency is key to building lasting visibility on LinkedIn.

CHAPTER VII
Advanced Tips for Beginners

7.1 Using Keywords for SEO on LinkedIn

7.1.1 What Are Keywords?

Keywords are fundamental to making your LinkedIn profile discoverable, and they play a crucial role in optimizing your presence on the platform. They are the words and phrases that recruiters, hiring managers, and potential business connections use to find profiles like yours. By understanding what keywords are and how to use them, you can dramatically increase your visibility, network reach, and career opportunities on LinkedIn.

Understanding Keywords and Their Importance

At the most basic level, **keywords** are terms or phrases that are used to match search queries. Just like Google, LinkedIn uses an algorithm to search and rank profiles, posts, and content based on keywords. The more relevant and frequently used the keywords in your profile, the higher your profile will rank in LinkedIn's search results.

For example, if a recruiter is searching for a "Marketing Manager" with experience in "SEO" and "Google Analytics," they will use these keywords in their search query. If these keywords appear in your profile, there's a higher chance that your profile will be recommended or visible in search results.

The importance of keywords lies in their ability to **connect you to the right opportunities**. Whether you're looking for a new job, trying to network, or aiming to showcase your skills, the right keywords will make sure the right people find you.

Types of Keywords

There are different types of keywords that you should be aware of to optimize your LinkedIn profile:

- **Core Keywords:** These are the primary keywords that describe your profession, skills, and industry. For example, if you're an accountant, keywords like "Accounting," "CPA," "Financial Reporting," and "Tax Preparation" would be core keywords.

- **Secondary Keywords:** These are additional terms that describe your competencies and qualifications. For example, "Project Management," "Data Analysis," "Financial Modeling," or "Business Strategy" might be secondary keywords for an accountant looking to expand their career in corporate finance.

- **Long-Tail Keywords:** These are more specific, niche keywords that might describe a particular aspect of your profession. For example, instead of just "Marketing," you might use "Digital Marketing Specialist" or "SEO Specialist." Long-tail keywords tend to attract more targeted searches.

- **Industry-Specific Keywords:** Depending on your profession, there might be industry-specific terms or jargon that are commonly used in your field. For instance, in the tech industry, terms like "Agile," "JavaScript," "Cloud Computing," and "Machine Learning" are crucial.

Why Keywords Matter for Your LinkedIn Profile

When you think of LinkedIn as a search engine, you can understand why keywords matter. Keywords help your profile surface in relevant searches and boost your chances of being noticed by potential employers, clients, or collaborators. The more keywords you use, the better LinkedIn can index your profile, making it easier for recruiters and others to find you.

LinkedIn Search Algorithm: LinkedIn's search algorithm functions similarly to search engines like Google. When a recruiter searches for a job title, skill, or industry, LinkedIn scans your profile for relevant keywords. LinkedIn's algorithm favors complete profiles with keywords integrated throughout your experience, skills, summary, and other sections.

Increased Visibility: Using the right keywords increases the likelihood of appearing in search results when potential employers or collaborators are looking for someone with your skills and qualifications.

Appearing in Job Matches: Keywords help LinkedIn's job-matching algorithm suggest roles that align with your experience. So, if you want to be considered for specific jobs, using the relevant job titles, skills, and industry terms can make you more likely to appear in those recommendations.

How Keywords Impact Your LinkedIn Profile Sections

Now that you understand the basics of keywords, let's dive into how they impact different sections of your LinkedIn profile. By strategically placing keywords throughout your profile, you increase the chances of getting noticed by search algorithms.

1. Headline: The headline is one of the most important parts of your profile for SEO purposes. It appears right below your name and is what people first see when they search for you. Use this space wisely by including relevant keywords that reflect your expertise, current position, or career goals. For example, instead of just saying "Marketing Manager," try something like "Digital Marketing Manager | SEO & Content Strategy Expert | Helping Brands Grow Online."

2. Summary: Your summary is a key area to include keywords because it provides an opportunity to describe yourself in greater detail. Think of it as your elevator pitch. Make sure to naturally integrate keywords that describe your job function, core skills, and accomplishments. For example, if you're a "Software Developer," mention technologies you're proficient in, such as "Java," "Python," and "SQL."

3. Experience Section: In your job experience section, include job titles, responsibilities, and accomplishments that align with industry-specific keywords. For example, as a "Sales Manager," you might include keywords like "B2B Sales," "Lead Generation," "Sales Strategy," and "Revenue Growth."

4. Skills & Endorsements: The skills section is one of the easiest areas to optimize with keywords. Make sure you list the most relevant and important skills related to your profession. Skills such as "Project Management," "Leadership," and "Financial Analysis" should be listed here. The more endorsements you receive for those skills, the better.

5. Recommendations: Recommendations also play a key role in your profile's visibility. While you can't directly add keywords to the recommendations, you can encourage those who recommend you to use relevant keywords when describing your skills and abilities. The more keywords used by others, the more relevant your profile will be in searches.

How to Identify the Best Keywords for Your Profile

Identifying the best keywords for your profile is a crucial step in the optimization process. Here's how you can choose the right keywords:

- **Job Descriptions**: Look at job listings that align with your career goals and take note of the keywords used in the descriptions. For example, if you're targeting a role in digital marketing, the job descriptions may frequently mention "SEO," "PPC,"

"Social Media Strategy," or "Email Marketing." These are the types of keywords you should use.

- **Industry Research**: Explore LinkedIn profiles of professionals in your industry, particularly those who have similar roles or aspirations. See what keywords they use in their profiles and consider using similar terms.

- **LinkedIn's Suggested Skills**: LinkedIn provides suggested skills based on your job title and industry. These suggestions can be a good starting point for identifying the right keywords to include in your profile.

- **Tools for Keyword Research**: Use keyword research tools like Google Keyword Planner or LinkedIn's "Job Matching" feature to identify the most relevant and highly searched terms for your profession.

How to Use Keywords Strategically

Using keywords in your LinkedIn profile is not just about stuffing them in every section. They need to be integrated thoughtfully and naturally. Here's how to do it strategically:

- **Be Specific**: Avoid generic terms like "hard-working" or "motivated." Instead, use industry-specific keywords that describe your skills and experience in more detail.

- **Use Variations**: Don't just repeat the same keyword over and over again. Use variations to capture a wider range of search queries. For example, instead of just "Marketing," also include terms like "Content Marketing," "SEO Specialist," or "Digital Marketing Expert."

- **Balance Keywords with Personality**: While keywords are essential, it's important not to overdo it. Your profile should still sound like you, so keep the tone conversational while making sure to include relevant terms.

Common Mistakes to Avoid When Using Keywords

- **Keyword Stuffing**: Avoid overloading your profile with too many keywords. This can make your profile seem unnatural and may even result in LinkedIn penalizing your profile. Aim for a natural flow of information.

- **Using Irrelevant Keywords**: Make sure your keywords reflect your actual skills and experience. Using keywords that don't align with your background can hurt your credibility.

- **Ignoring Long-Tail Keywords**: Long-tail keywords may be more specific, but they often attract highly relevant searches. Don't just focus on broad, highly competitive keywords. Include long-tail versions to capture more niche audiences.

Conclusion

In summary, keywords are an essential part of your LinkedIn profile, playing a significant role in optimizing your profile for search and visibility. By carefully selecting and strategically placing keywords throughout your profile, you can increase your chances of being discovered by recruiters, employers, and potential business connections.

Make sure to research and use keywords that are relevant to your industry, profession, and career goals. By doing so, you'll ensure that your LinkedIn profile is working to its full potential, helping you connect with the right people and seize new opportunities.

7.1.2 Placing Keywords Strategically in Your Profile

Keywords are an essential part of LinkedIn's SEO (Search Engine Optimization) strategy. By placing the right keywords strategically throughout your LinkedIn profile, you can increase your chances of being discovered by recruiters, potential clients, or professionals in your industry. This section will guide you through the process of identifying, selecting, and placing keywords effectively across different sections of your LinkedIn profile.

Why Strategic Keyword Placement Matters

LinkedIn functions much like a search engine when it comes to profiles. Recruiters and professionals search for talent using specific keywords that match job roles, skills, and industries. For example, a recruiter searching for a "Data Analyst" might use keywords such as "data visualization," "SQL," or "Excel." If your profile contains these keywords in relevant sections, it's more likely to appear in their search results.

Strategic keyword placement also helps LinkedIn's algorithm understand your expertise, thereby improving your profile's visibility. The better the algorithm matches your profile to a search query, the higher your chances of being discovered.

Where to Place Keywords in Your LinkedIn Profile

Let's go through each section of your LinkedIn profile and identify how to incorporate keywords strategically without overloading or making the content unnatural.

1. Headline

The headline is the first thing people notice on your LinkedIn profile, and it plays a critical role in search results. By default, LinkedIn sets your current job title as your headline, but customizing it with keywords can significantly improve your visibility.

Tips for Adding Keywords to Your Headline:

- Focus on your primary expertise and include role-specific keywords.

- Combine multiple keywords in a natural sentence structure.

- Highlight unique skills or specialties that set you apart.

Examples:

- Instead of "Software Engineer," try "Full-Stack Software Engineer | Python, Java, Cloud Computing Specialist."

- Instead of "Marketing Specialist," try "Digital Marketing Expert | SEO, PPC, Content Strategy."

Dos and Don'ts:

- **Do**: Use separators like vertical bars (|) or bullet points (•) for clarity.

- **Don't**: Overstuff the headline with too many keywords, which can appear spammy.

2. About (Summary) Section

The "About" section is where you tell your story and summarize your professional background. It's also an excellent place to integrate multiple keywords while maintaining a conversational tone.

Tips for Adding Keywords to Your About Section:

- Begin with a compelling introduction that includes your primary role and expertise.

- Use bullet points or paragraphs to showcase your skills, strengths, and achievements.

- Naturally weave in keywords related to your industry, tools, certifications, and specialties.

Example Template:

"As a Data Analyst with expertise in [insert skill, e.g., SQL, Python, Tableau], I specialize in transforming complex datasets into actionable insights. My experience spans [insert industry, e.g., healthcare, finance], where I've delivered impactful solutions in areas like [insert specific focus, e.g., data visualization and predictive modeling]."

3. Experience Section

The Experience section is where you detail your past roles and achievements. This is one of the most important areas to include keywords because it gives recruiters specific insights into your capabilities.

Tips for Adding Keywords to the Experience Section:

- Use keywords in your job titles, especially for roles that match your current career goals.

- Incorporate relevant tools, methodologies, or skills in the job descriptions.

- Highlight achievements using action verbs and industry terms.

Example:
Job Title: "Digital Marketing Specialist | SEO and Social Media Strategy"
Description:

- Optimized SEO campaigns that increased website traffic by 45%.

- Managed paid ad campaigns on Google Ads, resulting in a 30% ROI improvement.

- Analyzed performance metrics using Google Analytics and presented actionable reports to stakeholders.

Dos and Don'ts:

- **Do**: Tailor job descriptions to match roles you're targeting.

- **Don't**: Use vague or generic phrases like "Handled various tasks."

4. Skills Section

The Skills section is specifically designed for keyword integration. LinkedIn allows you to add up to 50 skills, so make the most of this feature.

Tips for Adding Keywords to the Skills Section:

- Prioritize skills that are in-demand in your industry or target role.

- Use precise terms instead of broad categories. For example, "Data Visualization" is better than "Data."

- Regularly update your skills to reflect current trends in your industry.

Example:

- Instead of "Programming," use "Python Programming" or "Java Development."

- Instead of "Marketing," use "Social Media Marketing" or "Content Marketing Strategy."

Pro Tip: Ask for endorsements from colleagues and managers to increase the credibility of your skills.

5. Recommendations

Although recommendations are written by others, you can subtly influence the keywords they use.

Tips for Influencing Keywords in Recommendations:

- When requesting a recommendation, mention specific projects, tools, or skills you'd like them to highlight.

- Focus on recommendations that align with your target roles.

Example Request: "Could you mention my expertise in project management and my ability to use tools like Trello and Asana effectively?"

6. Education and Certifications

Your educational background and certifications are another place to include keywords.

Tips for Adding Keywords to Education and Certifications:

- Include course names, majors, or certifications that contain relevant keywords.

- Add detailed descriptions for certifications, especially if they include technical skills or industry knowledge.

Example:

- Certification: "Certified Scrum Master (CSM)"

- Description: "Completed comprehensive training in Agile project management and Scrum methodologies."

7. Projects and Publications

If you've worked on significant projects or published articles, include them in your profile with relevant keywords.

Tips for Adding Keywords to Projects and Publications:

- Use project titles and descriptions that include keywords relevant to your expertise.

- Highlight measurable outcomes to showcase the impact of your work.

Example:
Project Title: "E-Commerce Website Optimization | SEO and UX Improvements"
Description:

- Conducted SEO audits and implemented strategies that improved organic traffic by 60%.

Best Practices for Keyword Placement

1. **Keep It Natural:** Avoid keyword stuffing. Always prioritize readability and flow.

2. **Stay Relevant:** Focus on keywords that align with your target industry or role.

3. **Update Regularly:** As your career evolves, refine your keywords to match new goals and trends.

4. **Research Competitor Profiles:** Look at profiles of successful professionals in your field to identify commonly used keywords.

5. **Use Synonyms and Variations:** Incorporate variations of keywords to increase search coverage. For example, use "Project Management" and "Agile Project Management."

Conclusion

Strategic keyword placement is essential for optimizing your LinkedIn profile and increasing your visibility to recruiters and industry professionals. By carefully integrating relevant keywords into your headline, summary, experience, skills, and other sections, you can improve your profile's search ranking and attract the right opportunities.

Take the time to refine your profile, and remember that the key to success lies in balancing keyword optimization with genuine, engaging content.

7.2 Managing Privacy and Settings

7.2.1 Customizing Your Profile Visibility

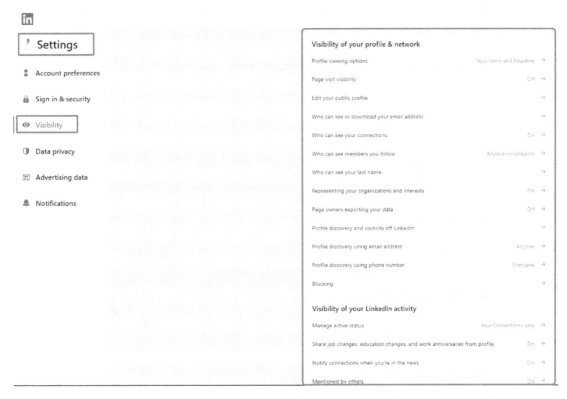

LinkedIn provides a range of privacy settings to help you control how your profile is viewed by others. Customizing your profile visibility is essential for maintaining a professional image while ensuring your personal information is secure. In this section, we will dive into everything you need to know about tailoring your LinkedIn profile visibility to suit your goals, whether you're a job seeker, a networker, or someone looking to maintain a private yet professional online presence.

Understanding Profile Visibility on LinkedIn

LinkedIn allows users to control their visibility in two main areas:

1. **How your profile appears to people within LinkedIn.**

2. **How your profile appears to people outside of LinkedIn (via search engines or shared links).**

Your profile visibility settings affect what others see when they view your profile, such as your name, photo, headline, activity, and contact information. Understanding these settings ensures that you strike the right balance between being discoverable by recruiters or potential clients and maintaining a level of privacy that you are comfortable with.

Step-by-Step Guide to Customizing Profile Visibility

Let's break down the steps to customize your profile visibility effectively:

Step 1: Accessing Privacy and Settings

1. Log in to your LinkedIn account.

2. Click on your profile picture in the top-right corner to open the dropdown menu.

3. Select **"Settings & Privacy"** from the menu. This will take you to LinkedIn's settings hub, where you can adjust various privacy-related options.

4. Navigate to the **"Visibility"** tab located on the left-hand side of the settings menu.

Step 2: Adjusting Public Profile Settings

LinkedIn allows you to control how your profile is displayed to people outside of LinkedIn, such as through Google or Bing searches. Here's how to manage it:

1. Under the **"Visibility"** tab, click on **"Edit your public profile"**.

2. You'll see a preview of how your profile appears to non-LinkedIn users.

3. Use the toggle buttons to show or hide specific profile sections, such as:

- o **Profile photo**: Decide whether to show your photo to everyone, your network only, or no one.

- o **Headline**: Choose whether to display your professional headline publicly.

- o **Summary and Experience**: Enable or disable visibility of your work history and achievements.

Tip: If you're actively seeking a job, keeping your headline and summary public can increase your chances of being discovered by recruiters. However, if you prefer privacy, consider hiding detailed information while keeping your headline visible.

Step 3: Controlling Who Can See Your Activity

1. Go back to the **"Visibility"** section under **"Settings & Privacy"**.

2. Locate the option labeled **"Profile viewing options"**.

3. Choose how you want to appear when viewing other people's profiles:

   - o **Public mode**: Your name and headline will be visible when you view someone else's profile.

   - o **Private profile characteristics**: Only your job title and company will be shown.

   - o **Private mode**: You will appear as an anonymous LinkedIn user.

Tip: Use public mode when you want others to know you're interested in connecting. Use private mode if you're conducting research or exploring profiles discreetly.

Step 4: Managing Your Network Visibility

Sometimes, you may not want your network to be notified every time you update your profile. LinkedIn allows you to control this:

1. Under the **"Visibility"** tab, select **"Visibility of your LinkedIn activity"**.

2. Turn off **"Share profile updates with your network"** if you don't want your connections to receive notifications about profile changes, such as updated job titles or new skills.

Example Use Case: If you're updating your profile multiple times in a short period, turning off notifications prevents unnecessary alerts to your connections.

Step 5: Adjusting Visibility of Contact Information

Your contact information includes your email address, phone number (if provided), and LinkedIn profile URL. Here's how to manage it:

1. Navigate to the **"Edit Contact Info"** section on your profile.

2. Adjust the privacy settings for each piece of contact information to control who can view it:

    o **Only You**: Keeps it completely private.

    o **Connections**: Allows only your 1st-degree connections to see it.

    o **Public**: Makes it visible to everyone.

Recommendation: Keep your contact information visible only to your connections unless you're a freelancer or entrepreneur actively seeking business opportunities.

Best Practices for Customizing Profile Visibility

1. **Showcase Relevant Information:** If you're job hunting, ensure your skills, experiences, and headline are public so recruiters can find you.

2. **Keep Personal Information Private:** Avoid making your email or phone number public to prevent spam or unwanted contact.

3. **Regularly Review Your Settings:** As your goals change, revisit your privacy settings to align them with your current objectives.

Common Mistakes to Avoid

1. **Over-Hiding Your Profile:** While privacy is important, making your profile too private might reduce your visibility to recruiters or networking opportunities.

2. **Ignoring Updates to LinkedIn Privacy Settings:** LinkedIn periodically updates its settings, so make it a habit to review them to stay in control.

3. **Sharing Too Much Information:** Avoid displaying sensitive details like your exact location or unnecessary contact information.

Practical Scenarios and Examples

- **Scenario 1: Job Seekers**: If you're looking for a job, enable "Open to Work" under your profile picture and make sure your profile headline and summary are public. Customize your contact info to only show your email address to connections.

- **Scenario 2: Freelancers and Entrepreneurs**: If you're a freelancer, consider making your summary and portfolio public to attract clients. You might also allow your LinkedIn profile URL to be visible to non-LinkedIn users.

- **Scenario 3: Passive Networkers**: For professionals who aren't actively seeking new opportunities, consider hiding your detailed activity updates and keeping your contact info private.

Conclusion

Customizing your LinkedIn profile visibility is about finding the right balance between being discoverable and maintaining your privacy. By tailoring your settings to suit your goals, you can ensure that the right people see your professional achievements without compromising your personal information. Whether you're job hunting, networking, or simply maintaining an online presence, LinkedIn's robust privacy settings give you the tools to take full control of how you appear to the world.

7.2.2 Managing Notifications and Communication Preferences

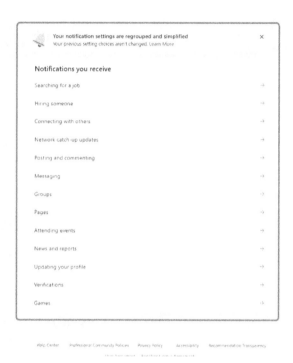

LinkedIn is a powerful platform for networking, job searching, and sharing content, but the constant notifications or overwhelming communication can sometimes feel intrusive. Managing your notifications and communication preferences effectively ensures that LinkedIn works for you in the way that best suits your needs. This section provides a step-by-step guide to customize these settings and create a more streamlined experience.

Understanding Notifications on LinkedIn

LinkedIn notifications help keep you informed about activities related to your profile, connections, posts, groups, job applications, and more. They are delivered through three main channels:

1. **On-Platform Notifications:** These appear in the notifications tab on LinkedIn.

2. **Email Notifications:** Sent to the email address associated with your LinkedIn account.

3. **Push Notifications:** Alerts sent to your mobile device if you have the LinkedIn app installed.

While notifications are useful, receiving too many can become distracting. That's why LinkedIn offers a variety of tools to manage what you want to be notified about and how.

Customizing Notification Settings

LinkedIn allows you to control notifications at both a granular and general level. Follow these steps to customize them effectively:

1. Accessing Notification Settings

1. Log in to your LinkedIn account.

2. Click on your profile picture at the top right corner of the homepage.

3. Select **Settings & Privacy** from the dropdown menu.

4. Navigate to the **Communications** tab on the left-hand side.

5. Under the **Notifications** section, you'll see a list of all notification types.

2. Choosing Notification Categories

LinkedIn breaks down notifications into several categories, such as:

- **Connections and Invitations:** Alerts about new connection requests or accepted invitations.

- **Content and Activity:** Updates when your posts, articles, or comments receive engagement.

- **Job Opportunities:** Notifications about jobs that match your preferences.

- **Network Updates:** Notifications about milestones (e.g., work anniversaries, new positions) in your network.

Each category can be toggled on or off based on your preferences. For instance, if you don't want to receive alerts about work anniversaries, you can disable them in the **Network Updates** section.

3. Managing Email Notifications

Email notifications are sent for various activities, such as job alerts, messages, or updates from groups. To manage them:

1. In the **Notifications** settings, click on **Email Frequency.**

2. You can choose from options like **Daily Digest, Weekly Digest, or Individual Emails.**

3. For minimal intrusion, select **Off** for categories you don't wish to receive via email.

4. Adjusting Mobile Push Notifications

Push notifications are helpful when you're on the go but can become overwhelming if not managed. To modify push notifications:

1. Open the LinkedIn app on your smartphone.

2. Tap your profile photo in the top left corner and go to **Settings.**

3. Under **Notifications**, customize which alerts you want to receive as push notifications.

4. Toggle off any notification types that are unnecessary or distracting.

Managing Communication Preferences

LinkedIn also gives you control over how and when you are contacted by other users. From deciding who can message you to limiting unsolicited communication, these settings ensure a balanced networking experience.

1. Controlling Who Can Message You

To manage who can contact you:

1. Go to **Settings & Privacy > Communications > Messages.**

2. Adjust the settings under **Who can send you messages:**

- o **Connections Only:** Restrict messages to your direct connections.

- o **Everyone on LinkedIn:** Allow messages from anyone on the platform.

- o **InMail Preferences:** If you have a Premium account, you can enable or disable receiving messages from InMail senders.

2. Filtering and Organizing Your Inbox

LinkedIn's messaging inbox includes tools to help you filter and prioritize messages.

1. Use the **Focused Inbox** feature, which separates important conversations from less relevant ones.

2. Archive old or irrelevant messages to keep your inbox tidy.

3. Block or report spammy messages by clicking the three dots in the top right corner of any message.

3. Managing Invitations and Requests

Some users may find connection requests overwhelming, especially if they receive them frequently. To manage this:

1. Navigate to **Settings & Privacy > Communications > Invitations.**

2. Enable or disable notifications for new connection requests.

3. Use the **My Network** tab to sort and respond to invitations in batches.

Tips for Minimizing Unnecessary Notifications

Here are some best practices to reduce distractions and focus on what truly matters:

1. **Prioritize Key Alerts:** Decide which notifications add value to your LinkedIn experience. For example, job seekers may prioritize job alerts, while content creators may focus on engagement notifications.

2. **Mute Group Notifications:** If you're part of active LinkedIn groups, mute their notifications to avoid being bombarded with updates.

3. **Limit Email and Push Notifications:** Unless you rely on LinkedIn for time-sensitive updates, set email and push notifications to a minimal level.

Balancing Engagement and Privacy

Managing notifications and communication preferences is about finding the right balance. If you disable too many notifications, you risk missing out on valuable opportunities. On the other hand, keeping too many enabled can lead to overload and reduce productivity. Periodically revisit your settings to ensure they align with your current LinkedIn goals.

Conclusion

Customizing your notifications and communication preferences is a crucial part of optimizing your LinkedIn experience. By tailoring these settings to your needs, you can focus on meaningful interactions, stay updated on career opportunities, and build a professional presence without feeling overwhelmed. With LinkedIn's robust settings, you have the power to make the platform work for you, not the other way around.

7.3 Avoiding Common Mistakes

7.3.1 Overloading Your Profile with Irrelevant Information

When creating or updating your LinkedIn profile, it's easy to fall into the trap of overloading it with information that may not serve your professional goals. While it's important to provide a detailed and complete profile, adding irrelevant or excessive details can confuse visitors, dilute your key message, and even turn away potential connections or recruiters. In this section, we'll explore why overloading your profile can be detrimental and how to avoid this common mistake.

Why Overloading Your Profile is Harmful

1. **Diluted Focus**: When your profile includes unnecessary details, it can confuse viewers about your professional identity. For example, if you're seeking a role in marketing but also highlight unrelated side jobs, it might give the impression that you're unfocused or uncertain about your career path. A recruiter who is quickly skimming your profile may struggle to identify your core competencies and move on to another candidate.

2. **Recruiter Fatigue**: Recruiters and hiring managers often spend just a few seconds scanning each profile. Overloading your profile with irrelevant information forces them to sift through unimportant details, making it harder for them to quickly assess your suitability for a role. This can lead to missed opportunities.

3. **Professionalism and Credibility**: Including too much information, especially if it is unrelated to your professional goals, can make your profile appear cluttered and unprofessional. For example, listing hobbies or personal anecdotes that have no relevance to your industry might distract or detract from your expertise.

4. **Search Engine Optimization (SEO) Challenges**: LinkedIn's algorithm uses keywords to rank profiles in search results. Adding irrelevant information may dilute the effectiveness of the keywords related to your industry or desired role, reducing your profile's visibility to recruiters and potential connections.

Identifying Irrelevant Information

Before you start editing your LinkedIn profile, it's important to identify the types of information that are unnecessary or out of place. Below are examples of common types of irrelevant content:

1. **Unrelated Work Experience**: While it's important to show a complete career timeline, you don't need to include detailed descriptions of every job, especially if they're unrelated to your current career path. For example, if you're now a software engineer, your first part-time job as a cashier likely doesn't need extensive detail.

2. **Unfocused Skills**: Listing too many unrelated skills can confuse viewers about your expertise. For example, if you're applying for a finance role, emphasizing skills like "Event Planning" or "Graphic Design" might dilute your credibility as a finance professional.

3. **Personal Interests and Hobbies**: While some hobbies can humanize your profile (e.g., leadership roles in volunteer activities), they should only be included if they're relevant to your personal brand or career. For instance, "Photography" may be relevant for a creative professional, but it's likely unnecessary for an accountant's profile.

4. **Excessive Use of Buzzwords**: Overloading your profile with buzzwords like "team player," "results-driven," or "innovative" without demonstrating these qualities in your experience can make your profile seem generic.

5. **Redundant Details**: Repeating information, such as the same achievements listed in multiple sections, can make your profile unnecessarily long and less engaging.

Tips for Avoiding Irrelevant Information

Now that we've identified what not to include, here are actionable steps to ensure your LinkedIn profile is focused, professional, and aligned with your career goals:

1. **Define Your Personal Brand**

- o Ask yourself: What do I want people to know about me when they visit my profile?

- o Focus on crafting a clear professional identity. For example, if you're an aspiring marketing professional, highlight your experience, skills, and achievements in marketing rather than unrelated areas.

2. **Tailor Your Profile to Your Career Goals**

   - o Customize your profile to align with your current or desired role. For example, if you're transitioning into data analysis, emphasize coursework, certifications, and experience in analytics, and minimize irrelevant details from past roles.

3. **Highlight Relevant Skills and Accomplishments**

   - o Focus on skills that are directly applicable to your industry or job target. Use examples and quantifiable achievements to back up your claims.

4. **Simplify Your Profile**

   - o Avoid using excessive text in sections like your Summary and Work Experience. Use bullet points and concise descriptions to convey key information.

   - o Example: Instead of writing "I was responsible for leading multiple teams and ensuring that projects were completed on time while also managing client relationships," write "Led cross-functional teams to deliver projects on time, achieving a 95% client satisfaction rate."

5. **Use Keywords Strategically**

   - o Identify the keywords commonly used in your industry and incorporate them naturally into your profile. Avoid keyword stuffing, which can make your profile appear robotic or inauthentic.

6. **Keep Your Work History Relevant**

   - o If you have a long career history, focus on the roles that are most relevant to your current goals. You can briefly mention older roles without going into excessive detail.

7. **Separate Personal from Professional**

   o If you want to showcase personal interests, do so in a way that complements your professional identity. For example, if you're in HR, mentioning volunteer work related to mentorship or community engagement might be relevant.

Examples of Streamlining Your Profile

Let's look at an example of how to revise a cluttered profile section:

Before:
"I worked at XYZ Café as a barista while attending college. I made coffee, cleaned the workspace, and interacted with customers. This job taught me how to work under pressure and deal with difficult customers."

After:
"While attending college, I developed customer service and time management skills as a barista at XYZ Café."

Why it Works: The revised version is concise and highlights transferable skills, making it relevant even if the role isn't directly tied to your current career.

Maintaining a Clean and Focused Profile

1. **Regular Updates**: Review your profile every few months to ensure that all information is current and relevant. Remove outdated roles, certifications, or projects that no longer reflect your career focus.

2. **Ask for Feedback**: Share your profile with a mentor, colleague, or recruiter for constructive criticism. They may notice irrelevant details that you overlooked.

3. **Think Like a Recruiter**: When editing your profile, put yourself in the shoes of someone scanning it. Ask yourself: Does this information add value to my story? If not, remove or reframe it.

Final Thoughts

Your LinkedIn profile is a powerful tool for showcasing your professional identity, but less is often more. By focusing on relevant, concise, and impactful content, you can create a profile that stands out to recruiters and connections while avoiding the common pitfall of overloading it with irrelevant information. Remember, every detail on your profile should serve a purpose: to communicate your expertise, accomplishments, and career goals effectively.

7.3.2 Misusing Connection Requests

When it comes to building your professional network on LinkedIn, connection requests are your primary tool. However, misusing connection requests is one of the most common mistakes beginners make. Whether you're trying to grow your network quickly or reach specific people, it's essential to approach this feature with strategy, professionalism, and respect. In this section, we'll explore common pitfalls and best practices to help you connect effectively and avoid damaging your reputation on the platform.

What Does It Mean to Misuse Connection Requests?

Misusing connection requests can take many forms, from sending too many generic requests to spamming strangers with irrelevant messages. Here are some common mistakes that users make:

1. **Sending Connection Requests Without Personalizing Them**

   o LinkedIn provides the option to include a short message with your connection request. Many users overlook this feature and send requests without any context. While this may work with people you know well, it often leaves strangers confused about why you're reaching out.

2. **Connecting Without a Clear Purpose**

   o Some users send requests simply to grow their network, without considering whether the connection is meaningful. This can lead to a cluttered network with little value for your professional goals.

3. **Sending Requests to People You Don't Know or Have No Shared Interests With**

   o Blindly connecting with random users, especially those outside your industry or location, can come across as spammy. It may also result in your requests being ignored or flagged.

4. **Overwhelming Recruiters or Influencers**

   o It's tempting to connect with recruiters, CEOs, or LinkedIn influencers to advance your career. However, sending them repeated requests or irrelevant messages can harm your credibility.

5. **Using Automation Tools to Send Bulk Requests**

   o Some users turn to automation tools to send hundreds of connection requests at once. While this may seem efficient, LinkedIn's algorithms can detect this behavior and may temporarily or permanently restrict your account.

Why Misusing Connection Requests Can Be Harmful

1. **Damages Your Professional Reputation**

   o LinkedIn is built on trust and professionalism. If your connection requests feel like spam or lack sincerity, you risk damaging your reputation within your industry.

2. **Reduces the Chances of Acceptance**

   o Generic or poorly thought-out requests are more likely to be ignored or rejected. LinkedIn tracks the acceptance rate of your requests, and a low acceptance rate may reduce your visibility on the platform.

3. **Leads to Account Restrictions**

   o LinkedIn monitors user behavior closely. If you send too many unsolicited or irrelevant connection requests, your account may be flagged for spam-like behavior, leading to restrictions.

4. **Missed Opportunities**

   o Misusing connection requests may close doors to meaningful connections, such as potential employers, collaborators, or mentors, who might have otherwise been willing to engage with you.

Best Practices for Sending Connection Requests

Now that we've covered what to avoid, let's focus on how to use connection requests effectively.

1. **Personalize Your Requests**

   o Always include a message when sending a request, especially to people you don't know personally. A personalized message should:

      ▪ Explain who you are.

      ▪ State why you want to connect.

      ▪ Highlight any shared interests or mutual connections.

   o For example:

"Hi [Name], I came across your profile while researching [industry/topic]. I noticed that we share a mutual interest in [specific area]. I'd love to connect and learn more about your work at [Company]."

2. **Connect with a Purpose**

   o Before sending a request, ask yourself why you want to connect with this person. Is it to learn from their experience? Explore potential collaborations? Avoid sending requests just to grow your network without a clear reason.

3. **Engage Before Sending a Request**

   o A great way to make your request stand out is to engage with the person's content before reaching out. Comment on their posts, like their updates, or share their articles. This shows genuine interest and makes your request more likely to be accepted.

4. **Target Relevant Connections**

   o Focus on connecting with people who align with your professional goals. This could include colleagues, industry peers, mentors, or individuals in companies you aspire to work for.

5. **Be Mindful of Timing**

   o Avoid sending requests at inappropriate times, such as immediately after someone changes their job title or posts a major announcement. Instead, wait for an appropriate opportunity to reach out.

6. **Follow Up After a Connection is Accepted**

   o Once your request is accepted, follow up with a polite message to thank them and start a conversation. Avoid pitching your services or asking for favors immediately after connecting.

Examples of Well-Written Connection Requests

1. **For Someone You Met at an Event:**

"Hi [Name], it was great meeting you at [Event]. I enjoyed our conversation about [Topic]. I'd love to stay connected and continue exchanging ideas."

2. **For a Colleague or Peer:**

"Hi [Name], I noticed we both work in [industry/field], and I admire your work at [Company]. I'd love to connect and learn more about your perspective on [specific topic]."

3. **For Someone You Admire:**

"Hi [Name], I've been following your work in [field] and found your recent article on [topic] very insightful. I'd be honored to connect and learn from your experience."

How to Handle Declined or Ignored Requests

It's important to remember that not all connection requests will be accepted, and that's okay. Here's how to handle declined or ignored requests professionally:

1. **Don't Take It Personally**

   o People may decline requests for various reasons, such as a full inbox or a preference for connecting only with close contacts.

2. **Wait Before Resending**

   o If your request is ignored, wait a few months before trying again, and make sure to personalize your message the second time.

3. **Respect Boundaries**

   o Avoid repeatedly sending requests to the same person. If they decline, move on and focus on other potential connections.

Final Thoughts on Connection Requests

Using connection requests effectively is about quality over quantity. A small, well-curated network of meaningful connections will provide far more value than a large, disconnected one. By personalizing your requests, targeting relevant people, and respecting professional boundaries, you'll build a LinkedIn network that supports your career goals and enhances your professional presence.

Take your time to build genuine relationships, and remember that LinkedIn is not just about numbers—it's about creating opportunities for meaningful collaboration and growth.

Conclusion

8.1 Recap: Building a Strong LinkedIn Foundation

As we near the end of this guide, it's important to consolidate all the knowledge and strategies we've covered so far. Building a strong LinkedIn foundation is essential for creating a lasting professional presence, maximizing your networking opportunities, and reaching your career goals. In this section, we'll recap the key components and steps required to set up and optimize your LinkedIn profile while offering additional tips to ensure your success on the platform.

1. Creating a Strong First Impression

Your LinkedIn profile is often the first touchpoint for recruiters, potential employers, clients, and collaborators. To make a positive and lasting impression, focus on the following:

- **Professional Profile Picture**: A high-quality, professional profile picture is a must. Choose an image where you appear approachable, confident, and appropriately dressed for your industry. Avoid using casual selfies, group photos, or blurry images.

- **Customizable Headline**: Your headline is one of the most visible parts of your profile. Instead of just listing your current job title, craft a headline that highlights your expertise and career goals. For example, instead of "Marketing Manager," try "Digital Marketing Specialist | Content Strategist | Helping Businesses Grow Through Creative Campaigns."

- **Personalized URL**: Customize your LinkedIn profile URL to make it clean and memorable. For example, change it from "linkedin.com/in/random1234" to "linkedin.com/in/yourname."

2. Crafting a Compelling Summary

The "About" section (or summary) is your chance to tell your professional story. A compelling summary includes:

- **A Personal Introduction**: Begin with who you are, your professional background, and what motivates you in your field. Share your passion and what makes you unique.

- **Highlight Key Achievements**: Mention specific accomplishments that demonstrate your skills and expertise. Use numbers or measurable outcomes to add credibility. For example, "Managed marketing campaigns that increased website traffic by 50% in 12 months."

- **State Your Goals**: End your summary by outlining your professional aspirations or the types of opportunities you're looking for. This helps viewers understand how they can collaborate with or assist you.

3. Detailing Your Professional Experience

Your experience section is where you highlight your work history in detail. To make this section stand out:

- **Use Action-Oriented Language**: Begin each bullet point with strong action verbs like "managed," "led," "created," or "developed."

- **Focus on Results**: Avoid simply listing your job duties. Instead, describe how you made an impact. For instance, instead of "Responsible for social media," write "Increased social media engagement by 200% by launching targeted campaigns."

- **Include Relevant Experience**: Tailor your experience to align with your current career goals. Highlight jobs, projects, or internships that are most relevant to your desired field.

4. Showcasing Skills and Endorsements

The skills section is a powerful way to demonstrate your expertise. Here's how to make the most of it:

- **List Key Skills**: Focus on listing skills that are in demand in your industry. Use LinkedIn's suggestions to find relevant keywords.

- **Get Endorsed**: Reach out to colleagues, classmates, or mentors and request endorsements for your skills. Offering to endorse their skills in return can be a helpful way to build mutual support.

- **Keep It Relevant**: Avoid listing too many skills that may dilute your expertise. Instead, prioritize the top 10-15 skills that align with your career goals.

5. Building and Maintaining Connections

Networking is one of the primary functions of LinkedIn. Building meaningful relationships can open doors to career opportunities.

- **Connect Strategically**: Always personalize your connection requests with a friendly note explaining why you'd like to connect. For example: *"Hi [Name], I noticed your expertise in [field] and would love to connect and learn more about your work."*

- **Engage Regularly**: Stay active by liking, commenting on, and sharing posts from your network. This keeps you visible and helps strengthen your relationships.

- **Join Groups**: LinkedIn groups allow you to connect with like-minded professionals. Participate in discussions to build credibility and expand your network.

6. Engaging with Content

Sharing and interacting with content is essential for staying relevant and building your personal brand.

- **Post Thoughtful Content**: Share updates about your career, industry insights, or articles you've written. Adding a personal touch or opinion helps spark engagement.

- **Publish Articles**: LinkedIn's publishing platform allows you to write long-form content. Use this feature to establish yourself as a thought leader in your field.

- **Support Others**: Comment on and share posts from your network. This not only builds goodwill but also keeps you top-of-mind for others.

7. Optimizing for Job Opportunities

LinkedIn is a powerful tool for job seekers. To make your profile recruiter-friendly:

- **Enable "Open to Work"**: Use the "Open to Work" feature to signal your availability to recruiters. You can customize this setting to control who sees it.

- **Use Keywords Strategically**: Optimize your profile with industry-specific keywords to appear in recruiter searches. For example, a graphic designer might include "Adobe Photoshop," "UI/UX design," and "brand identity."

- **Tailor Your Profile for Roles**: If you're targeting a specific type of job, align your profile's content—summary, experience, and skills—with the job descriptions of those roles.

8. Leveraging LinkedIn Analytics

Your LinkedIn dashboard provides valuable insights into your profile's performance.

- **Track Profile Views**: Monitor who is viewing your profile and use this information to identify potential connections or recruiters.

- **Measure Content Engagement**: Check the analytics for your posts to see what type of content resonates with your audience. Use these insights to refine your strategy.

9. Avoiding Common Mistakes

Many LinkedIn users inadvertently make mistakes that can harm their professional image. To avoid this:

- **Don't Be Too Formal or Too Casual**: Strike a professional yet approachable tone in your communications and profile content.

- **Avoid Overloading with Information**: Keep your profile concise and focused. Recruiters and potential connections should be able to understand your strengths at a glance.

- **Be Consistent**: Ensure your profile aligns with your resume and other professional materials. Inconsistencies can create confusion or doubt.

10. Final Tips for Long-Term Success

Building a strong LinkedIn presence is not a one-time task. It requires ongoing effort and consistency.

- **Update Your Profile Regularly**: Keep your profile up to date with new skills, certifications, and accomplishments.

- **Network Intentionally**: Set aside time each week to connect with new people, engage with content, and participate in groups.

- **Be Authentic**: Let your personality shine through. People are more likely to connect with you when they see the real person behind the profile.

By following these foundational steps and regularly refining your profile and strategy, you'll be well-positioned to make the most of LinkedIn. Whether you're a job seeker, entrepreneur, or professional looking to grow your network, your strong LinkedIn foundation will open doors to new opportunities and meaningful connections.

8.2 Next Steps: Growing Beyond the Basics

As you've built a solid foundation on LinkedIn by creating a strong profile, growing your network, and engaging with content, the next phase involves taking your LinkedIn presence to the next level. This section will guide you through advanced strategies and approaches to amplify your visibility, establish yourself as a thought leader, and leverage LinkedIn for long-term career growth.

Expanding Your Professional Network Strategically

Networking is the cornerstone of LinkedIn's success, but it's not just about numbers—it's about quality connections. Now that you've connected with colleagues, classmates, and industry professionals, focus on expanding your network strategically.

- **Engage with Industry Leaders:** Start by identifying thought leaders, influencers, and decision-makers in your industry. Follow their profiles, engage with their posts, and share their insights with your own commentary. Building relationships with these individuals can increase your credibility and expose your profile to a broader audience.

- **Participate in Industry Groups:** LinkedIn Groups are a great way to meet like-minded professionals and stay updated on trends in your industry. Join active groups related to your field, participate in discussions, and contribute value by sharing your knowledge.

- **Attend Virtual and In-Person Events:** LinkedIn often highlights industry events and webinars on your feed. Attending these events and connecting with attendees can broaden your professional reach. Be sure to follow up with personalized connection requests.

Establishing Yourself as a Thought Leader

Positioning yourself as an authority in your niche can elevate your professional reputation. To achieve this, focus on consistently sharing valuable content and building your personal brand.

- **Create Original Content:** Write articles, share insights, and post updates related to your expertise. For example, if you're in marketing, you could share tips on campaign optimization or highlight trends in consumer behavior. Original content helps showcase your knowledge and attracts like-minded professionals.

- **Use Multimedia to Engage Your Audience:** Visual content, such as infographics, videos, and slide decks, tends to perform well on LinkedIn. Use tools like Canva to create eye-catching visuals that complement your written posts.

- **Leverage LinkedIn's Publishing Platform:** LinkedIn allows users to write and publish long-form articles. Use this platform to share in-depth analyses, case studies, or how-to guides that align with your professional expertise.

- **Engage with Your Audience:** Thought leadership is not a one-way street. Respond to comments on your posts, ask questions, and foster meaningful conversations. The more interactive your content, the greater its reach.

Using LinkedIn for Career Development

LinkedIn is more than just a networking tool; it's a platform for discovering and seizing new career opportunities.

- **Set Career Goals and Align Your LinkedIn Strategy:** Define what you hope to achieve with your LinkedIn presence. Are you looking for a promotion? A new job? Freelance clients? Align your activities on LinkedIn with these goals by tailoring your content, connections, and messaging.

- **Leverage LinkedIn Learning:** One of the most underutilized features on LinkedIn is LinkedIn Learning. Access courses and certifications to enhance your skills in your field, then showcase your new credentials on your profile.

- **Track Job Trends:** Use LinkedIn's "Jobs" section not just to find current openings but also to identify trends in your industry. Pay attention to in-demand skills and incorporate them into your professional development plans.

- **Engage with Recruiters and Hiring Managers:** Building relationships with recruiters can help you learn about opportunities before they're advertised. Be proactive in reaching out, and keep your communication professional and concise.

Building a Personal Brand

Your personal brand is how others perceive you professionally. On LinkedIn, it encompasses your profile, the content you share, and how you engage with your network.

- **Consistent Messaging:** Ensure that your profile, posts, and comments align with the image you want to project. For instance, if you want to be seen as an innovative entrepreneur, share updates about industry trends, new business strategies, and success stories.

- **Use a Professional Voice:** The tone and language you use on LinkedIn matter. Aim for a tone that's professional but approachable, and avoid overly casual language or jargon that might alienate readers.

- **Optimize Your Profile for Branding:** Regularly update your headline and summary to reflect your current goals and achievements. Include multimedia elements like videos or portfolio links to enhance your profile's appeal.

- **Leverage Recommendations:** Ask colleagues and clients for recommendations that emphasize your key skills and strengths. These testimonials enhance your credibility and give potential connections or employers a reason to trust you.

Engaging in Thoughtful Interactions

One of the most effective ways to grow your LinkedIn presence is by being an active and thoughtful participant on the platform.

- **Commenting with Value:** When commenting on posts, add meaningful insights rather than generic responses. For example, if someone shares an article on leadership, you could contribute by sharing a personal anecdote or an additional resource.

- **Supporting Others:** Congratulate connections on their achievements, endorse their skills, and celebrate their milestones. Supporting others strengthens relationships and encourages reciprocation.

- **Avoiding Spammy Behavior:** Overposting, sharing irrelevant content, or sending generic messages can hurt your reputation. Always focus on providing value in your interactions.

Exploring LinkedIn's Advanced Features

LinkedIn offers a variety of tools and features that can help you achieve your professional goals more effectively.

- **Analytics and Insights:** Use LinkedIn's profile and post analytics to understand what content resonates with your audience. Monitor metrics like post impressions, profile views, and engagement rates to refine your strategy.

- **LinkedIn Sales Navigator:** For professionals in sales or business development, LinkedIn Sales Navigator offers advanced tools for finding leads and building relationships.

- **Showcase Pages and Company Pages:** If you're an entrepreneur or manage a business, consider creating a LinkedIn Page to highlight your company. Post updates, share your mission, and engage with your audience.

- **Using LinkedIn Events:** Host webinars or networking events directly on LinkedIn to connect with a targeted audience. Promote these events on your feed and through your network.

Measuring and Reflecting on Progress

As you grow beyond the basics, it's important to periodically assess your LinkedIn strategy and adjust as needed.

- **Set Key Performance Indicators (KPIs):** Examples include increasing profile views by 20% over the next quarter or gaining 10 new industry-specific connections each month.

- **Reflect on Content Performance:** Review which types of posts perform best and focus on creating more of what resonates with your audience.

- **Solicit Feedback:** Ask trusted colleagues or mentors to review your profile and provide suggestions for improvement.

By implementing these advanced strategies, you'll not only maximize the value of LinkedIn but also position yourself as a standout professional in your industry. Whether your goal is to land your dream job, expand your business, or build a personal brand, the steps outlined here will help you achieve long-term success on the platform.

8.3 Recommended Resources for Further Learning

LinkedIn is a dynamic and ever-evolving platform, and mastering its use requires continuous learning and adaptation. In this section, we will explore various resources that can help you deepen your understanding of LinkedIn and enhance your skills for personal and professional growth. These resources include LinkedIn's built-in learning tools, external training courses, books, blogs, podcasts, and other tools that will enable you to stay ahead in using LinkedIn effectively.

LinkedIn Learning: Your First Stop for Growth

LinkedIn Learning is a treasure trove of educational content tailored for professionals at all levels. As LinkedIn's own e-learning platform, it provides a wide range of courses designed to improve your skills and help you make the most out of the platform. Here's why LinkedIn Learning is invaluable:

- **LinkedIn-Specific Courses**: Courses like "Building Your LinkedIn Profile for Job Seekers," "Networking Strategies for LinkedIn," and "Personal Branding on LinkedIn" are specifically designed to help you master the platform.

- **Skill Development**: LinkedIn Learning also offers courses on soft skills (e.g., communication, leadership, and negotiation) and technical skills (e.g., project management, data analysis, and digital marketing) that align with your professional goals.

- **Interactive Learning**: With video tutorials, quizzes, and downloadable resources, LinkedIn Learning provides an engaging way to learn at your own pace.

- **Integration with Your Profile**: Once you complete a course, you can add a certificate to your LinkedIn profile to showcase your new skills to potential employers or clients.

To get started, simply click on the "Learning" tab at the top of the LinkedIn homepage. While LinkedIn Learning is a paid feature, many employers provide free access as part of their employee benefits, so be sure to check with your organization.

Books on LinkedIn Mastery and Personal Branding

Books offer a deep dive into strategies and insights that can help you use LinkedIn more effectively. Here are some highly recommended titles:

- **"How to Write a KILLER LinkedIn Profile... And 18 Mistakes to Avoid" by Brenda Bernstein**: This book is a step-by-step guide for optimizing your LinkedIn profile, complete with actionable tips and examples.

- **"LinkedIn Riches: How to Use LinkedIn for Business, Sales, and Marketing!" by John Nemo**: Ideal for entrepreneurs and professionals, this book focuses on using LinkedIn to generate leads and grow your business.

- **"The LinkedIn Code: Unlock The Largest Online Business Social Network to Get Leads, Prospects & Clients" by Melonie Dodaro**: This book dives into using LinkedIn strategically for networking and business development.

- **"Personal Branding for Dummies" by Susan Chritton**: While not exclusively about LinkedIn, this book is an excellent resource for building your personal brand, which can be amplified through LinkedIn.

Blogs and Websites for LinkedIn Insights

Reading blogs and websites dedicated to LinkedIn and professional development can provide fresh ideas, industry updates, and practical tips. Here are some notable ones:

- **LinkedIn Blog**: The official LinkedIn blog (blog.linkedin.com) shares updates about new features, user success stories, and tips for optimizing your profile.

- **Social Media Examiner**: This website frequently publishes articles on LinkedIn marketing and networking strategies.

- **Melonie Dodaro's Blog**: As a LinkedIn expert, Melonie Dodaro offers valuable tips and strategies through her blog (topdogsocialmedia.com).

- **HubSpot Blog**: HubSpot's marketing and sales blog includes helpful articles on how to leverage LinkedIn for business growth and personal branding.

Podcasts on LinkedIn and Professional Growth

Podcasts are an excellent way to learn about LinkedIn while commuting, exercising, or relaxing. Here are some podcasts that provide actionable advice and inspiration:

- **"The LinkedIn Lounge Podcast"**: This podcast focuses on building your professional brand and optimizing your LinkedIn presence.

- **"LinkedInformed Podcast"**: Hosted by Mark Williams, this podcast shares the latest LinkedIn news, tips, and insights for users at all levels.

- **"The GaryVee Audio Experience"**: While not exclusively about LinkedIn, Gary Vaynerchuk's podcast covers personal branding, social media strategies, and professional networking.

- **"Smart Passive Income" by Pat Flynn**: This podcast explores ways to build online connections and leverage platforms like LinkedIn for growth.

Online Communities and Forums

Joining online communities and forums allows you to exchange ideas, ask questions, and learn from experienced professionals. Some options include:

- **LinkedIn Groups**: Look for groups related to your industry or profession. Groups like "LinkedIn Tips & Tricks" or "Professional Networking Group" can be helpful for learning and networking.

- **Reddit**: Subreddits like r/LinkedIn and r/careeradvice are great places to find discussions and advice.

- **Quora**: Search for questions about LinkedIn and follow topics to receive valuable insights from experts.

YouTube Channels for Tutorials and Tips

YouTube offers a wide variety of LinkedIn-related tutorials, ranging from basic profile setup to advanced marketing strategies. Some popular channels include:

- **LinkedIn Learning**: The official YouTube channel features free previews of their courses.

- **Simpletivity**: This channel covers LinkedIn tips, productivity hacks, and professional growth.

- **CareerVidz**: A channel dedicated to job search strategies, LinkedIn tips, and career advice.

- **Skillshare YouTube Channel**: While primarily promoting Skillshare courses, this channel occasionally shares tips for using LinkedIn effectively.

Workshops and Webinars

Attending workshops and webinars can provide hands-on learning opportunities and allow you to interact with instructors in real time. Many of these events are hosted by LinkedIn experts or career coaches.

- **LinkedIn Live Events**: LinkedIn itself hosts webinars and live sessions on topics like job searching, profile optimization, and networking.

- **Career Development Workshops**: Universities, professional organizations, and career centers often host LinkedIn-specific workshops.

Experiment and Learn by Doing

While resources are invaluable, nothing beats learning by doing. Experimenting with LinkedIn's features, engaging with your network, and consistently updating your profile will provide practical experience that accelerates your growth. Here's how you can create a personal learning plan:

- **Weekly Goals**: Dedicate time each week to explore a new feature or strategy, such as posting an article or joining a group.

- **Feedback Loop**: Seek feedback from peers or mentors on your profile or networking strategies.

- **Track Progress**: Use LinkedIn Analytics to monitor the impact of your efforts.

Building a Long-Term Growth Plan

Learning about LinkedIn is not a one-time activity; it is an ongoing process. To sustain your growth:

- **Stay Updated**: Follow LinkedIn's updates and announcements to learn about new features.

- **Expand Your Network**: Continuously connect with professionals in your field and beyond.

- **Invest in Yourself**: Consider enrolling in advanced courses, attending conferences, or hiring a coach to refine your LinkedIn strategies.

By leveraging these recommended resources, you can transform your LinkedIn experience from a basic platform for professional connections into a powerful tool for career growth and personal branding. Continue learning, experimenting, and engaging with your network, and you'll unlock LinkedIn's full potential.

Acknowledgements

I would like to extend my heartfelt thanks to all the readers who have chosen *LinkedIn for Beginners: A Step-by-Step Guide*. Your decision to pick up this book means more than words can express, and I am truly honored to have had the opportunity to share this knowledge with you.

I would like to express my gratitude to the countless professionals who have inspired and shaped my understanding of LinkedIn and its role in personal and career development. Your expertise, insights, and real-world experiences have helped me create a comprehensive guide that I hope will make a difference in your journey.

A special thank you goes to the LinkedIn team for continuously improving and evolving the platform, making it an indispensable tool for millions of professionals worldwide. Your innovation and dedication to connecting people and fostering professional growth have been a key driving force behind this book.

To my family and friends, thank you for your unwavering support and encouragement throughout the writing process. Your belief in me and your patience during this journey has been invaluable.

Lastly, I would like to acknowledge the readers who have provided feedback, shared their experiences, and motivated me to keep improving this book. Your voices are an essential part of this work, and I hope it serves you well as you take the next steps in building your LinkedIn presence and advancing in your career.

Thank you again for your trust in this book. I wish you all the best as you continue to grow and succeed on LinkedIn.

Warm regards,